DEVELOPMENTAL NEUROPSYCHOLOGY, 26(1),
Copyright © 2004, Lawrence Erlbaum Associates, Inc

Using Developmental, Cognitive, and Neuroscience Approaches to Understand Executive Control in Young Children

Kimberly Andrews Espy
Department of Family and Community Medicine
Southern Illinois University School of Medicine

The 7 articles in this special issue address the nature of executive control in young children. Executive control is framed in a developmental context, where the unique aspects of cognition in this age range are considered. The set of articles demonstrates the multidisciplinary approaches to study cognition in young children that includes application of cognitive, neuroscience, and developmental paradigms in typically developing youngsters, as well as those affected by clinical conditions, such as traumatic brain injury, exposure to low levels of lead in the environment, and prematurity. Although much work remains to be done, these study results are illustrative of the dynamic work in this exciting developmental period.

At first glance, it would appear to be an oxymoron to study executive control in young children between ages 2 and 6 years. By definition, children of this age act "in the moment"—that is, they are impulsive, repetitive, inattentive, and cannot keep salient information in mind. It is precisely this kind of unmodulated behavior that is difficult to label *executive,* a term usually reserved for purposeful, planned, goal-directed action. In fact, the behavior of preschoolers resembles that of Phineas Gage, EVR (Eslinger & Damasio, 1985), and other famous patients with circumscribed lesions to the prefrontal cortex and related systems. Like many things with preschoolers, the first blush view may not be the most accurate representation.

Besides the remarkable "dysexecutive" behavioral presentation of young children, there also have been scientific impediments to considering executive control

Requests for reprints should be sent to Kimberly Andrews Espy, Department of Family and Community Medicine, MC 6503, Southern Illinois University School of Medicine, 600 Agriculture Dr., Carbondale, IL 62901–6503. E-mail: kespy@siumed.edu

in young children. Pioneering neuropsychologists, such as Brenda Milner (1963), demonstrated such compelling dissociations between knowledge and action in patients with prefrontal damage on the Wisconsin Card Sorting test (WCST; Heaton, Chelune, Talley, Kay, & Curtiss, 1993) that WCST performance became the sine qua non for executive functioning. Following this metaphor to its conclusion leads to a teleological error—young children cannot have executive abilities because they cannot complete the WCST. The emergence of *pediatric* neuropsychology has been critical in forcing the consideration of childhood cognition in a developmental context—that is, children are quantitatively, and qualitatively, different from adults—precisely because abilities are in an active state of change (e.g., Dennis, 1987; Fletcher & Taylor, 1984). Developmentalists consistently have shown that preschoolers generally do not suffer from a lack of abilities, but rather from the ability to deploy these abilities in particular contexts (e.g., Flavell, 1999)—that is, they lack basic metacognitive awareness of when, and how, to apply their knowledge and to deploy particular strategies effectively.

With this context in mind, the study of executive control in young children has burgeoned recently—driven by the confluence of several factors. First, several psychiatric and neurodevelopmental conditions become prominent in the preschool age range, in particular, Attention Deficit Hyperactivity Disorder. Therefore, it might be useful to be able to better identify children at risk for such disorders earlier in development, so as to reduce morbidity severity. In a related vein, understanding the genesis of the cognitive underpinnings of a disorder will shed light on the complex interplay among cognitive processes, development, and the social environment, which dynamically shape the pathways to adverse outcome later in life.

Second, paralleling these developments was the application of basic neuroscience techniques to elucidate brain–behavior relations in primates. Goldman-Rakic (1987) elegantly demonstrated that various manipulations to the dorsolateral prefrontal cortex fundamentally alter goal-directed behavior of the monkey, with outcome varying with respect to when during development these lesions occurred (Goldman, 1974). These monkeys demonstrated the same repetitive, perseverative behavior as that shown by patients with prefrontal damage evidence. Given the context of the limitations of primate cognition, perhaps these neuroscience tasks could be adapted for use with humans, with the added advantage of a more direct link to brain function than was available with traditional, standardized clinical instruments. Diamond (1985) first pioneered the application of such paradigms with infants, demonstrating striking parallels between infant search behavior and that of prefrontally lesioned monkeys. Such studies opened the door to the application of various paradigms from different disciplines to study executive control in preschool children. Just as Fletcher stressed in his 1996 *Developmental Neuropsychology* special series, "Executive Functions in Children," "the goal is to use cognitive tasks to understand the nature of brain function in children and brain dysfunction in CNS disorders specific to children" (p. 3), not to rely excessively on adult paradigms, findings, or principles. Children are not little adults, nor are pre-schoolers little children. Understanding brain behavior relations in the very young requires the use of innovative paradigms from multiple disciplines that capitalize on the unique, developmentally salient interests of this age range, taking into account the real limitations in verbal and motoric facility and in the variable attention span (e.g., Espy, 1997; Espy, Kaufmann, Glisky, & McDiarmid, 2001).

This historical context is the backdrop of this special issue. The seven articles demonstrate different measurement techniques that can be used to better understand the nature and organization of executive control in young children. Smidts, Jacobs, and Anderson (this issue) present their findings on the development of a concept generation task for use in early childhood. The task has its origins in adult neuropsychology, but Smidts et al. use a decidedly developmental approach for test development. Isquith, Gioia, and Espy (this issue), on the other hand, discuss the adaptation of a childhood paper-and-pencil instrument that can be completed by parents or teachers to assess divergent executive abilities. Rennie, Bull, and Diamond (this issue) use experimental methods to manipulate salient task demands to explicate the cognitive processes that underlie performance on the Dimensional Change Card Sort (DCCS) task (Zelazo, Reznick, & Pinion, 1995), a task used in the developmental psychology literature to demonstrate the development of sorting behavior. Finally, Senn, Espy, and Kaufmann (this issue) demonstrate the use of quantitative statistical techniques to investigate different models of executive control organization through systematically comparing structural models that are premised on tasks adapted from neuroscience, cognitive, and developmental disciplines. These studies share careful operationalization of the executive process under study and draw on cognitive or neuroscience models or both (Smidts et al., Rennie et al., and Senn et al.), or use a more empirical approach through psychometrics (Isquith et al., Senn et al., and Espy, McDiarmid, Cwik, Stalets, Hamby, & Senn, this issue).

Another purpose of the selected articles is to highlight the central role of executive control in outcomes that matter in the proximal day-to-day lives of young children. Although brain–behavior relations are interesting in their own right, and certainly important scientifically, it is the behavior–behavior relations (Fletcher & Taylor, 1984), that is, relations between cognitive processes and outcomes, such as behavior or academic achievement, that concern parents, educators, and policymakers. Isquith et al. (this issue) focus on behaviors in the everyday context, as conceived by both parents and teachers. Espy et al. (this issue) relate differing executive processes to early proficiency in mathematics, as measured by a widely used, standardized clinical instrument. These studies represent a first step in understanding the complex dynamics that underlie more proximal outcomes, such as behavior and academic achievement, in young children.

In a related vein, the final goal was to illustrate how executive control is altered by various CNS disorders of childhood, namely traumatic brain injury in the Ewing-Cobbs, Prasad, Landry, Kramer, and DeLeon article (this issue), and exposure to low levels of lead in the environment in the Canfield, Gendle, and Cory-Slechta article (this issue). In both articles, the paradigms used to assess executive control draw heavily from developmental cognitive neuroscience fields to effectively illustrate substantive variations in outcome. Despite the clinical orientation of these articles, the specific tasks chosen are driven by empirical theory. Clearly, even in investigations with young children, the time is past for the practice of administering a large battery of standardized tests and looking for differences post hoc. Isquith et al. (this issue) take a different tack, empirically contrasting the ratings of everyday executive behavior among children with various clinical conditions using analysis of scale profiles.

These seven articles represent a sampling of the exciting findings that are beginning to emerge from studies of executive control in young children. Clearly, much work remains to be done to truly explicate the developmental trajectories of the differing facets of executive control in this age range, with the next logical step being the use of longitudinal designs. One cautionary note: Because of the unique assessment methods used to assess executive control in young children, it will be necessary to formally establish the relation to subsequent abilities at school age and beyond. It may appear, for example, that the executive abilities required to complete the DCCS task at age 4 are isomorphic with those required for adequate performance on the WCST at age 8. In reality, the task demands and the organization of executive abilities may differ both qualitatively and quantitiatively, rendering a level of complexity that makes such relations less than intuitive and meriting careful study.

Although the studies here used empirical or strong theoretical justifications or both for task selection to test specific hypotheses, further refinement of the relations between executive tasks and executive constructs is necessary. Clearly, these complex tasks are multifactorial, that is, different abilities are required for smooth, purposeful, goal-directed behavior. What remains to be clarified is whether executive abilities are truly fractionated, or whether differing task demands engage a unitary executive control process—or some combination therein. In children, and particularly young children, where maturation is so rapid, the overlay of developmental change makes this issue more complicated. In the adult neuroimaging literature, it is clear that task characteristics, such as salience, novelty, reward, expectancy, affect the degree of frontal engagement (e.g., Barch et al., 1997; Casey et al., 2001; Petersen, van Mier, Fiez, & Raichle, 1998; Rogers, Owen, Middleton, Williams, & Pickard, 1999). In children, it is difficult to fully equate tasks with respect to these issues, posing unique challenges in the measurement of executive abilities in the developmental context.

Finally, there remain significant barriers to determining the true developmental brain representations of behavior in this age range. With the current scanning set-ups, young children are not suitable candidates to participate in functional magnetic resonance imaging (fMRI) studies that have expanded so elegantly this knowledge base in adults and even in children. High-density event-related (brain) potential recordings may offer the best hope currently, although the spatial precision is not ideal, particularly considering that fMRI findings show that cognitive functions may be subserved by more diffuse brain areas in school-age children in comparison to adults (e.g., Casey et al., 1995). Nonetheless, these seven articles represent real advances in explicating the nature of executive control in young children.

ACKNOWLEDGMENTS

This research was supported, in part, by the Pediatric Neuropsychology/Developmental Cognitive Neuroscience Award from the Rita Rudel Foundation; a research grant from the Blowitz–Ridgeway Foundation; and the Special Research Program award from the Southern Illinois University Office of Research Development and Administration.

REFERENCES

Barch, D., Braver, T., Nystrom, L., Forman, S., Noll, D., & Cohen, J. (1997). Dissociating working memory from task difficulty in human prefrontal cortex. *Neuropsychologia, 35,* 1373–1380.

Canfield, R. L., Gendle, M. H., & Cory-Slechta, D. A. (2004/this issue). Impaired neuropsychological functioning in lead-exposed children. *Developmental Neuropsychology, 26,* 513–540.

Casey, B. J., Cohen, J., Jezzard. P., Turner, R., Noll, D. C., Trainor, R. J., et al. (1995). Activation of the prefrontal cortex in children during a non-spatial working memory task with functional MRI. *Neuroimage, 2,* 221–229.

Casey, B. J., Forman, S., Franzen, P., Berkowitz, A., Braver, T., Nystrom, L, et al. (2001). Sensitivity of prefrontal cortex to changes in target probability: A functional MRI study. *Human Brain Mapping, 13,* 26–33.

Dennis, M. (1987). Using language to parse the young damaged brain. *Journal of Clinical and Experimental Neuropsychology, 9,* 723–753.

Diamond, A. (1985). Development of the ability to use recall to guide action, as indicated by infants' performance on AB. *Child Development, 56,* 868–883.

Eslinger, P. J., & Damasio, A. R. (1985). Severe disturbance of higher cognition after bilateral frontal lobe ablation: Patient EVR. *Neurology, 35,* 1731–1741.

Espy, K. A. (1997). The shape school: Assessing executive function in preschool children. *Developmental Neuropsychology, 13,* 495–499.

Espy, K. A., Kaufmann, P. M., Glisky, M. L., & McDiarmid, M. D. (2001). New procedures to assess executive functions in preschool children. *Clinical Neuropsychologist, 15,* 46–58.

Espy, K. A., McDiarmid, M. M., Cwik, M. F., Stalets, M. M., Hamby, A., & Senn, T. E. (2004/this issue). The contribution of executive functions to emergent mathematic skills in preschool children. *Developmental Neuropsychology, 26,* 465–486.

Ewing-Cobbs, L., Prasad, M. R., Landry, S. H., Kramer, L., & DeLeon, R. (2004/this issue). Executive functions following traumatic brain injury in young children: A preliminary analysis. *Developmental Neuropsychology, 26,* 487–512.

Flavell, J. H. (1999). Cognitive development: Children's knowledge about the mind. *Annual Review of Psychology, 50,* 21–45.

Fletcher, J. M. (1996). Executive functions in children: Introduction to the special series. *Developmental Neuropsychology, 12,* 1–3.

Fletcher, J. M., & Taylor, H. G. (1984). Neuropsychological approaches to children: Towards a developmental neuropsychology. *Journal of Clinical Neuropsychology, 6,* 39–56.

Goldman, P. S. (1974). An alternative to developmental plasticity: Heterology of CNS structures in infants and adults. In D. Stein, J. Rosen, & N. Butters (Eds.), *Plasticity and recovery of function in the central nervous system* (pp. 149–174). New York: Academic.

Goldman-Rakic, P. S. (1987). Circuitry of primate prefrontal cortex and regulation of behavior by representational knowledge. In F. Plum & V. Mountcastle (Eds.), *Handbook of physiology* (Vol. 5, pp. 373–417). Bethesda, MD: American Physiological Society.

Heaton, R. K., Chelune, G. J., Talley, J. L., Kay, G. G., & Curtiss, G. (1993). *Wisconsin Card Sorting Test manual.* Odessa, FL: Psychological Assessment Resources.

Isquith, P. K., Gioia, G. A., & Espy, K. A. (2004/this issue). Executive function in preschool children: Examination through everyday behavior. *Developmental Neuropsychology, 26,* 403–422.

Milner, B. (1963). Effects of different brain lesions on card sorting. *Archives of Neurology, 9,* 90–100.

Petersen, S., van Mier, H., Fiez, J., & Raichle, M. (1998). The effects of practice on the functional anatomy of task performance. *Proceedings of the National Academy of Sciences, 95,* 853–860.

Rennie, D. A. C., Bull, R., & Diamond, A. (2004/this issue). Executive functioning in preschoolers: Reducing the inhibitory demands of the Dimensional Change Card Sort Task. *Developmental Neuropsychology, 26,* 423–443.

Rogers, R., Owen, A., Middleton, H., Williams, E., & Pickard, J. (1999). Choosing between small, likely rewards and large unlikely rewards activates inferior and orbital prefrontal cortex. *Journal of Neuroscience, 19,* 9029–9038.

Smidts, D. P., Jacobs, R., & Anderson, V. (2004/this issue). The Object Classification Task for Children (OCTC): A measure of concept generation and mental flexibility in early childhood. *Developmental Neuropsychology, 26,* 385–401.

Senn, T. E., Espy, K. A., & Kaufmann, P. M. (2004/this issue). Using path analysis to understand executive function organization in preschool children. *Developmental Neuropsychology, 26,* 445–464.

Zelazo, P. D., Reznick, J. S., & Pinion, D. E. (1995). Response control and the execution of verbal roles. *Developmental Psychology, 31,* 508–517.

DEVELOPMENTAL NEUROPSYCHOLOGY, 26(1), 385–401
Copyright © 2004, Lawrence Erlbaum Associates, Inc.

The Object Classification Task for Children (OCTC): A Measure of Concept Generation and Mental Flexibility in Early Childhood

Diana P. Smidts
Faculty of Psychology and Education
Department of Clinical Neuropsychology
VU University, Amsterdam, The Netherlands

Rani Jacobs
Department of Psychology
University of Melbourne, Victoria, Australia
Murdoch Children's Research Institute
Parkville, Victoria, Australia
Royal Children's Hospital
Parkville, Victoria, Australia

Vicki Anderson
Department of Psychology
University of Melbourne, Victoria, Australia
Murdoch Children's Research Institute
Parkville, Victoria, Australia

In this study, the development of concept generation and mental flexibility was investigated in 84 Australian children between 3 and 7 years of age, using the Object Classification Task for Children (OCTC), a newly developed executive function test for use with young children. On this task, which was adapted from the Concept Generation Test (Levine, Stuss, & Milberg, 1995) and the Concept Generation Test for

---

Requests for reprints should be sent to Diana P. Smidts, Faculty of Psychology and Education, Department of Clinical Neuropsychology, VU University, Amsterdam, The Netherlands. E-mail: dp.smidts@psy.vu.nl

Children (Jacobs, Anderson, & Harvey, 2001), children were asked to categorize 6 plastic toys according to 3 predetermined groupings (i.e., color, size, and function). The test included 3 performance levels, each providing increasing levels of structure for the child. Findings from the OCTC show meaningful age-related changes in performance across age groups, with older children being less dependent on additional structure to complete the task, in comparison to younger children. Furthermore, findings from this study suggest that the ability to generate concepts emerges between 3 and 4 years of age, continuing to develop beyond the age of 7 years. A developmental spurt in cognitive flexibility was observed around 4 to 5 years of age, with refinement of this capacity occurring between 5 and 7 years of age. Results suggest that the OCTC is a useful measure of conceptual reasoning skills in early childhood.

The term *executive function* is often used as a label for a set of psychological processes necessary for adaptive and future-oriented behavior. Although cognitive capacities included vary across definitions, the construct of executive function generally denotes a range of "high-level" thought processes, such as planning, problem solving, initiation of action, self-monitoring, inhibition of automatic responses, and self-regulation. These psychological processes allow the individual to coordinate the activities required to attain a goal: to formulate intentions, develop action plans, implement strategies to execute those plans, monitor performance, and evaluate actions (e.g., Glosser & Goodglass, 1990; Levin et al., 1991; Luria, 1973; Stuss, 1992; Stuss & Benson, 1987). In addition, executive skills are also implicated in social–emotional processes, such as the modulation of emotions, personal and social decision making, perspective taking, affect, and social self-awareness (e.g., Anderson, Bechara, Damasio, Tranel, & Damasio, 1999; Anderson, Damasio, Tranel, & Damasio, 2000; Barrash, Tranel, & Anderson, 2000; Benton, 1991; Damasio, 1998; Eslinger, Biddle, & Grattan, 1997; Eslinger & Damasio, 1985; Eslinger, Grattan, Damasio, & Damasio, 1992; Stuss & Alexander, 2000). Thus, executive function is an umbrella term that encompasses multiple functional processes that are necessary for adaptive and future-oriented behavior.

Conceptual reasoning skills, which fall within the domain of executive function, are required in a number of cognitive activities, such as distinguishing what is relevant from what is irrelevant, following general rules, and making use of existing knowledge in a new situation. According to Siegler (1991), conceptual processes encompass the capacity to perceive an abstract concept, or set of concepts, and then shift flexibly between competing concepts or dimensions. Findings from case studies and neuroimaging research suggest that these processes are largely mediated by the frontal lobes, in particular the dorsolateral region of the prefrontal cortex (e.g., Lombardi et al., 1999; Stuss et al., 2000). It is believed that both left and right dorsolateral regions of the prefrontal cortex are involved in cognitive flexibility (e.g., Alexander & Stuss, 2000; Grattan & Eslinger, 1991); however, lateralization of shifting behavior has also been observed. For example, decreased verbal fluency has been associated with damage to the left dorsolateral area (e.g., Borkowski, Benton, & Spreen, 1967; Butler, Rorsman, Hill, & Tuma, 1993; Laine, 1988), whereas impaired performance in nonverbal divergent thinking has been associated with damage to the right dorsolateral area (e.g, Guilford, Christensen, Merrifield, & Wilson, 1978).

The Wisconsin Card Sorting Test (WCST; Berg, 1948; Grant & Berg, 1948) is a neuropsychological task, which has been widely used to assess cognitive processes that are believed to be mediated by the dorsolateral prefrontal cortex (e.g., Cicerone, Lazar, & Shapiro, 1983; Lombardi et al., 1999; Nelson, 1976; Stuss et al., 2000). Other tests of conceptual skills include the Category Test (Halstead, 1947; Reitan & Wolfson, 1993), Identification of Common Objects (commonly referred to as the "Twenty Questions Test"; Laine & Butters, 1982), Raven's Progressive Matrices (Raven, 1960; Raven, Court, & Raven, 1976), the Color Form Sorting Test (Goldstein & Scheerer, 1941, 1953; Weigl, 1941), and the Contingency Naming Test (Taylor, Albo, Phebus, Sachs, & Bierl, 1987). Whereas some of these tests focus primarily on abstract concept formation (i.e., Category Test and Raven's Progressive Matrices), others also include a requirement to shift between competing concepts (i.e., Contingency Naming Test, Twenty Questions Test, and WCST).

A number of traditional adult-based tasks have also been applied in child neuropsychological studies to investigate the development of conceptual reasoning skills in children. Using the WCST, for example, Chelune and Baer (1986) found that children between 6 and 10 years showed marked improvements in their performance, with children older than 10 years performing at adult level. These findings were replicated by Welsh, Pennington, and Groisser (1991), who demonstrated that adult-level skill on the WCST was attained by age 10, with considerable improvement occurring between the ages of 7 and 8 years. Similar results were reported by Levin et al. (1991), who found that the number of more efficient and goal-directed "constraint-seeking" questions on the Twenty Questions Test increased significantly between the ages of 7 and 15 years. Taken together, these findings support the proposition that conceptual reasoning skills develop rapidly during the middle childhood years.

Although a number of studies have investigated conceptual reasoning skills in middle childhood, the development of these cognitive processes in children younger than 7 years has received relatively little attention. Interest in this area has recently burgeoned; however, there remains a paucity of appropriate measures to assess concept generation and cognitive flexibility in young children. Most traditional measures that purport to tap these capacities have been developed for older children and adults. As a result, many are inappropriate or irrelevant for use with children younger than 7 years, where many lower order skills have not yet emerged (e.g., language, literacy, number skills). Adult measures often require a number of complex instructions, thereby placing a large demand on working memory capacity and receptive language {151} skills that are relatively immature in young children. Furthermore, traditional measures are not particularly sensitive to developmental changes in early childhood (e.g., Chelune & Baer, 1986), and therefore, little normative data with respect to the performance of young children are available. Recently, a number of researchers have attempted to overcome these difficulties by developing new, developmentally appropriate assessment tools to evaluate the maturation of conceptual reasoning skills in young children. For example, to investigate inhibition and switching processes in preschoolers, Espy (1997) used the Shape School, a storybook that requires the child to name figures, according to particular (inhibition and shifting) rules. Regarding switching efficiency, Espy found that performance improved significantly between 4 and 5 years of age. Similar findings were reported by Jacques and Zelazo (2001), who investigated switching processes in children between 3 and 5 years using a task called the Flexible Item Selection Task (FIST). This test requires children to select two cards from a set of three cards, according to a common dimension (i.e., size, number, shape, or color). Then, using the same set of cards, children have to select a different pair of cards that match each other on a different dimension. Jacques and Zelazo found that 3-year-olds had difficulty identifying a common dimension in two nonidentical cards, whereas 4-year-olds performed as well as 5-year-olds on this task. Selecting a different pair of cards (so that one card needed to be sorted according to two different dimensions), however, appeared to be very difficult for 4-year-olds, with 5-year-olds outperforming them on this task. Thus, it appears that these skills are developing rapidly during the preschool period, with children between the ages of 3 and 4 years becoming capable of identifying a common dimension in two nonidentical items, and the ability to switch between different concepts emerging after the age of 4 years.

Although the studies by Espy (1997) and Jacques and Zelazo (2001) have provided important insights about the developmental course of conceptual reasoning skills in preschoolers, there is still a gap in our understanding of how these cognitive processes develop across the relatively broad age range of early childhood—from age 3 through age 7. The aim of this study was to investigate the development of conceptual reasoning in children between 3 and 7 years, using a new task with parameters appropriate for children in this age range. This test, the Object Classification Task for Children (OCTC) was based on the paradigms of the Concept Generation Test (CGT; Levine, Stuss, & Milberg, 1995) and the Concept Generation Test for Children (CGT–C; Jacobs, Anderson, & Harvey, 2001), which was developed for children between 7 and 15 years. In these conceptual reasoning tasks, participants are required to generate a number of "sorts" according to some common feature. Whereas the CGT is a pencil-and-paper task of sorting behavior, the task devised by Jacobs et al. uses pictorial stimuli that can be manipulated by children. In this task, children are required to sort pictures according to six predetermined groupings of varying complexity, such as animal habitat and direction of lines. As with the CGT, the CGT–C has three conditions with increasing structure to allow for greater fractionation of the underlying cognitive processes contributing to conceptual reasoning skills, including sorting behavior and mental flexibility. Although the OCTC is similar to these concept-generation tasks, it differs in the following ways: (a) The OCTC uses plastic toys, which can be manipulated by the child and are thought to be more appealing to young children than diagrams or graphics; (b) it has two practice trials, which allow for investigating whether children are able to make two groups without the requirement of identifying a common feature; (c) the OCTC contains two different settings (i.e., a setting with four toys and a setting with six toys), which allow for the examination of conceptual reasoning skills in very young children; and (d) it has only three predetermined groupings (i.e., color, size, and function). It was hypothesized that younger children would perform more poorly on the task, due to the relative immaturity of conceptual reasoning skills. It was also predicted that there would be age-related differences in the ability to generate concepts and in the capacity to shift between concepts. Finally, it was postulated that older children would require less additional structure than younger children to perform successfully on this task.

METHOD

Participants

The sample consisted of 84 children, aged between 3 years 1 month and 7 years 9 months. This sample was divided into five age groups: 3-year-olds (n = 19), 4-year-olds (n = 19), 5-year-olds (n = 14), 6-year-olds (n = 22), and 7-year-olds (n = 10). Children were selected from several local child care centers, kindergartens, and primary schools in the metropolitan area of Melbourne, Australia. Inclusion criteria were: (a) aged between 3 years 0 months and 7 years 11 months at time of testing; (b) no previous history of developmental, neurological, or psychiatric disorder; and (c) English as a first language. Informed consent, based on agency ethics procedures, was obtained from parents or guardians of children who participated in the project. From all families approached, 68% agreed to participate in the study. Table 1 outlines the demographic characteristics of the sample.

TABLE 1
Demographic Characteristics of Sample

Age Group	n	Number of Boys	Age in months		Socioeconomic Status	
			M	SD	M	SD
3-year-olds	19	10	42	2	4.4	1.5
4-year-olds	19	10	53	3	4.6	1.1
5-year-olds	14	7	67	3	4.4	1.1
6-year-olds	22	13	77	3	4.2	1.1
7-year-olds	10	4	89	3	3.9	1.0

Note.   No significant group differences were found regarding gender or socioeconomic status.

Socioeconomic status (SES) was obtained using Daniel's Scale of Occupational Prestige (Daniel, 1983), a widely used measure to assess the class position of occupations in Australian society. This scale rates SES from 1 to 7, with a lower score representing a higher SES.

Materials and Instructions

Practice trials.   As a practice trial and introduction to the task, children were given two distinct bathtub toys (i.e., a yellow mouse with blue ears and a purple dinosaur with orange toes). After the child had examined the toys, the experimenter showed the child two toys identical to the first two and said

> See these toys? They are the same as the ones you have there, you see? The toys that are the same go together. Can you put the toys that go together on this side of the table (examiner points to one side of the table) and the other two that go together on that side of the table (examiner points to other side of the table)?

If the child did not understand these instructions, the examiner helped the child by asking

> So can you tell me which toys are the same? (Examiner waits for child to respond.) See, they go together because they are the same. And the other two also go together because they are the same as well. Now put these toys (examiner points to one pair of toys) on this side of the table and put the other two toys on that side of the table.

After the child had correctly placed the two matching pairs on either side of the table, the examiner showed the child two different sets of toys (i.e., a brown bear wearing a green hat and a blue fish with white eyes) and provided the following instructions, "Okay, now let's do the same thing with these toys. Can you put the ones that go together on this side of the table and the other two that are the same on that side of the table?" These practice trials were always presented with the same pairs of toys in the same order across all children in the sample.

Test trials.   After the two practice trials, the examiner showed the child six plastic toys that could be sorted into two groups in three different ways (i.e., on the basis of color, size, or function). The six toys were a big red plane, a big red car, a big yellow car, a small red plane, a small yellow plane, and a small yellow car. The examiner provided the following instructions:

Okay, now let's do the same thing with these toys. Can you make two groups for me? But something has to be the same about the toys in each group. Can you put one group on this side of the table and the other ones that go together on that side of the table?

If the child did not know what to do, or sorted the toys incorrectly, the examiner removed two toys, so that there were only four toys left (i.e., all cars). The OCTC was then administered using four toys, which could be sorted according to color or size. Thus, the OCTC could be administered with either six toys (Setting 1) or four toys (Setting 2), depending on the child's understanding and execution of task instructions when first shown the test toys.

Design and Procedure

Children who met the selection criteria described previously were administered the OCTC on an individual basis in a single session at their respective child care center, kindergarten, or primary school.

The OCTC included three conditions, each providing increasing levels of structure for the child: (a) free generation, where the child was required to generate categories with no clues or structure; (b) identification, where the examiner constructed the category for the child, and the child was asked to describe the rule used for the sort; and (c) explicit cueing, where the child received explicit instructions to group the toys. In the CGT–C (Jacobs et al., 2001), there was also a cued generation condition, where the child was given the rule for the sort and was asked to construct the categories according to that rule. In the OCTC, however, this condition was omitted, as the rule given by the examiner had to be provided in a manner similar to the explicit cueing condition so the child could understand the instructions. The level of structure within the two possible settings (i.e., six toys or four toys) was considered an indication of the child's capacity for conceptual reasoning.

Free generation condition.   After the child had grouped the toys, he or she was asked, "So, can you tell me what's the same about these toys? [Examiner points to a group of toys.] And what's the same about these toys? [Examiner points to other group of toys.]" Responses were recorded verbatim. In the free generation condition, the child received 3 points for sorting correctly and 1 point for a correct verbal response. If the child did not group the toys according to one of the three dimensions, a score of 0 was given. If the child sorted the toys correctly, but gave an incorrect verbal response, a score of 3 was given. After the child had generated two groups, the examiner mixed up the toys, and the child was asked, "Can you make two groups for me again? But now something else has to be the same about the toys." After the child had grouped the toys according to a second dimension, he or she was once again asked, "So, what's the same about these toys? And what's the same about the other toys?" If children were able to correctly sort the toys by all three predetermined groupings, the task was deemed complete. The total number of points available for a setting with four toys is 8 (i.e., 6 points for two correct sorts and 2 points for the correct verbal responses). The total number of points available for a setting with six toys is 12 (i.e., 9 points for three correct sorts and 3 points for three correct verbal responses).

Identification condition.   Children who were unable to correctly sort the toys using all three predetermined groupings in the free generation condition proceeded to the identification condition. In this condition, more structure was provided by constructing the category for the child and asking him or her to describe the rule used for the sort. Any of the groupings not correctly sorted in the free generation condition were administered in the identification condition. The examiner generated the groupings, and the child was asked, "See these two groups of toys? Can you tell me what's the same about these toys? [Examiner points to a group of toys.] And what's the same about these? [Examiner points to other group of toys.]" Responses were recorded verbatim. In the identification condition, the child received 2 points for a correct verbal response. If the child gave an incorrect verbal response, a score of 0 was given.

Explicit cueing condition.   Children who failed to identify all sorts provided by the examiner proceeded to the explicit cueing condition, in which any of the groupings not correctly identified were administered. For instance, if the child did not correctly identify the sort according to color in the identification condition, the examiner asked the child, "Can you put all the red ones on this side of the table and all the yellow ones on that side of the table?" A score of 1 was given for each correct sort. If the child was not able to sort the toys, a score of 0 was given.

Statistical Analysis

A one-way analysis of variance was employed to investigate the main effect of age on the total number of points scored on the OCTC. Post hoc Tukey least significant difference pairwise comparisons were conducted to examine differences in performance between age groups. To further explore the relation between age and the total number of points on the OCTC, a linear trend analysis was performed. A frequency analysis was also conducted for each condition within each shifting attempt.

RESULTS

All of the children, including the 3-year-olds, passed the second practice trial of the OCTC. Although some children did not understand the instructions the first time they were given, they were able to successfully complete the second trial once the examiner had provided further instruction.

TABLE 2
Means, Standard Deviations, Ranges, *F* Ratio, and *p* Value of Total of
Points on the Object Classification Task for Children Across Age Groups

Variables	Age Group					*F Ratio*	*p Value*
	3	*4*	*5*	*6*	*7*		
M	3.3	3.8	7.0	8.2	10.5	$F(4, 79) = 27.98$	.000
SD	2.3	2.7	2.0	2.1	1.6		
Range	0–7	0–7	4–10	5–12	7–12		

Effects of Age

Table 2 presents the results for the total of points, summed over all conditions, on the OCTC across age groups.

It was found that there was a main effect of age, $F(4, 79) = 27.98, p < .01$. Thus, it appears that performance on the OCTC increases as a function of increasing age. In particular, post hoc analysis revealed a significant increase in mean total of points between the 3- and 5-year-olds ($p < .01$) and between the 5- and 7-year-olds ($p < .01$). Figure 1 shows the data points for performance on the OCTC.

A Pearson correlation of the data revealed that age in months and total of points were significantly related, $r = .75, n = 84, p < .01$, two-tailed. A regression analysis was performed to explore the underlying trend of the relation between age and total of points. It was found that this relation can be expressed by a straight line that underlies this analysis. The equation for this line is given by: $Y = 0.17x - 4.49$, where Y is the outcome determined by this equation, and x is the age in months.

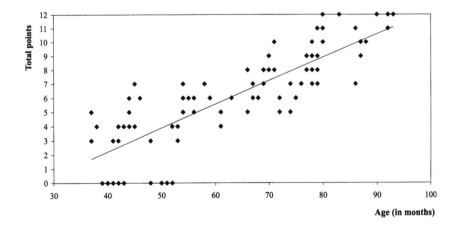

FIGURE 1   Data points and line of best fit for performance on the OCTC.

Thus, there is a linear trend for the data of the OCTC, with increasing performance as a function of increasing age.

Frequency Analysis

Although all children older than 4 years were able to sort six toys (Setting 1), some 3- and 4-year-olds were administered the OCTC with four toys (Setting 2). Figure 2 presents the proportion of 3- and 4-year-old children across the two settings of the OCTC.

There were 7 out of 19 children (37%) from the 3-year-old group who could sort the toys within a setting with six objects. Of the 12 children in Setting 2 (i.e., four toys), only 5 children (42%) could sort the toys correctly. As shown in Figure 2, 47% of the 4-year-olds could sort the toys in a setting with six objects. Of the 10 children in Setting 2, only 5 children (50%) could sort the toys correctly. Thus, for most children in the 3- and 4-year-old groups, the OCTC appeared to be too difficult using six toys. When the OCTC was administered with four toys, about half of the children could sort the toys correctly. However, none of these children were able to group the objects for a second time, according to a different feature.

Although all children older than 4 years were able to group six objects, when asked to group the toys for a second time, some children were dependent on structure provided by the examiner (i.e., identification or explicit condition). Figure 3 shows the proportion of children in each condition for the first switch (i.e., second sort) across age groups.

As shown in Figure 3, most 3- and 4-year-olds required explicit directions to group the toys for a second time and were not able to sort the toys independently. It must be noted that the only 3-year-old who grouped the objects without additional

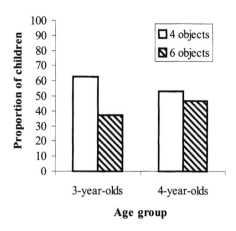

FIGURE 2 Proportion of 3- and 4-year-old children across settings of the OCTC.

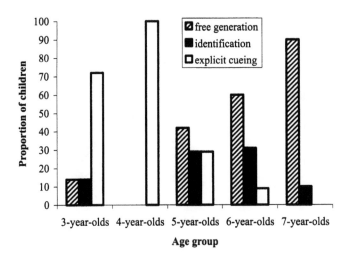

FIGURE 3   Proportion of children in each condition for first switch on the OCTC across age groups.

structure (i.e., free generation condition) appeared to be unaware that he had sorted the objects correctly. Although all 4-year-olds required explicit instructions to group the toys, 5-year-olds required less structure to do so. In particular, 42% of the children in this age group could sort the objects without additional structure, 29% of the children could identify a second concept when the examiner had grouped the toys for them, and the remaining 29% of the children required explicit instructions. A chi-square analysis revealed that there were significantly more children in the 7-year-old group who could sort the toys independently, when compared to the 5-year-olds, χ^2 (1, $n = 24$) = 5.54, $p < .05$. No other significant differences were found across age groups or conditions.

Figure 4 shows the proportion of children in each condition for the second switch (i.e., third sort) across age groups.

As shown in Figure 4, all children from the 3- and 4-year-old groups required explicit instructions to group the toys for a third time. In contrast, older children required less structure to perform this task. In particular, a chi-square analysis showed that there were significantly more 7-year-olds who could group the toys independently, when compared to 5-year-olds, χ^2 (1, $n = 24$) = 5.71, $p < .05$. No other significant differences were found for any of the age groups or conditions.

A few children ($n = 5$) generated valid sorts that were not included in the three predetermined groupings. These sorting categories included little wheels–big wheels and moving wheels–nonmoving wheels. These categories were considered as correct groupings. No child generated extra sorts in addition to correctly generating all three predetermined sorts.

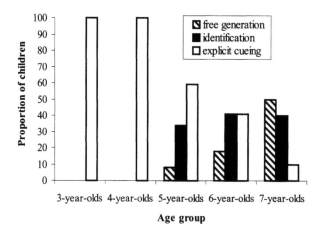

FIGURE 4   Proportion of children in each condition for second switch on OCTC across age groups.

DISCUSSION

Although several studies have investigated the development of conceptual reasoning skills in children older than 7 years, relatively little is known about how these processes mature in younger children. The assessment of conceptual reasoning skills in this age group has been hampered by the paucity of appropriate neuropsychological measures to assess these skills in young children. In this study, the development of concept generation and mental flexibility was investigated in children between 3 and 7 years, using the OCTC, a newly developed executive function test for use with young children. On the OCTC, which was adapted from the CGT (Levine et al., 1995) and the CGT–C (Jacobs et al., 2001), children were required to sort six nonidentical toys according to three predetermined groupings (i.e., color, size, and function). Findings from this study confirm our hypotheses and suggest that the OCTC is a useful measure of conceptual reasoning skills in young children. In particular, the results from this task reveal age-related changes in overall performance across the entire age range, providing a clear picture of developmental changes in concept generation and mental flexibility during early childhood. The two settings of the OCTC (i.e., four toys and six toys), and the use of different levels of structure within these settings, allowed for a detailed analysis of the performance of children between 3 and 7 years. The greatest improvement in performance was observed between the 4- and 5-year-old groups, indicating a rapid developmental progression of concept generation and mental flexibility in the period between 4 and 5 years of age.

Even the youngest children passed the practice trials, indicating that they were capable of grouping four objects according to overall appearance, although the majority of 3-year-olds experienced difficulty sorting the test toys according to a particular feature. This finding suggests that 3-year-olds have difficulty identifying a common feature within a group of nonidentical objects. Even when the number of dimensions was reduced to two (i.e., color and size) in a setting with only four toys, most children from the 3-year-old group were unable to perform the task. In contrast, almost half of the children in the 4-year-old group could identify a common dimension within a group of six toys, suggesting that 4-year-old children have less difficulty generating concepts, when compared to 3-year-olds. The results from this study show that all children older than 4 years were able to sort six toys according to a certain feature, indicating that these children are able to identify a common dimension within a group of different objects. Similar findings were reported by Jacques and Zelazo (2001), who used the FIST to investigate abstraction and cognitive flexibility in preschoolers. Jacques and Zelazo showed that, despite good performance on the criterial trials, where children were required to match identical cards, 3-year-olds performed poorly when required to identify a common dimension in two nonidentical cards. Jacques and Zelazo reported that, in contrast to 3-year-olds, most 4-year-olds experienced no difficulty recognizing how two nonidentical cards could match according to a particular feature. Thus, between the ages of 3 and 4 years, there appears to be a developmental change in the ability to abstract information from nonidentical items. This finding is consistent with the notion that young children primarily use concrete information as the basis for categorization (e.g., Flavell, 1985; Inhelder & Piaget, 1964). It is believed that it is not until later in life that categorization occurs on the basis of more abstract, conceptual–lexical information (e.g., Bruner, Olver, & Greenfield, 1966).

The results of the OCTC showed that, when required to spontaneously shift between concepts, none of the 4-year-old children were successful. All children from this age group required explicit instructions to group the toys, suggesting that 4-year-olds are unable to group six toys according to a second, different dimension. The majority of 5-year-olds were able to identify a second concept, albeit with additional structure provided by the examiner. In their study on abstraction and cognitive flexibility, Jacques and Zelazo (2001) found that 4-year-olds did worse on the shifting component of the FIST when compared to 5-year-olds, in keeping with our finding that there appears to be a developmental progression in mental flexibility between the ages of 4 and 5 years.

The OCTC was also used to assess children's ability to shift multiple times between different dimensions. Results from this study show that older children require less structure in completing the task when compared to younger children, suggesting a refinement of cognitive flexibility skills between the ages of 5 and 7 years. A better performance on the OCTC is reflected by the ability to shift between an increasing number of concepts, and to generate a dimension more complex than the fundamental concepts of color and shape. However, even the oldest children in our sample experienced difficulty generating a third concept without any additional structure provided, although the majority of these children could independently group the toys according to a second dimension. Thus, although 7-year-olds may be able to shift between *two* concepts, they appear to experience difficulty when they are required to shift between *three* concepts. These findings suggest that conceptual reasoning skills continue to develop beyond the age of 7 years. Support for this notion has come from a recent study conducted by Jacobs et al. (2001), who investigated the development of conceptual reasoning in children between the ages of 7 and 15 years, using the CGT–C, a similar, but more complex task than the OCTC. It was found that unstructured sorting and shifting was most difficult for children younger than 9 years, with only the oldest age group performing in line with adult expectations. Thus, it appears that the developmental course of conceptual reasoning follows a progression that is characterized by periods of growth spurts between 4 and 5 years and between 7 and 9 years. The ability to shift, as measured by the OCTC, appears to undergo different developmental gains when compared to other executive processes, such as inhibition, where growth spurts have primarily been identified in children younger than 6 years (Smidts & Anderson, 2003).

It must be noted that the failure of 3-year-old children to group the test toys could also be due to limited knowledge about the semantic components (i.e., color, size, and function) of the objects. Older children may perform better on the task because they have an established understanding of physical and functional properties of objects. Ample evidence exists for the notion that during early childhood, children acquire a range of linguistic capacities, such as increased vocabulary and use of grammatical rules, which are believed to be key processes in efficient functioning and essential for learning (e.g., Chen-Hafteck, 1997; Farrar & Maag, 2002; D. Molfese & V. Molfese, 2000). A study investigating the relation between verbal responses and sorting behavior on the OCTC is currently in progress.

Alternatively, younger children may have experienced difficulty shifting between concepts due to the immaturity of other skills within the domain of executive function. For example, older children may perform better on the task because they are able to selectively attend to the features of the objects and exercise more inhibitory control over their behavior, skills that are necessary to shift between concepts. Several developmental studies have shown that during early childhood, children become more capable in exercising inhibitory control over their behavioral actions (e.g., Becker, Isaac, & Hynd, 1987; Passler, Isaac, & Hynd, 1985). More research with the OCTC, however, is required to investigate these issues.

In summary, analysis of age trends in performance on the OCTC identifies a developmental course of conceptual reasoning skills in early childhood. In particular, results from this study suggest that the ability to generate concepts emerges between the ages of 3 and 4 years, continuing to develop beyond the age of 7 years.

Further, a developmental spurt in mental flexibility was observed around 4 to 5 years of age, with refinement of this capacity occurring between 5 and 7 years of age. Findings from this study show that the OCTC, which was specifically designed for use with children between 3 and 7 years, and did not show any floor or ceiling effects, appears to be a useful tool for the investigation of concept generation and mental flexibility in early childhood, and it may be a useful adjunct to the paucity of executive function tests available for this age range.

ACKNOWLEDGMENTS

This research was supported, in part, by a scholarship from the Murdoch Children's Research Institute in Melbourne, Australia, to Diana P. Smidts. This work was part of a PhD research project, which was conducted by Diana P. Smidts.

REFERENCES

Alexander, M. P., & Stuss, D. T. (2000). Disorders of frontal lobe functioning. *Seminars in Neurology, 20,* 427–437.

Anderson, S. W., Bechara, A., Damasio, H., Tranel, D., & Damasio, A. (1999). Impairment of social and moral behavior related to early damage in human prefrontal cortex. *Nature Neuroscience, 2,* 1032–1037.

Anderson, S. W., Damasio, H., Tranel, D., & Damasio, A. (2000). Long-term sequelae of prefrontal cortex damage acquired in early childhood. *Developmental Neuropsychology, 18,* 281–296.

Barrash, J., Tranel, D., & Anderson, S. W. (2000). Acquired personality disturbances associated with bilateral damage to the ventromedial prefrontal region. *Developmental Neuropsychology, 18,* 355–381.

Becker, M. G., Isaac, W., & Hynd, G. (1987). Neuropsychological development of non-verbal behaviors attributed to the frontal lobes. *Developmental Neuropsychology, 3,* 275–298.

Benton, A. L. (1991). Prefrontal injury and behavior in children. *Developmental Neuropsychology, 7,* 275–281.

Berg, E. A. (1948). A simple objective technique for measuring flexibility in thinking. *Journal of General Psychology, 39,* 15–22.

Borkowski, J. G., Benton, A. L., & Spreen, O. (1967). Word fluency and brain damage. *Neuropsychologia, 5,* 135–140.

Bruner, J., Olver, R. R., & Greenfield, P. M. (1966). *Studies in cognitive growth.* New York: Wiley.

Butler, R. W., Rorsman, I., Hill, J. M., & Tuma, R. (1993). The effects of frontal brain impairment on fluency: Simple and complex paradigms. *Neuropsychology, 7,* 519–529.

Chelune, G. J., & Baer, R. A. (1986). Developmental norms for the Wisconsin Card Sorting Test. *Journal of Clinical and Experimental Neuropsychology, 8,* 219–228.

Chen-Hafteck, L. (1997). Music and language development in early childhood: Integrating past research in the two domains. *Early Child Development & Care, 130,* 85–97.

Cicerone, K. D., Lazar, R. M., & Shapiro, W. R. (1983). Effects of frontal lobe lesions on hypothesis sampling during concept formation. *Neuropsychologia, 21,* 513–524.

Damasio, A. R. (1998). The somatic marker hypothesis and the possible functions of the prefrontal cortex. In A. C. Roberts, T. W. Robbins, & L. Weiskrantz (Eds.), *The prefrontal cortex* (pp. 36–50). New York: Oxford University Press.

Daniel, A. (1983). *Power, privilege and prestige: Occupations in Australia.* Melbourne: Longman-Cheshire.

Eslinger, P. J., Biddle, K., & Grattan, L. M. (1997). Cognitive and social development in children with prefrontal cortex lesions. In N. A. Krasnegor, G. R. Lyon, & P. S. Goldman-Rakic (Eds.), *Development of the prefrontal cortex: Evolution, neurobiology, and behavior* (pp. 295–335). Baltimore: Brookes.

Eslinger, P. J., & Damasio, A. R. (1985). Severe disturbance of higher cognition after bilateral frontal lobe ablation: Patient EVR. *Neurology, 35,* 1731–1741.

Eslinger, P. J., Grattan, L. M., Damasio, H., & Damasio, A. R. (1992). Developmental consequences of childhood frontal lobe damage. *Archives of Neurology, 49,* 764–769.

Espy, K. A. (1997). The Shape School: Assessing executive function in preschool children. *Developmental Neuropsychology, 13,* 495–499.

Farrar, M. J., & Maag, L. (2002). Early language development and the emergence of a theory of mind. *First Language, 22,* 197–213.

Flavell, J. H. (1985). *Cognitive development* (2nd ed.). Englewood Cliffs, NJ: Prentice Hall.

Glosser, G., & Goodglass, H. (1990). Disorders in executive control functions among aphasic and other brain-damaged patients. *Journal of Clinical and Experimental Neuropsychology, 12,* 485–501.

Goldstein, K., & Scheerer, M. (1941). Abstract and concrete behavior: An experimental study with special tests. *Psychological Monographs, 53*(2), 151.

Goldstein, K. H. & Scheerer, M. (1953). Tests of abstract and concrete behavior. In A. Weidner (Ed.), *Contributions to medical psychology* (Vol. 2, pp. 702–730). New York: Ronald.

Grant, D. A., & Berg, E. A. (1948). A behavioral analysis of degree of reinforcement and ease of shifting to new responses in a Weigl-type card-sorting problem. *Journal of Experimental Psychology, 38,* 404–411.

Grattan, L. M., & Eslinger, P. J. (1991). Frontal lobe damage in children and adults: A comparative review. *Developmental Neuropsychology, 7,* 283–326.

Guilford, J. P., Christensen, P. R., Merrifield, P. R., & Wilson, R. C. (1978). *Alternate uses: Manual of instructions and interpretation.* Orange: CA: Sheridan Psychological Services.

Halstead, W. C. (1947). *Brain and Intelligence.* Chicago: University of Chicago Press.

Inhelder, B., & Piaget, J. (1964). *The early growth of logic in the child.* New York: Harper & Row.

Jacobs, R., Anderson, V., & Harvey, S. (2001). Concept Generation Test as a measure of conceptual reasoning skills in children: Examination of developmental trends. *Clinical Neuropsychological Assessment, 2,* 101–117.

Jacques, S., & Zelazo, P. D. (2001). The Flexible Item Selection Task (FIST): A measure of executive function in preschoolers. *Developmental Neuropsychology, 20,* 573–591.

Laine, M. (1988). Correlates of word fluency performance. In P. Koivuselkä-Sallinen & L. Sarajärvi (Eds.), *Studies in languages* (No. 12). Joensuu, Finland: University of Joensuu, Faculty of Arts.

Laine, M., & Butters, N. (1982). A preliminary study of the problem-solving strategies of detoxified long-term alcoholics. *Drug and Alcohol Dependence, 10,* 235–242.

Levin, H. S., Culhane, K. A., Hartmann, J., Evankovich, K., Mattson, A. J., Harward, H., et al. (1991). Developmental changes in performance on tests of purported frontal lobe functioning. *Developmental Neuropsychology, 7,* 377–395.

Levine, B., Stuss, D. T., & Milberg, W. P. (1995). Concept generation: Validation of a test of executive functioning in a normal aging population. *Journal of Clinical and Experimental Neuropsychology, 17,* 740–758.

Lombardi, W. J., Andreason, P. J., Sirocco, K. Y., Rio, D. E., Gross, R. E., Umhau, J. C., et al. (1999). Wisconsin Card Sorting Test performance following head injury: Dorsolateral fronto-striatal circuit activity predicts perseveration. *Journal of Clinical & Experimental Neuropsychology, 21*(1), 2–16.

Luria, A. R. (1973). *The working brain.* New York: Basic Books.

Molfese, D., & Molfese, V. (2000). The continuum of language development during infancy and early childhood: Electrophysiological correlates. In C. Rovee-Collier, L. P. Lipsitt, et al. (Eds.), *Progress in infancy research* (Vol. 1, pp. 251–287). Mahwah, NJ: Lawrence Erlbaum Associates, Inc.

Nelson, H. E. (1976). A modified card sorting test sensitive to frontal lobe defects. *Cortex, 12,* 313–324.

Passler, M. A., Isaac, W., & Hynd, G. W. (1985). Neuropsychological development of behavior attributed to frontal lobe functioning in children. *Developmental Neuropsychology, 1,* 349–370.

Raven, J. C. (1960). *Guide to the standard progressive matrices.* London: Lewis.

Raven, J. C., Court, J. H., & Raven, J. (1976). *Manual for Raven's progressive matrices.* London: Lewis.

Reitan, R. M., & Wolfson, D. (1993). *The Halstead–Reitan Neuropsychological Test Battery: Theory and clinical interpretation.* Tucson, AZ: Neuropsychology Press.

Siegler, R. S. (1991). Developmental sequences within and between concepts. *Monographs of the Society for Research in Child Development, 46*(2), 84.

Smidts, D. P., & Anderson, V. (2003). Developmental trajectories for executive skills in preschool children. *Journal of the International Neuropsychological Society, 9,* 562–563.

Stuss, D. T. (1992). Biological and psychological development of executive functions. *Brain and Cognition, 20,* 8–23.

Stuss, D. T., & Alexander, M. P. (2000). Executive functions and the frontal lobes: A conceptual view. *Psychological Research, 63,* 289–298.

Stuss, D. T., & Benson, D. F. (1987). The frontal lobes and control of cognition and memory. In E. Perecman (Ed.), *The frontal lobes revisited* (pp. 141–158). New York: IRBN Press.

Stuss, D. T., Levine, B., Alexander, M. P., Hong, J., Palumbo, C., Hamer, L., et al. (2000). Wisconsin Card Sorting Test performance in patients with focal frontal and posterior brain damage: Effects of lesion location and test structure on separable cognitive processes. *Neuropsychologia, 38,* 388–402.

Taylor, H. G., Albo, V., Phebus, C., Sachs, B., & Bierl, P. (1987). Postirradiation treatment outcomes for children with acute lymphoblastic leukemia: Clarification of risks. *Journal of Pediatric Psychology, 12,* 395–411.

Weigl, E. (1941). On the psychology of so-called processes of abstraction. *Journal of Normal and Social Psychology, 36,* 3–33.

Welsh, M. C., Pennington, B. F., & Groisser, D. B. (1991). A normative-developmental study of executive function: A window on prefrontal function in children. *Developmental Neuropsychology, 7,* 131–149.

DEVELOPMENTAL NEUROPSYCHOLOGY, 26(1), 403–422
Copyright © 2004, Lawrence Erlbaum Associates, Inc.

Executive Function in Preschool Children: Examination Through Everyday Behavior

Peter K. Isquith
Department of Psychiatry
Dartmouth Hitchcock Medical School

Gerard A. Gioia
Pediatric Neuropsychology Program
Center for Neurosciences and Behavioral Medicine
Children's National Medical Center, Washington, DC

Kimberly Andrews Espy
Department of Family and Community Medicine
Southern Illinois University School of Medicine

Clinical assessment of executive function in preschool-age children is challenging given limited availability of standardized tasks and preschoolers' variable ability to participate in lengthy formal evaluation procedures. Given the benefits of ecological validity of measuring behavior by rating scales, the Behavior Rating Inventory of Executive Function (Gioia, Isquith, Guy, & Kenworthy, 2000) was modified for use with children ages 2 through 5 years to assess executive functions in an everyday context. The scale development process, based on samples of 460 parents and 302 teachers, yielded a single 63-item measure with 5 related, but nonoverlapping, scales, with good internal consistency and temporal stability. Exploratory factor analyses identified 3 consistent factors: Emergent Metacognition, Flexibility, and Inhibitory Self-Control across parent and teacher samples. In a second study with a mixed sample of preschool children with various developmental disorders, parents and teachers rated these preschool children as having greater executive difficulties in most domains than matched controls. Such rating-scale methodology may be a useful complementary tool by which to reliably assess executive functions in preschool children via everyday behaviors in the natural environment.

Requests for reprints should be sent to Peter K. Isquith, Department of Psychiatry, Dartmouth Hitchcock Medical School, One Medical Center Dr., Lebanon, NH 03756–0001. E-mail: peter.k.isquith@dartmouth.edu

Although the development of executive functions in children has become an active topic of discussion and research over the past 2 decades (e.g., Fletcher et al., 1996; Passler, Isaac, & Hynd, 1985; Welsh, Pennington, & Grossier, 1991), less attention has been devoted to the structure, organization, and development of executive functions in infants and preschool-age children (Espy & Kaufmann, 2002). One prominent view of preschooler's behavior is that young children are not able to exert higher order control of pertinent cognitive processes, emotional responses, and behavioral impulses. Historically, they are perceived as lacking inhibitory control, exhibiting significant distractibility, being inflexible in their ability to solve problems, and not organizing, planning, or monitoring their problem-solving behaviors. This "dysexecutive" behavior suggests that the study of executive functions in preschool-age children may not be particularly fruitful given the potential for a broad range of normal variability in these functions. However, the developmentally oriented neuropsychologist, whether focused on clinical service delivery or research investigation, has an inherent interest in the earliest roots of disorders that are evident in later childhood and adolescence. Through the study of the executive functions in preschoolers, the earliest forms or precursors of executive regulation can be defined and described. For example, better understanding of the roots of poor inhibitory control, later manifested in attention deficit hyperactivity disorder (ADHD), has potential implications for early detection and intervention of this disorder. Furthermore, a variety of disorders involving executive dysfunction, such as ADHD, autism spectrum disorders (ASD), and prematurity, may first manifest in the preschool years. Other acquired injuries, such as traumatic brain injury (TBI; see Ewing-Cobbs et al., this issue), when incurred in this age range may have greater or different impact on outcome than when such injuries are sustained later in life. Better characterization of this dysfunction at the earliest point of diagnosis is critical to a full understanding of the disorder, and it also can lead to important early interventions. The purpose of this article is to examine the potential for the assessment of executive function as manifested in the everyday behavior of preschool-age children, based on the premise that measurement of executive functions is possible when a developmentally appropriate behavioral repertoire is sampled (Wellman, 1988). We employed parental and teacher ratings of everyday behaviors that preschoolers display to explore the putative regulatory control of behavior, emotion, and cognitive problem-solving in this age range.

The development of attentional control, future-oriented, intentional problem solving, and self-regulation of emotion and behavior is considered to begin in infancy (Diamond, 1985; Haith, Hazan, & Goodman, 1988) and continues into the preschool period (Espy, Kaufmann, McDiarmid, & Glisky, 1999; Welsh, Pennington, & Grossier, 1991). For example, early manifestations of executive functions, such as goal-directed, planful problem-solving behaviors in infants, have been demonstrated with the use of object permanence and object retrieval paradigms

(Diamond, 1985, 1990). In toddlers, executive self-control abilities, such as maintaining an intentional action and inhibiting behavior incompatible with attaining a goal, undergo active development (Kochanska, Murray, & Coy, 1997; Vaughn, Kopp, & Krakow, 1984). Thus, early intentional self-control behaviors are present in infants and toddlers and contribute to goal-directed problem solving. Executive self-control at these early ages is, however, variable, fragile, and bound to the external stimulus situation, with increasing stability achieved between 18 and 30 months of age (Ruff & Rothbart, 1996).

In preschool-age children, executive functions can be differentiated by using developmentally appropriate tasks, such as those adapted from developmental cognitive neuroscience. For example, working memory, flexibility, and inhibition skills can be discriminated in preschool children (Espy, Kaufmann, McDiarmid, et al., 1999; Hughes, 1998). Furthermore, the developmental trajectories of these executive functions differ (Espy, 1997; Espy, Kaufmann, McDiarmid, & Glisky, 2001). Fundamental executive functions, such as inhibition and working memory, develop earlier, whereas the more complex processes, such as systematic problem solving and planning, have a more protracted course (Espy, 1997; Espy et al., 2001). As is the case with most dimensions of psychological and neuropsychological development, the emergence and development of executive control functions likely varies across individuals in terms of the age of onset, the rate of development, the level of proficiency at any given age, and the shape of the trajectory of skill acquisition. There is growing evidence that different neurological and behavioral disorders in preschoolers result in unique patterns of executive function disturbance (Diamond, Prevor, Callendar, & Druin, 1997; Espy, Kaufmann, & Glisky, 1999; Espy et al., 2003; Grodzinsky & Diamond, 1992; McEvoy, Rogers, & Pennington, 1993), such as is found in school-age children and adolescents (Gioia, Isquith, Kenworthy, & Barton, 2002; Ozonoff & Jensen, 1999; Pennington & Ozonoff, 1996; Sergeant, Guerts, & Oosterlaan, 2002).

Historically, clinical assessment of the executive functions in any age group has been challenging because of their fluid, dynamic nature (Denckla, 1994). This problem is particularly acute in preschool children (Espy & Kaufmann, 2001), in part because of the variable nature of behavior and limitations in motor and verbal proficiency in this age range. Aside from the NEPSY Developmental Neuropsychological Assessment (NEPSY; Korkman, Kirk, & Kemp, 1998) attention–executive subtests, there are few validated, standardized measures of executive function designed for this age group, limiting ease of clinical assessment and comparison across studies (Espy & Kaufmann, 2001). The structured nature of the typical individual assessment situation, be it for clinical or research purposes, also may limit opportunities for observing executive functions, regardless of the age of the child tested (Silver, 2000). Nevertheless, active development of new performance measures of executive function specific to this age group is underway (e.g., Diamond et al., 1997; Espy et al., 2001).

Examination of everyday behavior is a complementary approach to assessing executive functions in preschool children. The child's everyday environments, both at home and at school or day care, are important venues for observing routine manifestations of the executive functions. This methodology recently has been employed in the measurement of executive function in school-age children and adolescents with the development of the Behavior Rating Inventory of Executive Function (BRIEF; Gioia, Isquith, Guy, & Kenworthy, 2000). The BRIEF is a parent- and teacher-completed rating scale with 86 items in eight, nonoverlapping, scales tapping eight theoretically-derived subdomains of executive function as observed through everyday behaviors in children ages 5 to 18 years. The individual scales form two broad factor-based indexes: Inhibit, Shift, and Emotional Control scales compose a Behavioral Regulation Index, whereas Initiate, Working Memory, Plan/Organize, Organization of Materials, and Monitor scales form a Metacognition Index. Studies to date suggest that the BRIEF exhibits appropriate internal consistency, temporal stability, and evidence of validity based on convergence or divergence with a variety of measures and on internal factor structure (Gioia et al., 2000). The instrument also captures profiles of executive functions that differ across common developmental and acquired disorders, including ADHD, ASD, TBI, and reading disorders (Gioia et al., 2002). Finally, it has been argued that such rating-scale methodology adds a complementary ecological validity dimension to clinical assessment of executive function (Gioia & Isquith, in press; Silver, 2000). Reliable reports of the child's everyday behavioral manifestations of executive dysfunction allow for a high degree of ecological validity in understanding their real-world needs relative to test performance in an office setting. On the other hand, rating scales have their own limitations in terms of providing a more global level of behavior and less process-specific information. Rater bias can influence the ratings, particularly if the parent or teacher has certain unreasonable expectations for the child's behavior. Nevertheless, capitalizing on parents and teachers as valuable sources of data high in ecological validity, we explored modification and application of the BRIEF for assessing executive functions in preschool-age children.

In consultation with colleagues in pediatric neuropsychology regarding executive function domains that might be assessed behaviorally in preschoolers, the consensus was that behavioral and emotional regulation would be relatively clear and measurable, but the more metacognitive aspects of executive function, such as planning, organizing, initiating, monitoring, and working memory, in preschoolers might be more difficult to capture. Further, given the high degree of variability in self-regulation considered typical among preschool-age children, we questioned whether or not it would be possible to discriminate between such typical variability and atypical levels of dysregulation. Therefore, the primary questions investigated were

1. Can reliable dimensions of executive functions, as expressed in everyday behaviors, be defined adequately, and are there individual differences in these behaviors related to age group and sex?
2. What is the structure of the relation between these reliable dimensions in young children?
3. Can such dimensions differentiate between normal variability and executive dysfunction evident in children diagnosed with clinical disorders?

Specifically, we hypothesized that (a) a reliable set of behaviors could be assembled into a set of internally consistent scales tapping relevant executive functions; (b) the behaviors defining these scales of executive functions would be stable over time; (c) evidence for validity of these scales could be demonstrated via construct-based factor analysis, and; (d) the variability of the behaviors, as captured via rating-scale methodology, would permit sufficient differentiation between clinical and nonclinical populations. We present two related studies to examine these questions and stated hypotheses.

STUDY 1: DEFINING BEHAVIORAL DOMAINS OF PRESCHOOL EXECUTIVE FUNCTION

Method

Participants.   Two samples of participants were used for this study. For initial scale development, ratings of children between the ages of 2 and 5 years were collected from 372 parents (196 boys, 176 girls; $M = 3.6$ years, $SD = 0.93$) from normative populations in the Midwest, mid-Atlantic, Northeast, and Southern regions of the United States. Children were recruited from numerous preschool programs and local health care facilities. Teachers for 201 of these children (102 boys, 99 girls; $M = 3.6$ years, $SD = 0.85$) also provided ratings. Data on children whose parents or teachers identified them as having any special education needs, as having attention, developmental, speech–language, or cognitive difficulties, or as prescribed psychotropic medications were not included in these analyses. Following scale refinement, a second sample from the same demographic regions and backgrounds was collected from 88 parents (50 boys, 38 girls) and 101 teachers (62 boys, 39 girls) for the purpose of replication. The two data sets—initial development and replication—combined represented a broad ethnic and socioeconomic status distribution in both the parent and teacher samples. Tables 1 and 2 present the ethnic and socioeconomic distributions for the sample, respectively.

Instrumentation.   The original pool of 129 items from the eight-scale BRIEF (Gioia et al., 2000) served as the basis for the development of a preschool version of the BRIEF. Many items were edited to reflect the larger preschool context of behavior, rather than a more limited set of school-related behaviors. For example, "homework" references were changed to "task" or "activity" references. A new set of items also was generated to reflect preschool-specific behaviors (e.g., "Plays carelessly or recklessly in situations where he/she could be hurt [e.g., playground equipment, swimming pool].". Eliminating poorly worded, redundant, and irrelevant items resulted in a reduced pool of 97 items.

TABLE 1
Ethnic Distribution of Parent and Teacher Normative Samples

Ethnic Group	Parent[a]		Teacher[b]	
	n	*%*	*n*	*%*
White	336	73.0	217	71.9
African American	64	13.9	37	12.3
Hispanic	22	4.8	14	4.6
Asian and Pacific Islander	14	3.0	6	2.0
Native American and Eskimo	3	0.7	2	0.7
Not specified	21	4.6	26	8.6

[a]$N = 460$. [b]$N = 302$.

TABLE 2
Parent and Teacher Normative Samples by SES

SES Classification	Parent[a]		Teacher[b]	
	n	*%*	*n*	*%*
Upper	87	18.9	71	23.5
Upper middle	133	28.9	88	29.1
Middle middle	121	26.3	73	24.2
Lower middle	72	15.7	37	12.3
Lower	46	10.0	20	6.6
Unassigned	1	0.2	13	4.3

Note.   SES calculated via Hollingshead Index (Hollingshead, 1975). SES = socioeconomic status.
[a]$N = 460$. [b]$N = 302$.

Results

Scale refinement. Individual item distributions were examined and items with high means and wide dispersion indexes were eliminated. Member scales then were examined via iterative item-total correlations. Items with low correlations (< .40) were poor contributors and were removed from the scales. Finally, principal factor analysis with orthogonal rotation was used to clarify scale structure. The convergence of results prompted the removal of two of the scales included in the original BRIEF, Initiate and Monitor, and the combination of the Organization of Materials and the Plan/Organize scales. The initial scale-development process thus yielded a single 63-item rating form for both parent and teacher or day care provider raters. Five executive domains emerged: Inhibit (16 items), Shift (10 items), Emotional Control (10 items), Working Memory (17 items), and Plan/Organize (10 items).

For the purpose of independent replication, additional data were collected from a second sample of parents ($N = 88$) and teachers ($N = 101$) as described previously, using the refined 63-item scale. For the purpose of comparison, mean scores for each of the five executive domains defined by the 63-item scale were calculated from the original 97-item scale, using the same items as in the 63-item scale and compared to the mean scores from the 63-item scale. Multivariate analysis of variance (MANOVA) revealed no significant differences (all $ps > .10$, $\eta^2 < .02$) in mean ratings for any of the five executive domains between the initial (97-item form) and replication (63-item form) samples, for either the parent or teacher raters. Therefore, the data from both samples were combined for subsequent analyses. Table 3 presents representative items within each scale for the combined parent and teacher samples, along with item-total correlations. Scale means by sex for the combined samples of 460 parent ratings and 302 teacher–caregiver ratings are depicted in Table 4. Mean item responses with a possible range of 1 to 3 were used for each scale to maintain the same metric across scales. Of note are the relatively low means for each scale, with small standard deviations, consistent with reasonable, but not excessive, normal variability. This variability is particularly relevant to Study 2, where the differentiation between clinical and normative samples is investigated.

Internal consistency. Cronbach's alphas (1951) for parent ratings on the preschool BRIEF scales and total score were as follows: Inhibit $\alpha = .90$, Shift $\alpha = .85$, Emotional Control $\alpha = .86$, Working Memory $\alpha = .88$, Plan/Organize $\alpha = .80$, and total score $\alpha = .95$. Cronbach's alphas for teacher ratings were Inhibit $\alpha = .94$, Shift $\alpha = .90$, Emotional Control $\alpha = .91$, Working Memory $\alpha = .94$, Plan/Organize $\alpha = .97$, and total score $\alpha = .97$. Interestingly, parental ratings of Plan/Organize behaviors were somewhat lower than the rest of the scales. Overall, these results are consistent with excellent internal consistency.

TABLE 3
Sample Items and Item-Total Correlations by Scale for Parent and Teacher Ratings

Scale	Item	Item-Total Correlations Parent[a]	Item-Total Correlations Teacher[b]
Inhibit			
	Is unaware of how his or her behavior affects or bothers others	.51	.71
	Is impulsive	.61	.70
	Has trouble putting the brakes on his or her actions even after being asked	.66	.75
Shift			
	Becomes upset with new situations	.61	.59
	Is upset by a change in plans or routines	.57	.75
	Has trouble "joining in" at unfamiliar social events	.62	.66
Emotional control			
	Becomes upset too easily	.67	.78
	Mood changes frequently	.65	.74
	Small events trigger big reactions	.67	.74
Working memory			
	When given two things to do, remembers only the first or last	.44	.71
	Has trouble concentrating on games, puzzles, or play activities	.58	.74
	Has trouble with activities or tasks that have more than one step	.60	.75
Plan and organize			
	When instructed to clean up, puts things away in a disorganized, random way	.44	.60
	Has trouble thinking of a different way to solve a problem or complete an activity when stuck	.45	.68
	Gets caught up in the small details of a task or situation and misses the main idea	.41	.56

[a]$N = 460.$ [b]$N = 302.$

TABLE 4
Scale Means and Standard Deviations by Sex for Parent and Teacher Ratings

	Parent Ratings[a] Boys		Girls		Teacher Ratings[b] Boys		Girls	
Scale	M	SD	M	SD	M	SD	M	SD
Inhibit	1.53	.36	1.43	.33	1.45	.43	1.25	.30
Shift	1.46	.41	1.43	.35	1.40	.41	1.33	.35
Emotional control	1.51	.37	1.56	.40	1.38	.41	1.36	.41
Working memory	1.38	.30	1.34	.29	1.34	.37	1.23	.34
Plan and organize	1.52	.32	1.51	.34	1.38	.35	1.29	.33

[a]$N = 460.$ [b]$N = 302.$

Temporal stability.   Pearson correlations were calculated to examine the temporal stability of the preschool BRIEF in a sample of parent ratings ($n = 52$) over an average interval of 4.5 weeks (range 1–9 weeks). Correlations were Inhibit $r = .90$, Shift $r = .88$, Emotional Control $r = .87$, Working Memory $r = .85$, Plan/Organize $r = .78$, and total score $r = .90$. Similarly, a sample of teachers ($n = 67$) completed test and retest forms over an average of 4.2 weeks (range 2–6 weeks), with correlations of Inhibit $r = .94$, Shift $r = .65$, Emotional Control $r = .83$, Working Memory $r = .88$, Plan/Organize $r = .85$, and total score $r = .88$. Again, the temporal stability of parental ratings of Plan/Organize behaviors was somewhat lower than the rest of the scales, whereas teachers rated shifting behavior as somewhat less stable. These results are consistent with appropriate temporal stability.

Influence of child sex and age group.   The means presented in Table 4 were examined for sex and age differences in the parent and teacher rater samples. Results of a 2 (boys, girls) by 4 (2-, 3-, 4-, and 5-year-olds) MANOVA for the parent sample revealed small, but significant, main effects of sex, $F(5, 451) = 5.65, p < .001, \eta^2 = .06$, and of age, $F(15, 1349) = 1.90, p < .02, \eta^2 = .02$. Similarly, main effects of sex, $F(5, 293) = 5.86, p < .001, \eta^2 = .09$, and of age, $F(15, 875) = 1.66, p < .05, \eta^2 = .03$, also were evident in the teacher rater sample. In both rater samples, the interaction of age by sex was not significant. Examination of the univariate analyses in the parent sample revealed only one small difference between boys and girls on the Inhibit scale, $\eta^2 = .02$, with boys rated as having somewhat poorer inhibitory control than girls. In the teacher sample, boys similarly were rated as having greater inhibitory difficulties than girls, $\eta^2 = .06$, but also were rated as having poorer Working Memory, $\eta^2 = .02$, and Plan/Organize abilities, $\eta^2 = .01$. For parent ratings, small but significant differences between age groups were found on the Inhibit, $\eta^2 = .02$, Emotional Control, $\eta^2 = .02$, and Plan/Organize, $\eta^2 = .01$ scales, with 3-year-olds rated as having uniquely more difficulty in these domains in comparison to 2-, 4-, and 5-year-olds. Similarly, for teacher ratings, there were age-related differences on the Shift, $\eta^2 = .03$, and Emotional Control, $\eta^2 = .03$, scales, again with a slight elevation in problematic behavior in 3-year-olds relative to the other age groups.

Defining the structure of preschool executive function dimensions.   With the scales adequately defined, internally consistent, and temporally stable, we examined the internal structure of the five scales. That is, what are the relations between these five executive function dimensions, and do they reflect a single overarching dimension, or are they better conceptualized as overlapping dimensions or shared common factors? Defining the structural relations between the five executive function scales speaks to the validity of the construct. Evidence of this validity based on the internal structure of the preschool BRIEF is a complex issue because of the nature of the executive functions as higher order, "supervisory" functions.

Pragmatically, though, the executive problem-solving process argues for multiple executive processes to achieve multistep performance. Therefore, exploratory factor analyses with both the parent and teacher rater samples were conducted to investigate the preschool BRIEF scale structure.

To examine the underlying construct of the modified BRIEF as a measure of executive function in preschoolers, the exploratory factor analyses were conducted on the parent ($N = 460$) and teacher ($N = 302$) samples. Principal factor analysis was used as the exploratory method, with an oblique rotation (Promax) due to the likelihood of correlated factors. Decision criteria for the selection of an appropriate number of factors were based on conceptual and statistical considerations (Carroll, 1993). Our a priori conceptual model views executive function as a multidimensional construct (Miyake et al., 2000); therefore, a single factor model was not considered. Furthermore, a four-factor model was not considered because, with only 5 scales, one factor necessarily would be defined by only one scale. Analysis of the appropriate number of initial common factors was conducted by examining the eigenvalues, percentage of variance accounted for by the extracted factor, and scree plots (Gorsuch, 1983). The number of factors obtained was constrained to two or three primary factor solutions that were compared for interpretability of the differing factor structures. Subtests with factor loadings of >.35 were retained as measured indicators of the given factor.

For the parent sample, a three-factor model was retained as the best model in the analyses. Although only the eigenvalue for a one-factor model exceeded 1.0, the second and third factors accounted for 16% and 11% of the variance, respectively. In the two-factor solution, there was not sufficient separation among the scales for adequate interpretability. Furthermore, there was a Heywood case, where the communality for one variable (Emotional Control) exceeded 1.0 (Gorsuch, 1983). In Table 5 are the factor loadings for the three-factor solution, which accounted for 87% of the variance. Examination of the solution indicated that two scales, Working Memory and Plan/Organize, loaded exclusively on the first factor, with a secondary loading of the Inhibition scale. This factor was labeled *Emergent Metacognition* to reflect the developing metacognitive aspects of executive function in this age range. The Shift and Emotional Control scales defined a second factor, named *Flexibility,* capturing behavioral rigidity and emotional modulation. The Inhibit and Emotional Control scales defined a third factor *Inhibitory Self-Control,* reflecting the primary contribution of the Inhibit scale along with emotional modulation difficulties. The three factors were correlated moderately with values ranging from 0.46 to 0.66.

The same principal factor analysis performed on the data from the teacher sample produced a three-factor solution similar to that in the parent sample, accounting for 92% of the variance. The factor loadings for this solution are presented in Table 5. Examination of the solution indicated that, again, the Working Memory and Plan/Organize scales loaded on the first factor, labeled Emergent Metacognition.

TABLE 5
Factor Loadings for a Three-Factor Model for Parent and Teacher Ratings

Scale	Parent Sample[a]			Teacher Sample[b]		
	Factor			Factor		
	1	2	3	1	2	3
Working memory	.97			.87		
Plan and organize	.61			.86		
Shift		.65			.81	
Emotional control		.37	.63		.55	.53
Inhibit	.39		.59			.74
Factor correlations (r)						
Factor 2	.46			.47		
Factor 3	.59	.66		.55	.66	
Cumulative % of variance		87%			92%	

Note. Factor loadings greater than .35 are retained on a factor. Factor 1 = emergent metacognition; Factor 2 = flexibility; Factor 3 = inhibitory self-control.
[a]$N = 460$. [b]$N = 302$.

The Shift and Emotional Control scales again defined the second factor, named *Flexibility.* The Inhibit and Emotional Control scales again defined the third factor, labeled *Inhibitory Self-Control.* Similar to that with the parent rater sample, the factors were correlated moderately, ranging from 0.47 to 0.66.

Discussion

These results suggest that dimensions of executive function that are consistent with current developmental theories can be defined adequately, coherently articulated, and consistently measured via parent and teacheror caregiver ratings of children's everyday behaviors. Further, there is preliminary evidence of construct validity based on exploratory factor analyses. The scale development processes resulted in modification of the original BRIEF for preschool-age children with a 63-item measure composed of five scales: Inhibit, Shift, Emotional Control, Working Memory, and Plan/Organize. Each of the scales demonstrated strong internal consistency and temporal stability. Thus, the behavioral and emotional regulation dimensions identified in older school-age children with the BRIEF also were evident in younger children using the resulting preschool modification of the BRIEF. In contrast, the more metacognitive scale dimensions were reduced from five in older school-age children to two in this younger group. In keeping with our pediatric neuropsychologist colleagues' views, behavioral inhibition, flexibility, and emotional regulation were adequately clear and measurable as reflected in the scale consistency indexes. The metacognitive aspects of executive functions appear to be less differentiated, or more intertwined, in young children. The scale development process yielded a broad Working Memory scale and a combined Plan/Organize scale; yet the more subtle domains of initiation and self-monitoring were not evident in this age range as independent scales. Overall, a reliable set of internally consistent scales that tap executive functions in a representative sample of preschool-age children were developed.

Age and sex differences were small but significant given the large sample sizes. Not surprisingly, boys were rated as having somewhat poorer inhibitory control and, in school settings, greater difficulty with working memory, planning, and organization. Three-year-old children were rated as having somewhat greater difficulties with self-regulation compared with 2-, 4-, and 5-year-old preschoolers, although the magnitude of these differences was small.

Exploratory factor analyses revealed that the relation between the five preschool executive function scales was represented best by the three common factors. The scales form three related factors: Inhibitory Self-Control, Flexibility, and Emergent Metacognition. Similar solutions were derived for the parent and teacher rating samples separately, further supporting the underlying structure across raters and respective settings. These findings provide evidence of validity based on the internal structure of the preschool BRIEF, consistent with the third hypothesis.

STUDY 2: DIFFERENTIATION OF PRESCHOOL EXECUTIVE FUNCTIONS IN CLINICA AND NORMATIVE GROUPS

With a preschool modification of the BRIEF adequately articulated and initially supported, we examined whether the scale was sufficiently sensitive to detect atypical variations in behavior in preschool-age children with clinically diagnosed disorders that might be expected to include deficits in executive function. We hypothesized that the variability in executive functions between clinical and normative populations could be captured via differences in parent and teacher ratings.

Method

Participants.   Parent ratings for a mixed sample of 50 children between 2 and 5 years of age who were diagnosed clinically with either ADHD, an ASD, or a language disorder (excluding speech articulation disorders) were drawn from a larger pool of children referred for neuropsychological assessment. Teachers also completed ratings for a subset of the clinical sample ($N = 20$). Children in the clinical sample were matched individually with a nonreferred child from a local preschool based on the child's sex, age, and ethnicity and the mother's education level. A sample of children with varied diagnoses was used in this preliminary study to include children with a wide variety of executive disturbance. This procedure enabled initial examination of whether the preschool BRIEF was sensitive, but not specific, to individual differences in executive functions.

Results

Mean scores across all items within a scale (as opposed to scale sums), with a possible range of 1 to 3 for each scale, were calculated to facilitate comparisons across scales. In keeping with the results from the factor analyses conducted in Study 1, summary scores also were calculated for each of the Inhibitory Self-Control, Flexibility, and Emergent Metacognition factor-derived indexes. These summary scores were simple means across all items of the indexes' scales, again with a range of 1 to 3. Figures 1 and 2 show the mean parent and teacher ratings, respectively, for clinical and control groups on the preschool BRIEF scales. Error bars indicate 1 *SD*.

Parent sample.   MANOVA with the control versus the clinical group as the between-subject factor and scales or indexes as dependent variables revealed significant group main effects and large effect sizes for all variables (η^2 ranged from .16 to .43). Executive behaviors in the clinical group were rated consistently as more problematic than in the normative sample, across all domains assessed by the preschool BRIEF.

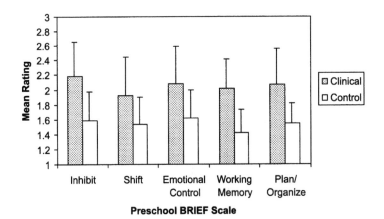

FIGURE 1   Mean parent ratings on BRIEF scales for clinical ($N = 50$) and matched control groups.

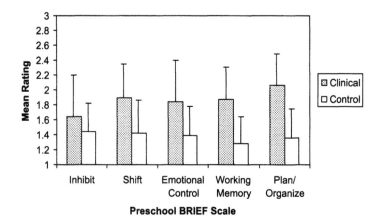

FIGURE 2   Mean teacher ratings on BRIEF scales for clinical ($N = 20$) and matched control groups.

Teacher sample. A similarly structured MANOVA revealed significant group main effects for all variables, except the Inhibit scale, with large effect sizes (η^2 ranged from .19 to .44). Executive behavior in the clinical group was rated consistently as more problematic than in the normative control group in the majority of the preschool BRIEF domains assessed, with the exception of Inhibitory Control ($\eta^2 = .05$, *ns*).

Discussion

This preliminary examination of sensitivity of the modified BRIEF is limited in scope and generalizability by the small sample sizes and mixed diagnoses included in the clinical groups. Despite these limitations, there was sufficient variability in executive function behaviors between children diagnosed with clinical disorders and nonreferred typically developing children to detect group differences. Indeed, the effect sizes were moderate to large, suggesting that self-regulatory difficulties may be measured well via rating-scale methodology. Children with ADHD, ASD, or language disorders were rated by parents and teachers as having greater difficulty in most domains of executive function relative to matched peers. The differences in ratings were not accounted for by a child's age, sex, or ethnicity, or by parent education. Interpreted cautiously in light of the stated limitations, the study serves, however, as an initial test of the sensitivity of the modified BRIEF and as a pilot for future examination of profiles of executive function in preschoolers with specific clinical disorders.

CONCLUSIONS

A complementary method of assessing the executive functions in preschool children via their everyday behavior as reported by their parents and teachers or day care providers was investigated. This literature on the ontogenetic aspects of executive function is relatively small, but growing, demonstrating that aspects of the executive functions likely are evident in infancy (Diamond, 1985; Haith et al., 1988), with continued development in the preschool period (Espy et al., 1999; Kochanska et al., 1997). Different disorders that may be evident in the preschool period may present with specific profiles of executive dysfunction (Diamond et al., 1997; Espy et al., 1999, 2003). Capturing the typical development of self-regulatory functions and atypical variations early in the course of development may prove useful in detecting difficulties and developing interventions during the critical years before elementary school entry. Assessment of executive functions in this age group is, however, challenging. Although executive functions can be measured via developmentally appropriate tasks, such as those adapted from developmental cognitive neuroscience (e.g., Espy et al., 1999, 2001), few such tasks are standardized, with known psychometric properties suitable for use by clinicians for individual, clinical assessment. These studies examined whether rating-scale methodology could reliably and consistently capture typical executive functions in preschool-age children, the internal structure of such executive function scales, and whether this method might be useful in detecting atypical executive functioning in children with developmental disorders.

In the first study, the existing executive function rating-scale measure, designed originally for school-age children and adolescents, was edited for use with preschool-age children. The scale development process yielded five scales reflecting subdomains of executive function consistent with the extant literature: Inhibitory Control, Flexibility, Emotional Modulation, Working Memory, and Planning/Organization. Finer gradations of metacognitive self-regulation, such as initiation and self-monitoring, were not internally consistent and could not be reliably defined as distinct subdomains. Multiple domains of executive function can be measured via parent and teacher ratings in a consistent and reliable manner, but they represent less differentiated, more intertwined abilities than what is observed in school-age children.

Furthermore, the overall scale structure and relations among the five scale dimensions revealed by exploratory factor analysis of parent and teacher ratings in the second study yielded similar three-factor solutions across raters: The Inhibit and Emotional Control scales formed an Inhibitory Self-Control factor, Shift and Emotional Control formed a Flexibility factor, and Working Memory and Plan/Organize formed an Emergent Metacognition factor. Interestingly, the Emotional Control dimension was associated comparably with both Inhibitory Control and Flexibility indexes, suggesting that the regulation of emotional response has general importance across a variety of executive domains and represents one of the key developmental tasks in this age range. The only difference among analyses conducted with the parent versus teacher rater samples was the contribution of the Inhibition scale. In the parent rater sample, Inhibition loaded both on the Emergent Metacognition and Inhibitory Control factors. Analysis of scale items revealed that several Inhibit Scale items contained referents to monitoring behavior relative to others or self. Given the less structured environment of the home setting in comparison to that of the school, these items may be related more prominently to emergent metacognitive skills in typically developing preschool children. That is, in the home, the child must use these emergent metacognitive skills to inhibit irrelevant or inappropriate behavior. In the school setting, the teacher and other authority figures may provide additional structure that, in turn, provides more explicit monitoring of behavior relative to peers. In preschool children with clinical disorders, where there is greater variability in behavior in the everyday context than in normative samples, the pattern of these relations among executive function scales and factors may differ.

Finally, the second study explored whether atypical variations in executive functions could be measured via a rating scale by comparing parent and teacher ratings of clinical versus nonclinical groups of matched children. In these samples, parents and teachers rated the clinical group of children as having more problematic executive behavior than the typically developing children across most domains measured. Interestingly, teachers did not rate behaviors measured by the Inhibit scale of children with mixed clinical disorders as differing from those of typically developing controls. The discrepancy from parental ratings may reflect the higher degree of structure in preschool classrooms that may limit the expression of disinhibition in that setting. Alternatively, these discrepant results across raters may be related to the small sample size of children with mixed diagnoses. Nevertheless, preliminary evidence that measurement of group differences is possible via rating-scale methodology was demonstrated.

In essence, the adaptation of the original BRIEF everyday behavior rating methodology to the measurement of executive behavior of preschoolers yielded an internally consistent, temporally stable instrument, with an internal structure consistent with the multidomain construct of executive functioning in preschool-age children (Espy et al., 1999; Hughes, 1998) that was sensitive to atypical variations in executive function development. Several general observations are relevant. The specificity of measurable executive function domains appears less differentiated in preschool-age children than in school-age children. Although the BRIEF assesses eight domains of executive functioning in older school-age children, this modification for preschool-age children resulted in a reduced set of five, more general, domains. Furthermore, there was greater cross-loading of the executive function scales on the factors in preschool children in comparison to that of older, school-age children (Gioia & Isquith, in press). Consistent with our hypotheses, the metacognitive domains of self-regulation were more difficult to uniquely measure in this age group. In this manner, these findings from rating-scale methodology parallel those of the general developmental literature: Fundamental executive functions, such as inhibition and working memory, develop earlier, whereas more complex functions involved in problem solving and planning, have a more protracted course (Espy et al., 2001). An alternative explanation for the reduced number of metacognitive domains is that overt molar behavioral rating methods are not sensitive in capturing these processes in young children.

These findings document a range of variability in behaviors thought to reflect executive functions, where the variability is constrained sufficiently to enable atypical performance to be captured adequately. It also is important to note that the preschool BRIEF ratings are not anchored behaviorally in an absolute scaling sense, but instead tap parents' and teachers' own expectations for typical development, and their internal norms by querying the degree to which certain behaviors are *problematic*. In this sense, the degree of latitude that parents and teachers allow for the more variable preschool behavior is captured in the ratings, as well as the child's actual executive behavior. Nonetheless, the rating-scale methodology allows for a systematic and reliable capture of children's everyday executive function and dysfunction in preschool-age children.

Reliable reports of the preschool child's everyday behavioral manifestations of executive dysfunction have the potential for a high degree of ecological validity in understanding their real-world abilities. On the other hand, this method also carries limitations, as the focus is on a more global view of executive function in the everyday context with less process-specific information. This behavioral rating methodology is viewed best as a tool that is complementary to developmentally appropriate cognitive performance tests that measure the specific executive function processes. Furthermore, rating-scale methods depend on informant ratings and, therefore, may be affected by rater biases, including atypical developmental expectations of behavior by parents or teachers. The inclusion of validity scales, as are incorporated in the BRIEF for school-age children and adolescents, can address some of these problems, at least in their extreme form. The clinical judgment of the clinician also remains paramount in identifying possible bias in the context of individualized clinical assessment.

The derived preschool modification of the BRIEF was sensitive to variations in executive dysfunction among clinically referred and typically developing children, despite the small group sizes and mixed diagnostic etiologies. The purpose of these current analyses was not to uncover unique patterns of executive dysfunction in children with specific neurodevelopmental disorders, for example, which could be used for diagnostic and other clinical purposes. Rather, the preschool BRIEF scale should be viewed as capturing and describing broad domains of executive function in the everyday context that are sensitive to individual differences in behavior. Further study with more specific diagnostic groups and larger sample sizes is warranted.

ACKNOWLEDGMENTS

We maintain financial interest in the BRIEF as developers of that instrument. No financial support was provided for any phase of this research. The publisher of the BRIEF did not have any input into this study and has not reviewed the manuscript.

We are grateful to Dennis L. Molfese and the reviewers for their helpful guidance in developing this article.

REFERENCES

Carroll, J. B. (1993). *Human cognitive abilities: A survey of factor-analytic studies.* New York: Cambridge University Press.

Cronbach, L. J. (1951). Coefficient alpha and the internal structure of tests. *Psychometrika, 16,* 297–334.

Denckla, M. B. (1994). Measurement of executive function. In G. R. Lyon (Ed.), *Frames of reference for the assessment of learning disabilities: New views on measurement issues* (pp. 117–142). Baltimore: Brookes.

Diamond, A. (1985). Development of the ability to use recall to guide action, as indicated by infants' performance on AB. *Child Development, 56,* 868–883.

Diamond, A. (1990). Developmental time course in human infants and infant monkeys, and the neural bases of inhibitory control in reaching. *Annals of the New York Academy of Sciences, 608,* 637–676.

Diamond, A., Prevor, M. B., Callendar, G., & Druin, D. P. (1997). Prefrontal cortex cognitive deficits in children treated early and continuously for PKU. *Monographs of the Society for Research in Child Development, 62*(4, Serial No. 252).

Espy, K., Stalets, M., McDiarmid, M., Senn, T., Cwik, M., & Hamby, A. (2003). Executive functions in low risk preschoolers born preterm: Application of cognitive neuroscience paradigms. *Child Neuropsychology, 8,* 83–92.

Espy, K. A. (1997). The Shape School: Assessing executive function in preschool children. *Developmental Neuropsychology, 13,* 495–499.

Espy, K. A., & Kaufmann, P. M. (2002). Individual differences in the development of executive functions in children: Lessons from delayed response and a-not-B tasks. In D. L. Molfese & V. Molfese (Eds.), *Developmental variations in learning: Applications to social, executive function, language and reading skills* (pp. 113–137). Mahwah, NJ: Lawrence Erlbaum Associates, Inc.

Espy, K. A., Kaufmann, P. M., & Glisky, M. L. (1999). Neuropsychologic outcome in toddlers exposed to cocaine in utero: a preliminary study. *Developmental Neuropsychology, 15,* 447–460.

Espy, K. A., Kaufmann, P. M, McDiarmid, M., & Glisky, M. L. (1999). Executive functioning in preschool children: a-not-B and other delayed response format task performance. *Brain and Cognition, 41,* 178–199.

Espy, K. A., Kaufmann, P. M., McDiarmid, M. D., & Glisky, M. L. (2001). New procedures to assess executive functions in preschool children. *Clinical Neuropsychologist, 15,* 46–58.

Ewing-Cobbs, L., Prasad, M. R., Landry, S. H., Kramer, L., & DeLeon, R. (2004/this issue). Executive functions following traumatic brain injury in young children. *Developmental Neuropsychology, 26,* 487–512.

Fletcher, J. M., Francis, D. J., Stuebing, K. K., Shaywitz, B. A., Shaywitz, S. E., Shankweiler, D. P. et al. (1996) Conceptual and methodological issues in construct definition. In G. R. Lyon & N. A. Krasnegor (Eds.), *Attention, memory and executive function* (pp. 17–42). Baltimore: Brookes.

Gioia, G. A., & Isquith, P. K. (in press). Assessment of executive function in traumatic brain injury from an ecological perspective. *Developmental Neuropsychology.*

Gioia, G. A., Isquith, P. K., Guy, S. C., & Kenworthy, L. (2000). *The Behavior Rating Inventory of Executive Function.* Lutz, FL: Psychological Assessment Resources.

Gioia, G. A., Isquith, P. K., Kenworthy, L., & Barton, R. (2002). Profiles of everyday executive function in acquired and developmental disorders. *Child Neuropsychology, 8,* 121–137.

Gorsuch, R. L. (1983). *Factor analysis* (2nd ed.). Mahwah, NJ: Lawrence Erlbaum Associates, Inc.

Grodzinsky, G., & Diamond, R. (1992). Frontal lobe functioning in boys with attention deficit hyperactivity disorder. *Developmental Neuropsychology, 8,* 427–445.

Haith, M. M., Hazan, C., & Goodman, G. S. (1988). Expectation and anticipation of dynamic visual events by 3.5-month-old babies. *Child Development, 59,* 467–479.

Hollingshead, A. B. (1975). *Four factor index of social status.* New Haven, CT: Yale University Press.

Hughes, C. (1998). Finding your marbles: Does preschoolers' strategic behavior predict later understanding of mind? *Developmental Psychology, 34,* 1326–1339.

Kochanska, G, Murray, K., & Coy, K. (1997). Inhibitory control as a contributor to conscience in childhood: From toddler to early school age. *Child Development, 68,* 263–277.

Korkman, M., Kirk, U., & Kemp, S. (1998). *NEPSY: a developmental neuropsychological assessment manual.* San Antonio, TX: Psychological Corporation.

McEvoy, R. E., Rogers, S. J., & Pennington, B. F. (1993). Executive function and social communicative deficits in young autistic children. *Journal of Child Psychology and Psychiatry, 34,* 563–578.

Miyake, A., Friedman, N. P., Emerson, M. J., Witzki, A. H., Howerter, A., & Wagner, T. D. (2000). The unity and diversity of executive functions and their contributions to complex "frontal lobe" tasks: a latent variable analysis. *Cognitive Psychology, 41,* 49–100.

Ozonoff, S., & Jensen, J. (1999). Brief report: Specific executive function profiles in three neurodevelopmental disorders. *Journal of Autism and Developmental Disorders, 29,* 171–177.

Passler, M. A., Isaac, W., & Hynd, G. W. (1985). Neuropsychological development of behavior attributed to frontal lobe functioning in children. *Developmental Neuropsychology, 1,* 349–370.

Pennington, B. F., & Ozonoff, S. (1996). Executive functions and developmental psychopathology. *Journal of Child Psychology and Psychiatry and Allied Disciplines, 37,* 51–87.

Ruff, H. A., & Rothbart, M. K. (1996). *Attention in early development: Themes and variations.* New York: Oxford University Press.

Sergeant, J. A., Guerts, H., & Oosterlaan, J. (2002). How specific is a deficit of executive functioning for attention-deficit/hyperactivity disorder? *Behavioural Brain Research, 130,* 3–28.

Silver, C. (2000). Ecological validity in neuropsychological assessment in childhood traumatic brain injury. *Journal of Head Trauma Rehabilitation, 15,* 973–988.

Vaughn, B. E., Kopp, C. B., & Krakow, J. B. (1984). The emergence and consolidation of self-control from eighteen to thirty months of age: Normative trends and individual differences. *Child Development, 55,* 990–1004.

Wellman, H. M. (1988). The early development of memory strategies. In F. E. Weinert & M. Perlmutter (Eds.), *Memory development: Universal changes and individual differences* (pp. 3–29). Hillsdale, NJ: Lawrence Erlbaum Associates, Inc.

Welsh, M. C., Pennington, B. F., & Grossier, D. B. (1991). a normative–developmental study of executive function: a window on prefrontal function in children. *Developmental Neuropsychology, 7*, 131–149.

DEVELOPMENTAL NEUROPSYCHOLOGY, 26(1), 423–443
Copyright © 2004, Lawrence Erlbaum Associates, Inc.

Executive Functioning in Preschoolers: Reducing the Inhibitory Demands of the Dimensional Change Card Sort Task

David A. C. Rennie and Rebecca Bull
School of Psychology
University of Aberdeen, Scotland

Adele Diamond
Center for Developmental Cognitive Neuroscience
University of Massachusetts Medical School

To investigate the role of inhibitory control in preschoolers' ability to switch sets, 3 conditions of the Dimensional Change Card Sort task (Zelazo, Reznick, & Pinon, 1995) were tested. In Condition B (novel response options, standard stimuli) action inhibition was reduced, but the need for attentional inhibition was maintained. In Condition C (novel stimuli, standard response options) demands on both action and attentional inhibition were reduced. Performance in these was compared to that in the standard condition (A). Rule complexity was comparable across conditions. All 21 children who passed preswitch (average age 37 months) were tested on all postswitch conditions, order counterbalanced. Although reducing demands on action inhibition (Condition B) did not significantly improve performance, when demands on both action and attentional inhibition were reduced (Condition C) almost all children (95%) successfully switched sets (even children only 2½ years old). Inadequate inhibition (of attention alone or both attention and action) appears sufficient to account for virtually all errors by preschoolers on this card sorting task.

Executive functioning (EF) is a highly complex set of processes essential to the everyday working of humans when controlled, rather than automatic, processing is required (Shallice, 1988). Although there is debate about what constitutes EF, these executive abilities, considered to be subserved by frontal systems, are evident in tasks such as the A-not-B (Piaget, 1954), Stroop (Stroop, 1935), and Wis-

---

Requests for reprints should be sent to Rebecca Bull, School of Psychology, William Guild Building, University of Aberdeen, Scotland AB24 2UB. E-mail: r.bull@abdn.ac.uk

consin Card Sorting (Heaton, Chelune, Talley, Kay, & Curtiss, 1993) tasks. Important processes subsumed under EF include forming abstract concepts, constructing and using a sequenced plan of action, focusing and sustaining attention or mental effort, manipulating information held in mind, cognitive and behavioral flexibility, being able to inhibit impulsive or inappropriate responses, and being able to self-monitor and detect errors as a task is being performed (Hughes, 2004; Liss et al., 2001). A marked improvement in EF occurs between the ages of 3 and 5 years that is particularly apparent on tasks that require holding information in mind plus inhibition (Diamond, 2002; Diamond & Taylor, 1996; Gerstadt, Hong, & Diamond, 1994; Zelazo & Jacques, 1996; Zelazo, Reznick, & Pinon, 1995).

Frye, Zelazo, and Palfai (1995) created the Dimensional Change Card Sort (DCCS) task to assess the extent to which young children are able to hold two sets of rules in mind, apply them, and switch between them. The DCCS task requires children to sort picture cards according to shape or color. Initially 3-year-olds have few problems with the task, but many have great difficulty when asked to switch sorting criteria, irrespective of which criterion was used first. From the age of 4 to 5 years and on, most children can successfully switch to sort by the second dimension. It is interesting that children who fail the postswitch phase of the test by sorting perseveratively (continuing to sort by the preswitch criterion) display an apparent dissociation between knowing the rules and using them (Zelazo, Frye, & Rapus, 1996). For example, 3-year-olds answer knowledge questions ("Can you show me where the red ones/blue ones (stars/trucks) go?") correctly pre- and postswitch, showing that they understand and know the rules. However, during the postswitch they do not apply the rules they have just indicated they know. Instead, they continue sorting by the previously correct dimension. In some ways this is reminiscent of Luria and Homskaya's (1964) observation that adults with frontal lobe damage who consistently verbalized the correct sorting rules, simultaneously sorted cards in such a way as to violate those stated rules. Recent studies examining the performance of children aged 3 to 5 years on other measures requiring holding information in mind plus inhibitory control support a dissociation between children's intact knowledge of rules for the task and their apparent lack of sufficient inhibitory control to correctly apply those rules—for example, go/no-go task (Dowsett & Livesey, 2000), delay gratification (Mischel & Mischel, 1983), and the windows task (Russell, Mauthner, Sharpe, & Tidswell, 1991).

Munakata (2001) and Munakata and Yerys (2001) maintained that this apparent dissociation can be explained in terms of graded knowledge representations, with strength of the representation being dependent on factors such as the stage of development of an individual. Munakata and Yerys suggested that stronger representations are required to resolve conflict, for example, in situations where there might be a conflict between a new rule (color) and an old rule (shape). Answering a standard knowledge question, such as "Where do red things go in the color game?" does not require conflict resolution. However, when children are asked, "Where does the red truck go in the color game?" after they have just played the shape game, they err in the verbal response as well as in their manual sorting response (Munakata & Yerys, 2001), suggesting that there is no dissociation between action and knowledge when the two measures are equated in terms of conflict.

Kirkham, Cruess, and Diamond (2003) argued from the same results that children succeed when memory, but not inhibition, is taxed (nonconflict situations), but fail when inhibition is required (conflict situations), indicating that it is the need for the exercise of inhibitory control that causes problems for the children. Certainly, children have not simply forgotten that the sorting criterion has switched or what it has switched to, as the experimenter emphasizes that rules have been changed and mentions what the new criterion is. Children are reminded of the sorting criterion on every trial, and in some studies are asked to restate the new rules during the task (Zelazo et al., 1995). Children's correct answers to the knowledge questions provide evidence of their intact recall of the rules, Kirkham et al. (2003) argued. Indeed, where children are required to remember more than two rules, but where no switching between sorting criteria is required, children are capable of maintaining the rules in memory and acting correctly (Zelazo & Frye, 1998).

Another theory attempting to account for children's difficulties on tasks such as the DCCS is the Cognitive Complexity and Control (CCC) theory (Zelazo & Frye, 1997, 1998). This theory posits a system of levels of rule use, with the level at which a child can function depending on age. According to the CCC theory, 2-year-olds can only operate at the lowest level. For example, they can correctly sort blue cards into a blue pile, but when given red cards they also put those in the blue pile. At around 3 years of age, children can use a pair of rules; for example, "Blue ones go here and red ones go there" *or* "Trucks go here and stars go there." It is not until 4 or 5 years of age, according to the CCC theory, however, that children are able to embed both sets of rules in a more complex hierarchical structure; for example, "In the color game, blue ones go here and red ones go there. In the shape game, however, trucks go here and stars go there." That is, if we are playing the shape game, a blue truck should be sorted with the red trucks, not with the blue stars. Thus according to the CCC theory, 3-year-olds do not change their mode of sorting when the sorting criterion changes because they are unable to effectively represent the hierarchical rule structure.

Manipulations of the DCCS task that seem to support the CCC interpretation of why 3-year-olds fail to switch sorting criteria on the DCCS task include the work of Jacques, Zelazo, Kirkham, and Semcesen (1999), who added an error-detection component to the task. By examining children critiquing a third party performing the task, Jacques et al. reasoned that the response control (inhibition) component of the task would be reduced, and thus the ability to apply the rules would be the main ability assessed. Children of 3 years failed the postswitch phase when undertaking it themselves *and* when critiquing a puppet performing the task. They failed to detect when the puppet sorted perseveratively, and they reported that the puppet was wrong when it correctly switched sorting criteria in the postswitch phase. Jacques et al.'s interpretation of this result was that the 3-year-olds' failure on the task occurs because they are unable to represent, manipulate, and reflect on the rules (i.e., their rule-use system is immature). The authors argued that if 3-year-olds' failure on the DCCS task were due to a lack of response control (inhibition), children would have been able to recognize that the puppet was sorting perseveratively. However, this does not preclude the possibility that failure was due to lack of attentional inhibition. Diamond and Kirkham (2001) proposed that a failure of attentional inhibition would be expected to produce the pattern of results obtained by Jacques et al (1999).

Recent findings seem incompatible with the complexity-of-rule-use interpretation. In particular, two recent studies have shown that 3-year-olds can succeed in switching even when they must hold two sets of rules in mind, each set having two subordinate rules apiece, just as is in the DCCS task, *as long as the children do not have to switch the dimension to which they are attending* (Brooks, Hanauer, Padowska, & Rosman, 2003; Perner & Lang, 2002). For example, 3-year-olds can reverse sorting rules, so that in the "sensible" game they sort trucks with trucks and stars with stars and then switch to sorting trucks with stars and stars with trucks in the "silly" game. This hierarchical, embedded rule structure would seem as complex as that in the DCCS task. Presumably there must be some other reason why 3-year-olds succeed here but not on the DCCS task. Indeed, there is considerable evidence (e.g., Roberts et al., 1994; Rogers, Andrews, Grasby, Brooks, & Robbins, 2000) that intradimensional shifts (shifts that stay within a single dimension, as in Brooks et al., 2003, and Perner & Lang, 2002), are often easier than extradimensional shifts (shifting from one dimension to another, as in the standard DCCS task). The question is, if intra- and extradimensional shifts do not differ in the complexity of rule structure, what is the critical difference that makes intradimensional shifting easier? Often the difficulty in an extradimensional shift is in thinking a bit "outside the box," in realizing that a different dimension might be relevant and in considering what that newly relevant dimension might be. That is not the case with the DCCS task, however, because participants do not have to deduce the relevant dimension, as the relevant dimension is restated by the examiner on every trial.

Diamond and Kirkham (2001; Kirkham et al., 2003) proposed that children fail the standard DCCS task because of "attentional inertia," that is, insufficient inhibitory control of attention to enable 3-year-olds to break their attentional focus on the initial sorting dimension. Contrary to other explanations, Diamond and Kirkham argued that before the stimulus appears, 3-year-olds are ready to perform correctly; they have clearly in mind what the new sorting criterion is, and the appropriate rules for that dimension. This is shown by their correct responses to the knowledge questions. The problem occurs, according to Diamond and Kirkham, when a stimulus card is presented that is relevant to both the pre- and postswitch sorting dimensions in incompatible ways (i.e., if sorting by Dimension 1, the card should go here, but if sorting by Dimension 2 the card should go there). Children's attention is pulled to the previously relevant dimension; they must then inhibit that pull. Children of 3 years are thus said to have difficulty redirecting their attention to a newly relevant sorting dimension when the values of the previously correct dimension are still present. They have a problem disengaging from a mindset (a way of thinking about the stimuli) that is no longer relevant, hence showing attentional inertia (see also, Allport, Styles, & Hsieh, 1994; Allport & Wylie, 2000). This theory can easily account for the findings of Jacques et al. (1999) because the cognitive set currently held by the children would drive what they expect the puppet to do, that is, to continue sorting by the dimension to which they had previously been attending.

Findings consistent with this point of view include those of Zelazo, Frye, Reznick, Schuster, and Argitis (1995, as cited in Zelazo & Jacques, 1996). They found that if the stimulus cards were changed only along the dimension that had previously been irrelevant, but maintained the values that had been relevant to sorting during the preswitch phase (e.g., sorting red and blue rabbits by color in the preswitch phase, and blue and red flowers by shape at postswitch), then children still had great difficulty on the postswitch trials and continued sorting according to the preswitch rule (color). Kirkham et al. (2003) argued that the reason for the difficulty is the presence of the previously relevant values of the previously relevant dimension. Zelazo et al. (1995, Expt. 3, cf Zelazo & Jacques, 1996) found that when the postswitch cards differed along both dimensions (color and shape), younger children were much more successful. Here, rule complexity was unchanged from the standard condition, but the previously relevant values of the preswitch dimension were no longer available to divert children's attention from what they should be focusing on postswitch. This finding would appear to be consistent with the "attentional inertia" hypothesis, but not with CCC theory.

According to Diamond and Kirkham (2001; Kirkham et al., 2003), the familiar target cards, each with a valid value on the previously relevant dimension, serve as attractors, pulling the child to think and act according to the previously relevant rules. Consistent with that idea, 3-year-olds succeed if the previously relevant values on the now irrelevant dimension are no longer present on the target cards or, indeed, when no target cards are present at all (Perner & Lang, 2002; Towse, Redbond, Houston-Price, & Cook, 2000). Because that manipulation does not change the complexity of the rule structure of the task, it is hard to see how CCC theory could account for such findings.

Kirkham et al. (2003) administered new conditions of the DCCS task that varied in inhibitory demand. In the "label" condition, for example, instead of the experimenter labeling the relevant sorting dimension of the test card on each trial, the child did so. Kirkham and colleagues reasoned that having children label the relevant dimension of the card to be sorted would help them inhibit attending to the previously relevant dimension and help them refocus their attention on the currently relevant dimension. Indeed, significantly more 3-year-olds were able to switch sorting dimensions. In another manipulation, inhibitory demand was increased by having children sort the cards into trays face up, rather than with the picture facing down. After the switch, a child might have to sort a blue truck by color but be faced with seeing a blue truck card under the red truck target card and a red star card under the blue star target card. Hence, the picture sitting in the tray should intensify the perceptual pull to continue sorting by the previous dimension. As predicted, fewer 4-year-olds were able to switch sorting dimensions in the face-up condition than in the standard condition or any other condition.

Another possible reason why 3-year-olds do not switch to sorting by the second dimension on the DCCS task might be that they are unable to inhibit the prepotent response of sorting by the previously correct stimulus-response mappings. Indeed, Towse et al. (2000) argued that the inhibitory failure is at the level of action. If an inability to inhibit a dominant response tendency were the reason 3-year-olds fail to switch on the DCCS task, one might expect that the more times they sorted by the first criterion the more likely they would be to perseverate. However, even after only one preswitch trial, most 3-year-olds fail to switch sorting criteria (Zelazo et al., 1995, as cited in Zelazo & Jacques, 1996; Zelazo et al., 1996). Their performance after one preswitch trial is not significantly different from their performance after six preswitch trials. That result is not devastating finding for this perspective, however, because a bias or conditioned tendency can be instilled by just one trial (e.g., Thompson, 1990). However, Jacques et al.'s (1999) findings would also be inconsistent with a response-inhibition interpretation.

Inhibition of action and inhibition of attention might reflect different processes, even though both involve *inhibition.* For example, Mayr and Keele (2000) proposed that there are two types of inhibitory processes involved in switching tasks. One, the need to resist goal-incongruent action tendencies (stimulus-response mappings), and two, the need to flexibly change attentional control settings. Bunge, Dudukovic, Thomason, Vaidya, and Gabrieli (2002) reported different patterns of maturation, and different patterns of neural activation, for interference suppression (inhibition of attention) and response inhibition (inhibition of action).

Our study looked at the effect of reducing the demand on inhibition of action, and of reducing the demand on inhibition of both action and attention, on preschoolers' performance of the DCCS task. The three conditions of the DCCS task varied in the level of inhibition required but maintained the same level of rule complexity (two rule sets, color and shape, each with two subordinate rules), and all used cards with stimuli that had both color and shape. In the standard DCCS condition (Condition A), blue trucks and red stars served as the stimuli, and a blue star and red truck were each pictured on one of the target cards. Each target card was mounted over one of the two sorting bins (see Figure 1).

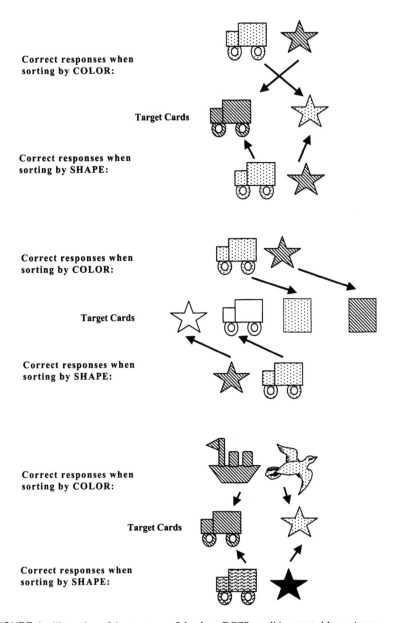

Correct responses when sorting by COLOR:

Target Cards

Correct responses when sorting by SHAPE:

Correct responses when sorting by COLOR:

Target Cards

Correct responses when sorting by SHAPE:

Correct responses when sorting by COLOR:

Target Cards

Correct responses when sorting by SHAPE:

FIGURE 1   Illustration of the structure of the three DCCS conditions tested here. Arrows show correct sorts. The top panel illustrates Condition A: Standard DCCS. The middle panel illustrates Condition B: Reduced Action Inhibition (univalent target cards). The bottom panel illustrates Condition C: Reduced Attentional and Action Inhibition (each stimulus card matched only one target card and along only one dimension; different stimulus cards used pre-and postswitch).

In Condition B, the response options were changed. Four sorting bins were used, and the target card mounted over each was unidimensional (i.e., "univalent:" colorless truck or star against a white background, or red or blue rectangle). The same stimulus cards as in Condition A were used. Because the stimulus cards still contained relevant values along both dimensions, if attention were not inhibited to the wrong dimension, a response option was available to sort by that wrong dimension. The advantage of Condition B over the standard condition is that the correct answers here for the postswitch trials were *not* answers that had been relevant (actively inhibited) during the preswitch phase. In Condition B, children still had to understand and remember which dimension was currently relevant, and they still had to switch the focus of their attention from one dimension to another, but different stimulus-response mappings were relevant pre- and postswitch so that the old stimulus-response mappings did not have to be overridden. Therefore, this condition decreased the possibility of perseveration at the level of action (see Figure 1).

In Condition C, the same response options (same target cards over the same two bins) as in the standard condition were used, but the stimuli were changed. The stimulus cards used here were yellow and green trucks and stars for sorting by shape, and red and blue birds and boats for sorting by color. Hence, any given stimulus card matched only one target card and did so along only one dimension; no inhibition was required because only one response option was relevant to any given stimulus card. Here, old stimulus-response mappings did not need to be inhibited (they were not an option postswitch), and attention to the previously relevant dimension did not need to be inhibited (no relevant values on the previously relevant dimension were presented during the postswitch phase). Hence, this condition reduced the necessity for inhibition at the level of attention and action (see Figure 1).

Our predictions were that (a) children of 3 years would fail the standard task (Condition A), that is, they would not switch sorting dimensions; (b) more 3-year-olds would succeed on Condition B (reduced demand on action inhibition) than Condition A, and a greater number of the younger children would succeed as well; (c) Condition C (reduced demand on attentional and action inhibition) should be the easiest condition; most 3-year-olds would pass (i.e., successfully switch sorting dimensions).

METHOD

Participants

Thirty-three children between the ages of 30 and 46 months ($M = 37$ months, $SD = 4$ months) were tested. There were 17 girls and 16 boys. All were British White children, with English as their first language, recruited through private day care centers located in lower middle-class areas in Aberdeen, Scotland. Children were tested following informed parental consent. Children with known developmental delays (as identified by the teacher) did not take part in the study. All children were tested in all DCCS conditions, with the order of conditions and initial stimulus dimension to be sorted (shape or color) counterbalanced within each gender and among the oldest half and youngest half of the children.

Materials

Laminated 15-cm × 12-cm test cards were sorted into 30-cm × 21-cm × 10-cm boxes. The height of the back of the boxes was raised to 24 cm to accommodate the laminated target cards, which were situated 12 cm above the level of the box and were always at the child's eye level during testing. On each of the cards used, the picture was situated in the middle of the card with a white background behind the picture and a black border on the edge of the card, except for the single-color cards in Condition B, which were the same size, but the entire card was of the color required. Target cards for Condition A were a blue star and a red truck, and the stimulus cards were a red star and a blue truck. Training cards were blue and red grapes and yellow trucks and stars. In Condition B, the four target cards were just the outline drawings of a truck or star (i.e., no color fill) against a white background, and entirely blue or entirely red cards. The stimulus cards and training cards were the same as in Condition A. The target cards in Condition C were the same as Condition A. The stimulus cards for Condition C were yellow trucks and green stars and red boats and blue birds. The training cards were red and blue grapes and colorless trucks and stars. Colorless rather than yellow training cards were used because the stimulus cards were colored yellow and introducing a new color into the task might have been confusing. The cards matched exactly those used by Kirkham et al. (2003) with the addition of colorless stimulus cards and cards that were entirely red or blue.

Design

The study incorporates a within-subjects design with three levels (standard, reduced response inhibition, and reduced attentional and response-inhibition DCCS conditions). There were four between-subject factors: condition order, dimension order (sorting by shape or color first), gender, and age. Children were randomly assigned to the order in which the conditions and the stimulus dimensions were presented. The dependent variable was the accuracy in sorting the card on each trial. Children were required to achieve five consecutively correct responses out of a total of six trials to pass the preswitch condition, and five consecutively correct responses out of six trials to pass the postswitch.

Procedure

Procedures Relevant to All Conditions

Children were asked to sort stimulus cards one at a time into sorting trays according to one of two criteria, color or shape, and then by the other criterion. Stimulus cards were always presented to the children face up and in the middle, between the target trays (between the two trays in Conditions A and C and between Trays 2 and 3 in Condition B). The children were given a short introduction to the task, followed by training on each dimension with stimulus cards that matched the target cards on only one dimension (for the color game the training cards had pictures of blue and red grapes, and for the shape game the training cards had pictures of the relevant shapes, trucks and stars, in a neutral color, yellow). Training took place once the child was comfortable and settled, with the experimenter giving the following instructions:

> Now we are going to play a card game. In this game we play the color (shape) or shape (color) game. In the color (shape) game all the blue ones (trucks) go in this tray (experimenter points), and all the red ones (stars) go in this tray (again, experimenter points).

These sentences were used again later in the session when the rules were restated between trials. Next, the child was asked, "Can you point and show me where the blue/red ones (trucks/stars) go?" (Child points, experimenter praises if correct, and restates the rules if incorrect.) "Here's a blue one (truck). Where does it go?" (Child sorts card by placing it face down in a tray. Experimenter praises if correct, and corrects the child if wrong.) "Here's a red one (star). Where does it go?" To pass the training and continue with the game, the child had to correctly sort four cards (two for each dimension) and was only allowed a total of eight attempts during training. All children passed the training phase.

Test trials began immediately after the last training trial with the experimenter saying, "Now we are going to keep playing the shape (color) game" and was based on the dimension last sorted (e.g., if the last training card was a yellow truck, the first test dimension would be shape). Half the children started with color first and half with shape; this was true for each of the three conditions (A, B, and C). When each test card was shown, the experimenter said, "Here is a truck (star, red one, blue one). Where does it go?"—always labeling the card along the currently relevant dimension. The cards were presented in a predetermined pseudorandom order.

After the trials at the first dimension (preswitch), the game was switched to the other dimension. This postswitch phase was initiated by the experimenter saying, "Now we are going to play the other game. Do you remember the color (shape) game?" The experimenter then restated the rules and asked knowledge questions to make sure the child knew how to sort the cards correctly according to the new dimension. All children answered the knowledge questions correctly. Testing on the second dimension continued until the child achieved five consecutive correct responses out of the six postswitch trials administered. During either phase (pre- or postswitch), if the child sorted incorrectly five times in a row, the experimenter reverted back to the training cards for the dimension currently in use and administered those cards until the child sorted both training cards correctly. After this, the experimenter continued with more postswitch trials. At the end of the testing each child was praised for his or her performance.

During the intertrial intervals, the experimenter alternated between restating the relevant rules or asking the child knowledge questions for each of the two currently relevant rules ("Can you tell me where the red ones/blue ones (stars/trucks) go?"). No feedback was given throughout the test trials on the sorting of any card. Feedback was only given to responses to knowledge questions between trials. Sorting by the first dimension continued until the child made five consecutive correct responses, or until the first six trials had been administered. Children who failed to pass the preswitch trials continued with the postswitch phase, although their data was not included in the postswitch analysis ($n = 12$) because preswitch failure indicated inadequate establishment of the prepotent response set. All children who passed preswitch also answered all knowledge questions correctly.

Condition Specific Procedures

Condition A.   This is the baseline condition, comparable to the original card sort procedure of Zelazo et al. (1996) and identical to that of Kirkham et al. (2003), described previously.

Condition B.   This is the univalent response or reduced action-inhibition condition, where the relevant response options changed from pre- to postswitch. Here, the inhibition that had been instituted during the preswitch ("Don't go to red, go to blue on this trial" or "Don't go to the truck, go to the star this time") did not have to be reversed. In this condition there were four trays on the table throughout training and testing, with univalent target cards (colorless star, colorless truck, blue card, red card) attached to them (see Figure 1). The trays faced the child in this order: star, truck, blue, red. In all other respects the procedure here was identical to that used in Condition A.

Condition C.   This is the reduced attentional and action-inhibition condition. Although each stimulus still had a color and a shape, any stimulus card only matched the target cards along one dimension. The stimulus cards were yellow trucks and green stars and red boats and blue birds. The training cards were red and blue grapes and colorless trucks and stars. The response trays and target cards were the same as in Condition A. Thus, for example, a green truck matched no target card by color, but matched the red truck target card by shape (see Figure 1). Therefore, this condition decreased the need for inhibition of an irrelevant dimension and did not require that stimulus-response mappings be changed. The procedure was the same as in Condition A except (a) the stimulus cards matched the target cards along only one dimension, and (b) the shape dimension was trained by using colorless trucks and stars and not trucks and stars in a neutral color.

RESULTS

Initial analyses examined the number of children correctly sorting five or more cards on preswitch trials for each condition to investigate whether there were any differences in performance across the different DCCS conditions prior to the category switch. This analysis also investigated whether any of the confounding variables (age, gender, condition order, and dimension presentation order [color vs. switch first]) had an effect on performance. Generalized estimating equations (GEEs) were carried out on the data to take account of the repeated measures structure of the data (see Table 1 for a summary of the results). The GEE model used an exchangeable correlation structure, binomial error and logit link.

This analysis showed that there was a marginal, nonsignificant difference in the number of children passing the preswitch phase across the three DCCS conditions ($Z = 4.94$, $p = .09$). A total of 12 children failed the preswitch phase (1 child failed Conditions A and B, 7 failed Condition A only, 2 failed Condition B

TABLE 1
Generalized Estimating Equations Analysis of
Dimensional Change Card Sort Task Pre- and Post
Switch Performance as a Function of Potential
Confounding Variables

Variable	Z Value	p Value
Pre switch ($N = 33$)		
Age	0.18	0.85
Gender	0.19	0.85
Condition order	5.93	0.05
Dimension order	0.11	0.91
Post switch ($N = 21$)		
Age	1.08	0.28
Gender	1.10	0.27
Condition order	1.21	0.55
Dimension order	0.54	0.59

Note. GEE = Generalized Estimating Equations; DCCS = Dimensional Change Card Sort Task only, and 2 failed Condition C only). Furthermore, the order in which the conditions were presented was related to the likelihood of passing each of the preswitch conditions ($Z = 5.93$, $p = .05$). Children were significantly more likely to pass the preswitch trials of Condition A if they had completed that condition first, rather than when it followed either of the remaining DCCS conditions. Thus, experience with the easier conditions appeared to have been helpful to children when subsequently tested on the standard DCCS condition. The preswitch trials for Condition A were slightly more complex (because of the bivalent target and response cards) than those for Conditions B and C. However, in all conditions, the stimulus cards were only labeled according to the currently relevant dimension. Children who failed a preswitch phase of any condition were removed from all postswitch analyses, leaving a sample of 21 children. The sex ratio and mean age of the remaining children did not differ from that of the total sample (50% girls, M age = 37 months, SD = 4 months).

To determine the most appropriate method for analyzing performance on the postswitch trials, the frequency and distribution of the number of correct responses in each condition were examined. Figure 2 shows that in the majority of cases, children's performance was consistent throughout postswitch (i.e., six correct sorts or no correct sorts). Very few children showed success on some trials and not others. Therefore, it is appropriate to treat success–failure as a dichotomous variable. Again, GEE analysis was conducted to check for any confounding effects in order of presentation of task conditions, order of sorting by stimulus dimension, age, or gender on success outcome in the three DCCS conditions. Children were deemed to have passed if they made at least five consecutively correct sorts within

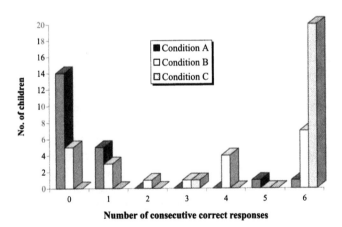

FIGURE 2   Number of children showing 0, 1, 2, 3, 4, 5, or 6 correct consecutive postswitch responses in Condition A (standard), Condition B (reduced action inhibition), and Condition C (reduced attentional and action inhibition).

six postswitch trials. None of the potentially confounding variables (or interactions among the variables) were found to have a significant effect on the likelihood of passing or failing the postswitch trials (see Table 1).

Observation of the raw data in Figure 2 shows that the number of children passing in each of the postswitch conditions differs dramatically, with only 2 children (10%) passing the postswitch in Condition A, 7 (33%) passing in Condition B, and 20 (95%) passing in Condition C. Due to the very low failure rate in Condition C and the very high rate of failure in Condition A, it was not possible to estimate the effect of condition using GEE to account for the repeat observations per child. However, a lower order Cochran's Q analysis was conducted, a test that is particularly suitable when the data are in a nominal scale or are dichotomized ordinal information (Siegel, 1956). This analysis revealed a significant difference in performance in the three postswitch conditions $Q(df = 2, N = 21) = 25.52, p < .001$. Analysis of each pairwise comparison using the McNemar Test revealed that children were significantly more likely to pass Condition C than Conditions A and B (all $ps < .001$: C vs. A, C vs. B, and C vs. A & B), but there was no significant difference in performance between Conditions A and B ($p = .18$).[1] The increase in numbers of children successfully switching dimensions in Condition C was not restricted to just the oldest children in the sample, but was seen even in children only 30 months old.

DISCUSSION

The failure rate for children around age 3 years on the postswitch phase of Condition A (standard DCCS procedure) was very high, indeed higher than predicted. It was expected that a majority would fail, as most children cannot switch dimensions on the standard DCCS test until about 48 to 60 months of age (Kirkham et al., 2003; Zelazo & Jacques, 1996; Zelazo et al., 1995), and the average age of children in this study was only 37 months. The higher than typical failure rate may have been due to the very young age of our participants. Reducing the need for action inhibition (Condition B) resulted in more children passing the task, but not significantly more than in the standard DCCS condition. When demands on both attentional and action inhibition were reduced (Condition C), significantly more

---

[1] Pairwise comparisons were conducted both (a) excluding all subjects who failed the preswitch phase in any of the three conditions and (b) only excluding those subjects who failed the preswitch phase of either of the two relevant conditions for each pairwise comparison. In all cases, performance in Condition C was significantly better at the $p < .001$ level than performance in Condition A or B. When only those participants who failed the preswitch phases of Conditions A or B were excluded from that pairwise comparison, the significance level improved from $p < .18$ to $p < .11$, but it still failed to reach the threshold for being considered statistical significant.

children succeeded at the postswitch phase than in Conditions A or B, with 95% of children successfully switching sorting dimensions, including children as young as 2½ years of age.

Before discussing the results for each condition in more detail, a few cautionary notes are necessary. First, the number of participants (21) who correctly sorted according to the initial sorting dimension in the preswitch phase was relatively small, and hence the number of participants who could be included in analyses of postswitch performance was comparably small. However, that sample size of 21 is larger than the number of participants tested in each condition in other DCCS studies—in some cases over twice as large. Furthermore, limited information regarding sociodemographics and other cognitive skills of the participants limits the generalizations that can be made to the population as a whole.

Performance on Condition A

In the standard condition of the DCCS task there is (a) a need to inhibit the stimulus-response mappings relevant preswitch (action inhibition) and replace them with opposing stimulus-response mappings postswitch and (b) a need to stop focusing on the properties of the dimension that had been relevant preswitch (attentional inhibition), instead focusing on the previously ignored dimension. Virtually all children failed to switch sorting dimensions in Condition A, which required inhibition at both the level of attention and action. This result is consistent with the myriad of previous findings using the standard DCCS task (e.g., Zelazo et al., 1996), although the failure rate here (90%) is particularly high. That might be due to the unusually young age of participants in this study (many not yet 3 years old). It is not until 4 or 5 years of age that children become skilled at extradimensional set shifting, even when no hypothesis testing or deduction is required to figure out which dimension is newly relevant.

Performance on Condition B

Condition B presented four univalent response options, each relevant to only one dimension (e.g., a colorless truck). Children could err by responding to the previously relevant sorting dimension, as each stimulus card matched one target card by shape and another by color. Because the stimulus cards still contained relevant values along both dimensions, children could focus on the wrong dimension if attention were not inhibited. More important, however, correct answers postswitch were not answers that had been relevant preswitch (thus they had not been actively inhibited or "negatively primed"). Also, because different responses (different stimulus-response mappings) were relevant pre- and postswitch, the need for action inhibition was greatly reduced. If children fail because of a difficulty inhibiting an action tendency, as opposed to difficulty refocusing attention onto the relevant dimension, then 3-year-old children should be more successful in this condition. The findings show that this was not the case, although the success rate was somewhat higher in this condition. It may be the case that because the locus of attention on the preswitch trials was spatially distinct from the postswitch trials (i.e., different sorting bins were used on the postswitch trials), the tendency to see the previous dimension as relevant may have been diminished. Therefore, we were not able to rule out the possibility that in some way, attentional inhibition (even if only to a small extent) was also reduced in this condition, accounting for the increase (although nonsignificant) in success rate.

Towse et al. (2000) also compared two-tray and four-tray conditions. Unlike here, they found most children succeeding when four sorting trays were used. However, they also found most children succeeding in the standard two-tray DCCS condition, making interpretation of their results difficult. The children in Towse et al.'s study were significant older (approximately 42–52 months of age) than the children tested here, which may account for why they performed so well in conditions resembling our Conditions A and B.

Performance on Condition C

Condition C reduced demands on both the attentional and action inhibition required for switching. Attentional inhibition was reduced because each stimulus card only matched one target card, and along only one valid dimension. For example, because the target cards were a blue truck and a red star, if the preswitch sorting dimension was color, children were shown stimulus cards with blue and red birds and boats. Both shape and color dimensions were shown, but only the color dimension matched any target card. At postswitch (shape), the child was presented with green and yellow trucks and stars. Now, the presented values on the previously correct dimension (color) were no longer valid. They did not match the color of any target card. The rule structure was the same as for Conditions A and B, however (two if, then rules for color and two if, then rules for shape).

In the terminology of Diamond and Kirkham (2001; Kirkham et al., 2003), there was no "attentional inertia" in Condition C. Their theory stated that depending on which criterion was used first, the child may become fixed on the "blueness" or the "truckness" of the stimuli and may have trouble inhibiting attention to that dimension. Because the values along the preswitch dimension changed (and were not valid—i.e., matched no target card) at postswitch, children should not have had difficulty inhibiting their focus on, for example, "blueness," as "blueness" at postswitch was no longer present. No postswitch stimulus card contained blue. Hence the switch to attending to the relevant dimension (e.g., "truckness") should have been easier.

Also, no remapping of stimulus-response associations was needed here. It was not the case that during preswitch one response was correct for a red bird stimulus and during postswitch another response was correct for that stimulus. The red bird stimulus was never presented during the postswitch phase. Because there was no overlap of stimulus cards pre- and postswitch, no response to any stimulus card needed to be remapped from the pre- to the postswitch phase.

By reducing the demand on attentional and action inhibition, more children could successfully make the switch from sorting by shape to color (or vice versa), with 95% of children passing the postswitch trials despite their young age. We are not able to conclude from these results whether such a high rate of success in this condition resulted from the reduction in attentional inhibition, or from the conjunction of reduced action and attentional inhibition. Clearly, the answer to this would be found by using a condition that only reduced attentional inhibition. Kirkham et al. (2003) constructed a condition that required switching the stimulus-response mappings (i.e., the action inhibition) but which made the correct sorting dimension at postswitch more salient by having the children label the stimulus card (see also, Towse et al., 2000). It was proposed that this modification reduced the attentional inertia to the previously correct dimension, and it did indeed result in better sorting performance. What can be concluded from these results is that inhibitory demands on attention alone, or the conjunction of attention plus action (although not action alone), can account for essentially all of the difficulty that 3-year-olds, and even 2½-year-olds have on the DCCS task. By reducing inhibitory demands in Condition C, virtually all the children were able to succeed.

A LARGER CONTEXT IN WHICH TO CONSIDER OUR RESULTS

Improvement in performance, produced by reducing demands on attentional inhibition, or attentional plus action inhibition, is in line with results with other cognitive tasks where demands on attentional inhibition were minimized by reducing the perceptual salience of the stimulus dimensions. For example, in an appearance–reality task, the perceptual salience of the stimulus was decreased by removing the object from view during questioning, resulting in significantly better performance by 3- or 4-year-old children (Herbele, Clune, & Kelly, 1999). Children of 3 or 4 years generally fail tests of liquid conservation (they tend to focus exclusively on the most perceptually salient of the two dimensions; Flavell, 1963). If the salience of the visual perception that the tall, thin container contains more liquid is mitigated by placing an opaque screen between the child and the containers before the child answers, children 3 to 4 years of age can succeed (Bruner, 1964). Similarly, manipulations that reduce the perceptual salience of the true state of affairs on false belief and theory of mind tasks enable children of 3 or 4 years to succeed (such as telling the children where the object is really hidden but never actually showing them; Zaitchik, 1991).

Reducing the inhibitory demands required for switching sorting criteria may be accomplished by removing the target cards (Perner & Lang, 2002; Towse et al., 2000), having children label the stimulus card themselves to refocus attention on the relevant dimension (Kirkham et al., 2003), or by eliminating the need to refocus attention by making values of the previously relevant stimulus dimension invalid (our study; Zelazo et al., 1995). In all of those conditions, children of 3 years are able to shift set and succeed at the task. Conversely, studies have shown that increasing demands on attentional inhibition can cause children of 3 or 4 years, who would otherwise succeed, to fail. Inhibitory demands imposed when shifting set are much less when the switch is intradimensional rather than extradimensional (as the former requires no attentional inhibition to a previously relevant dimension); 3-year-olds succeed at the former but not the latter (Brooks et al., 2003; Perner & Lang, 2002). However, Brooks et al. (2003) found that when a second dimension (color) was added to black-and-white line drawings that indicated shape, 3-year-olds then failed the reversal task, although color was never used or referred to in the experiment; it was simply present. Hanauer and Brooks (2003) found age-related improvements in children's ability to selectively attend to a visual Stroop task and ignore conflicting auditory cues (for example, hearing the word *purple* when *green* is the answer). They could correctly identify the colors when they were presented without conflicting stimuli, but they were unable to selectively attend to the visual stimuli when required to inhibit attention to auditory stimuli.

Most studies of attentional and action inhibition have begun testing at 3, 3½, or 4 years. It is interesting that in this study we found no difference in performance between 2½ and 3½ years. Children of 36 to 46 months performed as poorly as children of 30 to 35 months when inhibition was required, and children of 30 to 35 months performed as well as children of 36 to 46 months when demands on inhibition were reduced.

In summary, decreasing the inhibitory demands of the DCCS task enabled younger children to switch from a color task to a shape task or vice versa. The results of Condition C, in which inhibition was reduced at both the levels of attention and action, indicate that inadequate inhibitory control can account for a large proportion of the difficulty that children of 3 years have with the DCCS task. All 3-year-olds (indeed almost all 2½-year-olds) were able to succeed in making the switch when inhibitory control was not required (Condition C). With no inhibitory control required, this task essentially becomes a measure of the ability to hold rules in memory and to represent a hierarchical, embedded rule structure. Clearly, the evidence from this study, along with previous research findings, supports the idea that when the external environment is structured in such a manner as to reduce the inhibitory demands, children of 2½ to 3 years have the memory and representational skills to be able to learn, remember, and flexibly deploy rule sets.

ACKNOWLEDGMENTS

This research was completed in partial fulfillment for the BSc degree of David A. C. Rennie (University of Aberdeen, Scotland).

Sincere thanks go to all the staff and children from the participating nurseries; and to the staff at the Center for Developmental Cognitive Neuroscience at the Shriver Center, UMass Medical School, for their training of the tester, help with the preparation of the testing materials, and their support and inspiration, which contributed greatly to the production of this research. Thanks also to three anonymous reviewers for their insightful comments on a previous version of this manuscript.

REFERENCES

Allport, A., Styles, E. A., & Hsieh, S. (1994). Shifting intentional set: Exploring the dynamic control of tasks. In C. Umilta & M. Moscovitch (Eds.), *Attention and performance XV* (pp. 421–452). Cambridge, MA: MIT Press.

Allport, A., & Wylie, G. (2000). Task switching, stimulus-response bindings, and negative priming. In S. Monsell & J. Driver (Eds.), *Control of cognitive processes: Attention and performance XVII* (pp. 35–70). Cambridge, MA: MIT Press.

Brooks, P. J., Hanauer, J. B., Padowska, B., & Rosman, H. (2003). The role of selective attention in preschoolers' rule use in a novel dimensional card sort. *Cognitive Development, 18,* 195–215.

Bruner, J. S. (1964). The course of cognitive growth. *American Psychologist, 19,* 1–15.

Bunge, S. A., Dudukovic, N. M., Thomason, M. E., Vaidya, C. J., & Gabrieli, J. D. E. (2002). Immature frontal lobe contributions to cognitive control in children: Evidence from fMRI. *Neuron, 33,* 301–311.

Diamond, A. (2002). Normal development of prefrontal cortex from birth to young adulthood: Cognitive functions, anatomy, and biochemistry. In D. T. Stuss & R. T. Knight (Eds.), *Principles of frontal lobe function* (pp. 466–503). London, England: Oxford University Press.

Diamond, A., & Kirkham, N. (2001, October). Card sorting by children of 3 & 4 years and task switching by older children: Inhibition needed to overcome "attentional inertia." In *Rule use through the lens of the Dimensional Change Card Sort: What develops?* Symposium conducted at the meeting of the Cognitive Development Society, Virginia Beach, VA.

Diamond, A., & Taylor, C. (1996). Development of an aspect of executive control: Development of the abilities to remember what I said and to "Do as I say, not as I do." *Developmental Psychobiology, 29,* 315–334.

Dowsett, S. M., & Livesey, D. J. (2000). The development of inhibitory control in preschool children: Effects of "executive skills" training. *Developmental Psychobiology, 36,* 161–174.

Flavell, J. H. (1963). *The developmental psychology of Jean Piaget.* Princeton, NJ: Van Nostrand.

Frye, D., Zelazo, P. D., & Palfai, T. (1995). Theory of mind and rule-based reasoning. *Cognitive Development, 10,* 483–527.

Gerstadt, C. L., Hong, Y. J., & Diamond, A. (1994). The relationship between cognition and action: Performance of children 3.5–7 years on a Stroop-like day–night test. *Cognition, 53,* 129–153.

Hanauer, J. B., & Brooks, P. J. (2003). Developmental change in the cross-modal Stroop effect. *Perception and Psychophysics, 65,* 359–366.

Heaton, R. K., Chelune, G. J., Talley, J. L., Kay, G. G., & Curtiss, G. (1993). *Wisconsin Card Sorting Test Manual: Revised and Expanded.* New York: Psychological Assessment Resources.

Herbele, J., Clune, M., & Kelly, K. (1999, April). *Development of young children's understanding of the appearance reality distinction.* Paper presented at the biennial meeting of the Society for Research in Child Development, Albuquerque, NM.

Hughes, C. (in press). The development of executive functions. In B. Hopkins (Ed.), *Cambridge encyclopedia of child development.* Cambridge, England: Cambridge University Press.

Jacques, S., Zelazo, P. D., Kirkham, N. Z., & Semcesen, T. K. (1999). Rule selection versus rule execution in preschoolers: An error-detection approach. *Developmental Psychology, 35,* 770–780.

Kirkham, N. Z., Cruess, L., & Diamond, A. (2003). Helping children apply their knowledge to their behavior on a dimension-switching task. *Developmental Science, 6,* 449–467.

Liss, M., Fein, D., Allen, D., Dunn, M., Feinstein, C., Morris, R., et al. (2001). Executive functioning in high-functioning children with autism. *Journal of Child Psychology and Psychiatry, 42,* 261–270.

Luria, A. R., & Homskaya, E. D. (1964). Disturbance in the regulative role of speech with frontal lobe lesions. In J. M. Warren & K. Akert (Eds.), *The frontal granular cortex and behavior* (pp. 353–371). New York: McGraw-Hill.

Mayr, U., & Keele, S. (2000). Changing internal constraints on action: The role of backward inhibition. *Journal of Experimental Psychology: General, 129,* 4–26.

Mischel, H. N., & Mischel, W. (1983). The development of children's knowledge of self-control strategies. *Child Development, 54,* 603–619.

Munakata, Y. (2001). Graded representations in behavioral dissociations. *Trends in Cognitive Sciences, 5,* 309–315.

Munakata, Y., & Yerys, B. E. (2001). All together now: When dissociations between action and knowledge disappear. *Psychological Science, 12,* 335–337.

Perner, J., & Lang, B. (2002). What causes 3-year olds' difficulty on the dimensional change card sorting task? *Infant & Child Development, 11,* 93–105.

Piaget, J. (1954). *The construction of reality in the child.* New York: Basic Books.

Roberts, A. C., De Salvia, M. A., Wilkinson, L. S., Collins, P., Muir, J. L., Everitt, B. J., et al. (1994). 6-Hydroxydopamine lesions of the prefrontal cortex in monkeys enhance performance on an analog of the Wisconsin card sort test: Possible interactions with subcortical dopamine. *Journal of Neuroscience, 14,* 2531–2544.

Rogers, R. D., Andrews, T. C., Grasby, P. M., Brooks, D. J., & Robbins, T. W. (2000). Contrasting cortical and subcortical activations produced by attentional-set shifting and reversal learning in humans. *Journal of Cognitive Neuroscience, 12,* 142–162.

Russell, J., Mauthner, N., Sharpe, S., & Tidswell, T. (1991). The windows task as a measure of strategic deception in preschoolers and autistic subjects. *British Journal of Developmental Psychology, 9,* 331–349.

Shallice, T. (1988). *From neuropsychology to mental structure.* Cambridge, England: Cambridge University Press.

Siegel, S. (1956). *Nonparametric statistics for the behavioral sciences.* New York: McGraw-Hill.

Stroop, J. R. (1935). Studies of interference in serial verbal reactions. *Journal of Experimental Psychology, 18,* 643–662.

Thompson, R. F. (1990). Neural mechanisms of classical conditioning in mammals. *Philosophical Transactions of the Royal Society, B, 329,* 161–170.

Towse, J. N., Redbond, J., Houston-Price, C. M. T., & Cook, S. (2000). Understanding the dimensional change card sort: Perspectives from task success and failure. *Cognitive Development, 15,* 347–365.

Zaitchik, D. (1991). Is only seeing really believing? Sources of the true belief in the false belief task. *Cognitive Development, 6,* 91–103.

Zelazo, P. D., & Frye, D. (1997). Cognitive complexity and control: A theory of the development of deliberate reasoning and intentional action. In M. Stamenov (Ed.), *Language structure, discourse and the access to consciousness* (pp. 113–153). Philadelphia: Benjamins.

Zelazo, P. D., & Frye, D. (1998). Cognitive complexity and control: II. The development of executive function in childhood. *Current Directions in Psychological Science, 7,* 121–126.

Zelazo, P. D., Frye, D., & Rapus, T. (1996). An age-related dissociation between knowing rules and using them. *Cognitive Development, 11,* 37–63.

Zelazo, P. D., & Jacques, S. (1996). Children's rule-use: Representation, reflection and control. *Annals of Child Development, 12,* 119–176.

Zelazo, P. D., Reznick, J. S., & Pinon, D. E. (1995). Response control and the execution of verbal rules. *Developmental Psychology, 31,* 508–517.

DEVELOPMENTAL NEUROPSYCHOLOGY, 26(1), 445–464

Using Path Analysis to Understand Executive Function Organization in Preschool Children

Theresa E. Senn, Kimberly Andrews Espy, and Paul M. Kaufmann

Department of Family and Community Medicine
Southern Illinois University School of Medicine

There continues to be no consensus definition of executive functions. One way to understand different executive function components is to study abilities at their emergence, that is, early in development, and use advanced statistical methods to understand the interrelations among executive processes. However, to fully determine the constructs of interest, these methods often require complete data on a large battery of tasks, which are difficult to obtain with young children. Path analysis is an alternative statistical technique that requires only a single measure of each construct, yet still allows researchers to investigate complex relations among measures, to compare nested models, and to compare model fit across groups. Therefore, 117 preschool children (ages 2 years 8 months to 6 years 0 months) completed several executive function tasks. Path analysis was used to determine the relations between complex problem solving and working memory, inhibition, and set shifting processes. The best-fitting model included paths from working memory and inhibition to problem solving, and a correlation between working memory and inhibition. Interestingly, in younger children, inhibition was the strongest predictor of problem solving, whereas working memory contributed more strongly in older children. Suggestions for useful statistical methods to investigate the relations among executive functions in children are discussed.

The nature of executive functions and the relations among executive processes are far from resolved (Lyon & Krasnegor, 1996), with Borkowski and Burke (1996) concluding that "the greatest problem hindering research on executive functioning

Requests for reprints should be sent to Kimberly Andrews Espy, Department of Family and Community Medicine, MC 6503, Southern Illinois University School of Medicine, 600 Agriculture Dr., Carbondale, IL 62901–6503. E-mail: kespy@siumed.edu

(EF) is a failure to find consensus on a general definition of the construct. ... "
Cognitive neuropsychological approaches often have focused on more microlevel
components, such as working memory and response inhibition (e.g.,
Goldman-Rakic, 1987; Roberts & Pennington, 1996). In contrast, approaches
based on data from clinical patients often include more macrolevel constructs,
such as social judgment, self-regulation, planning, and problem solving (e.g.,
Damasio & Anderson, 1993).

One promising development has been the attempt to integrate these micro-
and macrolevel approaches, by examining the relations among these putative executive functions. These micro and macro approaches were developed from two
different historical traditions and may reflect differing perspectives by which to
view similar phenomena. For example, cognitive neuropsychological researchers
view perseveration as an inherent by-product of breakdown in working memory
and inhibition processes (e.g., Roberts & Pennington, 1996). In clinical neuropsychological approaches, lack of flexibility can be seen as a fundamental determinant of executive dysfunction in the social arena (e.g., Damasio & Anderson,
1993). One method of using both micro and macro approaches entails examining
the relations among microlevel variables (working memory, inhibition, and shifting) and investigating the impact that these functions have on more macro abilities, such as judgment, planning, and problem solving.

Previous studies have investigated relatively simple relations among these mi-
cro- and macrolevel executive functions. For example, in a sample of college students, Miyake et al. (2000) used structural equation modeling to examine the contributions of working memory, flexibility, and inhibition as predictors of
performance on a prototypic EF task, the Tower of Hanoi (TOH; Simon, 1975). In
TOH, the participant has to move rings on pegs in an initial state to reproduce the
configuration of a model, the end-goal state. The initial state of the rings deter-
mines the degree of difficulty of the problem, whereas the reproduction of the
model in the end-goal state can be achieved from as little as two moves for a relatively simple problem to as many as 7, 11, or more moves for a more complex
problem. On the basis of face validity, TOH often is considered a planning or problem-solving task in the clinical neuropsychological literature (Lezak, 1995),
where subjects plan and implement move sequences of progressive complexity to
achieve the end-goal state. TOH performance is impaired in patients with damage
to the frontal lobe (Goel & Grafman, 1995; Levin et al., 1994) and in those with altered dopaminergic neurotransmission (Owen, Doyon, Petrides, & Evans, 1996;
Welsh, Pennington, Ozonoff, Rouse, & McCabe, 1990). Several lines of evidence,
however, suggest that TOH can be better conceptualized as an inhibitory task. By
analyzing the strategy used to solve the TOH puzzles, Goel and Grafman found
that patients with diverse damage to the prefrontal cortex had difficulty making
moves that were counterintuitive, those that required backward movement in conflict with the longer term goal of peg configuration. Goel and Grafman interpreted

this difficulty as consistent with a lack of inhibition of prepotent (and more temporally salient) moves. In contrast, these patients did not have problems maintaining move "stacks," or sequences of moves, therefore suggesting a minimal contribution of working memory. Using a different approach, Welsh, Satterlee-Cartmell, and Stine (1999) compared the pattern of correlations between diverse executive function tasks and TOH performance in normal adults. TOH performance was related to errors on the Contingency Naming Task, Part B (Taylor, Albo, Phebus, & Sachs, 1987), and the Stroop Color and Conflict Scores (Golden, 1978), both of which are inhibitory type tasks, but it was unrelated to measures of working memory, such as Spatial Working Memory Test (Owen, Downes, Sahakian, Polkey, & Robbins, 1990) or Visual Memory Span (Wechsler, 1987). Therefore, Miyake et al. (2000) compared a model with paths from the three hypothesized latent executive functions (flexibility, working memory, and inhibition) to TOH performance, to a model with only a path from inhibition to TOH. In both models, correlations among working memory, flexibility, and inhibition were included. The fit of the model with one path from inhibition to TOH was equivalent to that of the full model; therefore, the simpler, inhibition-only model was preferred.

These results highlight the utility of a latent variable approach and the importance of considering multiple levels of executive functions to determine the true nature of executive function organization. Such layered approaches ultimately may provide a better understanding of a wider array of cognitive functions, their interrelations, and how they are disturbed by diverse neuropathology. These approaches have been underused in the neuropsychology (Francis, Fletcher, & Rourke, 1988) and cognitive neuroscience fields generally, perhaps related to the statistical sophistication, the diverse executive function battery necessary to fully identify latent constructs, and the large number of participants required. In particular, obtaining complete data on large test batteries in clinical populations can be difficult, due to a shortened attention span, fatigue, and an inability to understand directions on some tasks. Such problems also are evident in children with neurological, psychiatric, and developmental disorders and normally developing young children. In these populations, the simpler approach of path analysis could be used to better understand cognitive organization. Path analysis can be considered a special case of structural equation modeling, where observed performance on a specified test fully measures the latent construct of interest. Although this method does not take advantage of the shared variance among multiple measures to define the cognitive construct of interest, potential complex relations among multiple constructs can be tested using only one measure per construct. Importantly, the incremental fit of nested path-analysis models can be compared directly by removing one or more paths in the same manner that nested structural equation models are compared. If the chi-square values of the two models do not differ, the simpler model with fewer paths is preferred due to the principle of parsimony. Finally, path analysis can be used to compare cognitive organization across multiple groups to determine whether the same model fits the observed data from different groups equally well.

The purpose of this study was to illustrate how path analysis can be used to test hypothesized relations among executive functions in a population in which it is difficult to obtain complete data on multiple measures, that is, preschool children. A secondary purpose was to explore the nature of the organization among executive function constructs in preschool children. A multiple-group comparison analysis, using path analysis to compare model fit between younger and older children, also is illustrated. Models included both micro (i.e., working memory, inhibition, and flexibility) and macro (i.e., problem solving) executive functions to substantively address the relation among executive processes in this age range.

METHOD

Participants

Preschool children (ages 2 years 8 months to 6 years 0 months; M_{age} = 4 years 2 months, SD_{age} = 10 months) were recruited from birth announcements, local preschools, and the local health department. Among those preschool children participating in an ongoing cross-sectional study of executive function development (e.g., Espy, Kaufmann, Glisky, & McDiarmid, 2001; Espy, Kaufmann, McDiarmid, & Glisky, 1999), there were 117 children (60 boys, 57 girls) with complete data on all of the measures used here. The majority of the sample was White (n = 97), and the average maternal education of the sample was 15 years 8 months (SD = 2 years 8 months).

Procedure

The children were tested individually in a quiet room. The examiner, a trained graduate student, sat across from the child at a low table. A parent (usually the mother) was present in the room, completing questionnaires while the full battery of executive function tasks was administered, of which four tasks were selected for analysis here. The entire battery took approximately 60 to 90 min. A fixed task order was used, where tasks of different formats and cognitive demands were intermingled, to engage the child's maximal interest over the entire battery. The large number of tasks in the full battery and the need to separate tasks of similar format (e.g., tasks that used cups to hide rewards) prohibited counterbalancing. For a full description of the procedures and some of the other measures administered, see Espy et al. (2001, 1999).

Measures

Delayed alternation (DA; Espy et al., 1999).   DA was adapted from non-human animal neuroscience investigations (e.g., Goldman, Rosvold, Vest, & Galkin, 1971) for use with preschool children, as it has well-demonstrated relations to the dorsolateral prefrontal cortex and is considered a measure of working memory because a child holds information from a previous trial online to guide correct responding on the subsequent trial. In DA, a reward (small stickers, M&M Baking Bits®, colored Rice Krispies®, raisins, Cheerios®, or pennies) was hidden in one of two shallow wells on a testing board by the examiner, out of the child's sight. Both wells were covered by identical beige coffee cups. A pretrial was administered where neither well was baited, to determine the side of hiding on the test trials. After a 10-sec delay, the child retrieved the reward by displacing one of the cups, keeping the reward only if the correct cup were displaced. After correctly retrieving the reward, the reward was hidden in the opposite well. To obtain maximal rewards, the child had to search at alternating wells on each successive trial for 16 trials. The number of correct retrievals was scored.

Shape School (SS; Espy, 1997).   The SS is a Stroop-like task in a story-book format that includes different conditions designed to assess different executive functions. Here, the Inhibit condition was used to assess inhibition. First, the prepotent response was set up by having children name the color of 15 neutral-faced figures that are in line for a "school" activity. Then in the SS Inhibit condition, the child was presented again with the colored figures, some of whom had completed their work and were ready for the next activity (depicted with happy faces) and some who had not, shown with sad or frustrated faces. The child was instructed to name the color of the happy-faced figures, but not to name the colors of the sad-faced figures (to inhibit naming the figure color). An inhibition efficiency score was calculated (Efficiency = number correct/total time).

Spatial reversal (SR; Kaufmann, Leckman, & Ort, 1989).   Reversal tasks are prototypical flexibility tasks in the nonhuman animal neuroscience literature (Mishkin, 1964), which are believed to rely on ventromedial–orbitofrontal circuits for adequate performance (Watanabe, Kodama, & Hikosaka, 1997). In SR, the reward was hidden out of the child's sight, and the same wells used in DA were covered with beige coffee cups. First, there was a pretrial, where both wells were baited with a reward to establish the side of hiding for subsequent trials. Then, during the test trials, the reward was hidden in the same well (the side chosen during the pretrial) until the child correctly retrieved the reward on four consecutive trials; then the reward contingency was switched to the other well until the next consecutive four-trial set was achieved, where the contingency was reversed again. Sixteen trials were administered. An efficiency score was calculated, the number of correct four-trial sets divided by the total number of errors. SR was administered before DA for all children because the child initially experienced success on the pretrial, regardless of choice, and because it was hypothesized to be easier to search at a previously rewarded location consistently. There were four other tasks that were administered between SR and DA to minimize any carryover effects.

Tower of Hanoi (TOH; Welsh, Pennington, & Groisser, 1991).   TOH was chosen as a macro-outcome variable because it is a more complex task than DA, SS, or SR and is considered to require multiple abilities, including multiple-executive functions (Bull, Espy, & Senn, 2004; Pennington, Bennetto, McAleer, & Roberts, 1996). TOH typically is considered to measure problem solving or planning ability (e.g., Simon, 1975). Because preschool children do not evidence overt behaviors that typically are considered to reflect planning (e.g., pausing before implementing move sequences, implementing organized move sequences), TOH likely taps problem solving to a greater degree than planning in this age range. TOH is composed of three discs that fit over three pegs; the child must move the discs across the pegs according to certain rules to achieve a model configuration. A story was used to describe the rules and goals of the task, involving three monkeys (rings) of different sizes (Daddy, Mommy, and Baby) that jump among trees (pegs) (Klahr & Robinson, 1981). Six successively more difficult problems were administered, where the number of moves to solve the problem increased progressively. A child was given 2 points for correctly solving the two-move problem, 3 points for correctly solving the three-move problem, and so on. If the child solved the problem using the fewest possible number of moves, a bonus of 25% of the points was given for that problem (e.g., if the child correctly solved the two-move problem in two moves, the child's score was $2 + .25 \times 2 = 2.5$ points). A total TOH score was obtained by summing scores across the six TOH problems.

Design

The model included four constructs, working memory, inhibition, and mental flexibility, as predictors of problem solving. Each construct was defined by a single task: working memory by DA, inhibition by SS, mental flexibility by SR, and problem solving by TOH, based on extant animal neuroscience literature or previous studies or both. For example, results of animal neuroscience investigations suggest that performance on DA and reversal tasks depends on different prefrontal circuits (Goldman et al., 1971; Mishkin, 1964), and in preschool children these tasks load on different factors (Espy et al., 1999), with differing trajectories of age-related differences in task performance (Espy et al., 2001). Although preliminary in nature, performance on the SS Inhibit condition loads with the NEPSY—A Developmental Neuropsychological Assessment (Korkman, Kemp, & Kirk, 2001) Statue subtest (Cwik, 2002), and it has a different pattern of development in preschool children from a task hypothesized to rely on flexibility (Espy, 1997). Although a single index was chosen to assess each construct, as with most executive function tasks, performance likely is not determined by a single, discrete ability. For example, in addition to requiring inhibition, SS also likely demands a degree of working memory proficiency to hold the instructions in mind while successfully inhibiting the prepotent stimuli. Here, however, these measures (DA, SS, SR) were selected as primarily representing the microconstruct of interest, where these three microcomponents have been found in both exploratory (e.g., Espy et al., 1999; Hughes, 1998) and confirmatory (e.g., Miyake et al., 2000) factor analysis studies of executive functions.

Given that TOH is presumed to involve higher order planning or problem solving, and therefore depends on multiple abilities, including working memory, inhibition, and flexibility (Bull et al., 2004), a complex model of associations among these constructs may better predict performance than a model with single, direct effects from working memory, inhibition, and flexibility to problem solving (e.g., Miyake et al., 2000). In the complex model, flexibility was hypothesized to act as a mediator between working memory, inhibition, and problem solving. Diamond (1988) hinted at the potential mediating role of flexibility when she theorized that dual disturbances in working memory and inhibition may lead to perseveration (the inverse of flexibility). In other words, if an individual is not able to maintain information over time or inhibit prepotent responses or both, he or she will continue to inflexibly choose the incorrect response. This lack of flexibility in turn is related to problem solving by limiting the ability to flexibly choose among alternate problem-solving strategies. Direct effects also were hypothesized from working memory and inhibition to problem solving (full model; see Figure 1). Path coefficients, which indicate the strength and direction of the relations between the constructs, are included in the figure. The full model is similar to the model tested by Miyake et al. (2000), as a breakdown in either working memory or inhibition was postulated to impair problem solving. Finally, given the competitive balance between working memory and inhibition proposed by Roberts and Pennington (1996), a correlation between working memory and inhibition was posited. This model was just identified; that is, based on the number of measures there were 10 possible variances and covariances that could be estimated, and in this model 10 variances and covariances were estimated (five paths between constructs, one correlation, and four residual variances), resulting in 0 df for the model and a perfect model fit (see Loehlin, 1998, for a more thorough discussion of model identification).

However, simpler models may account for the observed data as well as more complex models. Therefore, several nested models were tested, where one or more paths were removed, while retaining the same structure in the rest of the model. The incremental fit of the nested models was determined by calculating the difference in chi-square values and degrees of freedom between the two models. If the difference was not significant at the critical p value, then the more parsimonious

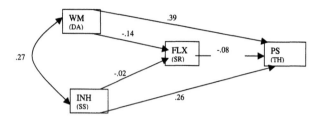

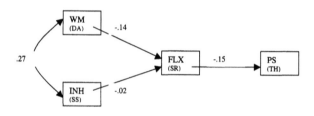

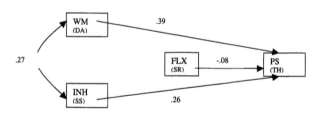

FIGURE 1   Top: Model 1, Full Model. Middle: Model 2, Flexibility as Mediator Only Model. Bottom: Model 3, Direct Paths Model.

model would be preferred. If the incremental difference in fit was significant, then the model with fewer paths fit the observed data more poorly and would be rejected. A model would not be considered nested if new, additional paths were added, and therefore differences in fit could not be compared by the difference in chi-square values and degrees of freedom. A theory-based and empirically driven rationale was used to develop all models.

In this vein, Model 2 tested whether the effects of working memory and inhibition on problem solving operated only through flexibility. Therefore, flexibility still was included as a mediator in Model 2, but the direct paths from working memory and inhibition to problem solving were dropped (see Figure 1), making it a nested model compared to the full model. Model 3 was similar to that of Miyake et al. (2000), including only direct paths from working memory, inhibition, and flexibility to problem solving, and a correlation between working memory and inhibition (see Figure 1). This model was nested in comparison to the full model, as the paths from working memory and inhibition to flexibility were dropped. However, this model was not nested within Model 2 because this model included additional paths from working memory and inhibition to planning. Therefore, the incremental fit could not be tested directly against Model 2. Unlike Miyake et al. (2000), working memory and inhibition were not hypothesized to correlate with flexibility, as the premise of the full model is that flexibility mediates the contributions of working memory and inhibition on problem solving.

Some researchers have postulated that only working memory and inhibition are central executive functions (e.g., Goldman-Rakic, 1987; Roberts & Pennington, 1996). In Model 4, the paths to and from flexibility were removed, leaving only the direct paths from working memory and inhibition to problem solving. The correlation between working memory and inhibition also was retained (see Figure 2).

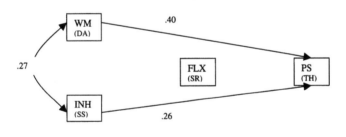

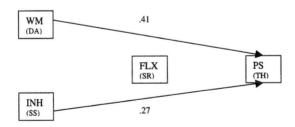

FIGURE 2   Top: Model 4, Working Memory & Inhibition Paths + Correlation Model. Bottom: Model 5, Working Memory & Inhibition Paths Only (independent) Model.

Although there is both theoretical (e.g., Roberts & Pennington, 1996) and empirical (e.g., Diamond, 1988; Espy et al., 1999) support for a correlation between working memory and inhibition, these executive functions may not be correlated, consistent with results by Hughes (1998) from a three-factor exploratory factor analysis. Therefore, to test the importance of this correlation, Model 5 included only direct paths from working memory and inhibition to problem solving without a correlation between working memory and inhibition (see Figure 2).

Because there is recent evidence (Miyake et al., 2000; Welsh et al., 1999) that inhibition is the primary contributor to TOH performance, at least in adults, Model 6 included only a direct path from inhibition to problem solving and a correlation between working memory and inhibition (see Figure 3). In contrast, other researchers have emphasized the centrality of working memory in solving the TOH (e.g., Simon, 1975) and in executive functions more generally (Kimberg & Farah, 1993; Pennington, 1997). In solving the TOH, children may work out the steps necessary to achieve the final goal mentally, placing demands on working memory. Therefore, Model 7 included only a direct path from working memory to problem solving, and a correlation between working memory and inhibition (see Figure 3).

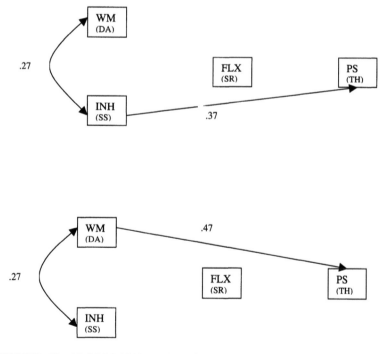

FIGURE 3   Top: Model 6, Inhibition Only Model. Bottom: Model 7, Working Memory Only Model

There are age-related differences in performance noted on some of the executive function tasks (Espy et al., 2001, 1999). Such performance differences may arise because of changes in proficiency. However, performance differences may not be a consequence of changes in proficiency, but rather differences in the nature of organization of executive control in children of different ages. Therefore, specifically testing different models of executive organization across children of varying ages can be informative. Here, an exploratory, multiple-group comparison was conducted to test whether executive function organization differed as a function of age group. The fit of the final model was tested against the observed data from children ≤ age 4 ($n = 46$) and that from children > age 4 ($n = 71$). First, a multiple-group model was run in which path coefficients were allowed to differ across the two groups. Then, the same structural model was run in which path coefficients were constrained to be equal across the two age groups. If the latter model fit the observed data more poorly, as determined by the incremental difference in chi-square values and degrees of freedom, then the model would be rejected, as it would not fit the observed data equally well for younger and older children.

These path analyses were conducted using Mplus version 2.1 (Muthen & Muthen, 1998), using maximum likelihood estimation procedures. The advantage of using Mplus or other structural equation modeling programs over conventional regression analyses (e.g., Pedhazur & Schmelkin, 1991), is that fit indexes are computed for the model as a whole, rather than providing path coefficients only. All variables had sufficient variability and appeared to be distributed approximately normally.

To determine model fit, several different goodness-of-fit indexes were used, as recommended by Hu and Bentler (1999). The chi-square, the root mean square error of approximation (RMSEA), and the comparative fit index (CFI) were used, where models with acceptable fit were defined as those with a nonsignificant chi-square (although caution must be used when interpreting chi-square, as it is highly dependent on sample size), with an RMSEA < .06, and a CFI ≥ .95 (Hu & Bentler, 1999). In addition, the models yield a percentage of variance that is accounted for in the dependent construct or variable (TOH) by the predictor constructs or variables. The residual variance—that not accounted for in the model—contains measurement error, subject-related error, and the influences of variables not included in the model.

RESULTS

Mean scores and standard deviations on each of the dependent measures are presented in Table 1. Note the psychometric characteristics of the measured task performance, where no performance floors or ceilings were observed, consistent with our previous reports (Espy, 1997; Espy et al., 2001). Goodness-of-fit indexes are

TABLE 1
Group Performance on Measured Variables

Variable	All Participants[a]		Age ≤ 4[b]		Age > 4[c]	
	M	SD	M	SD	M	SD
DA	9.94	2.31	8.97	1.93	10.57	2.33
SS	0.54	0.31	0.35	0.23	0.61	0.29
SR	0.39	0.27	0.42	0.30	0.37	0.26
TOH	13.66	8.78	8.61	5.24	16.93	9.09

Note. DA = Delayed Alternation number of correct retrievals; SS = Shape School-Inhibition Condition efficiency score; SR = Spatial Reversal efficiency score; TOH = Tower of Hanoi total score. [a]$N = 117$. [b]$n = 46$. [c]$n = 71$.

presented in Table 2. As can be seen in this table, the data were an acceptable fit for several of the models (i.e., Model 1, Model 3, and Model 4; Hu & Bentler, 1999). However, the real value of the approach demonstrated here lies in the direct testing of nested models to determine which competing models provide the best fit to the observed data. The incremental fit provides a more direct test of elements of model fit, with less of a reliance on the more qualitative goodness-of-fit indexes. A comparison of the chi-square values for the models is presented in Table 3.

TABLE 2
Goodness-of-Fit Indexes

Models	χ^2	RMSEA	CFI
1	$\chi^2(0) = 0.00$	.00	1.00
2	$\chi^2(2) = 37.46$	.39	0.06
3	$\chi^2(2) = 2.65$	.05	0.98
4	$\chi^2(3) = 3.62$	.04	0.98
5	$\chi^2(4) = 12.49$	.14	0.76
6	$\chi^2(4) = 25.93$	.22	0.52
7	$\chi^2(4) = 13.62$	.14	0.80

Note. RMSEA = root mean square error of approximation; CFI = comparative fit index.

TABLE 3
Comparison of Nested Models

Model Comparison	χ^2 Difference	df Difference	p Value
Model 2 versus Model 1	37.46	2	< .001
Model 3 versus Model 1	2.65	2	.27
Model 4 versus Model 3	0.97	1	.32
Model 5 versus Model 4	8.87	1	.003
Model 6 versus Model 4	22.31	1	< .001
Model 7 versus Model 4	9.64	1	.002

The difference in fit between Model 2 (flexibility as mediator only) and the full model was significant, indicating that the flexibility as mediator model did not adequately reproduce the observed data as well as the full model. The fit of Model 3 (only direct paths from working memory, inhibition, and flexibility) also was compared to that of the full model, resulting in a nonsignificant difference in chi-square. Because both models fit the data equally well, the more parsimonious model (Model 3) was the preferred model.

Model 4 (paths from working memory and inhibition only) was nested within both Model 3 and Model 1. Because Model 3 was preferred over Model 1, the incremental fit of Model 4 was compared to that of Model 3. The change in chi-square between Model 3 and Model 4 was nonsignificant; therefore, Model 4 was preferred due to parsimony. Model 5 was similar to Model 4 (direct paths from working memory and inhibition to problem solving), except the correlation between working memory and inhibition was dropped. Model 5 fit the observed data significantly more poorly than Model 4, indicating that working memory and inhibition are correlated. This correlation, therefore, was retained in the remaining models.

The fit of Model 6, with a path from inhibition only and a correlation between working memory and inhibition, was compared to that of Model 4. Model 6 did not fit the observed data as well as Model 4. Similarly, Model 7, with a path from working memory to problem solving only and a correlation between working memory and inhibition, was compared to Model 4. Model 7 also did not fit the observed data as well as Model 4. Across analyses, Model 4, then, was the preferred model because it was the simplest, most parsimonious model that best fit the observed data. The estimate or coefficient (similar to a beta weight in regression analyses) for the path from working memory to problem solving was .40, and was .26 for the path from inhibition to problem solving, with a correlation of .27 between working memory and inhibition. In preschool children, this final model accounted for 29% of the variance in TOH scores.

In the multiple-group comparison, path analyses were conducted to determine whether Model 4 fit the data equally well in younger and older children. First, path coefficients (working memory to problem solving; inhibition to problem solving; correlation between working memory and inhibition) were held equal across the two age groups, resulting in an overall $\chi^2(9) = 19.27$. Then, path coefficients were allowed to differ across the two age groups, resulting in an overall $\chi^2(6) = 5.1$. The difference, $\chi^2(3) = 14.17$, between the models was significant ($p < .01$), indicating that the value of the path coefficients differed for younger and older children in Model 4 (see Figure 4). Among younger children, inhibition was the strongest predictor of problem-solving performance, with a path coefficient of .44. Working memory contributed relatively little to problem solving (path coefficient = −.05) in younger children. In contrast, among older children, working memory was the main contributor to problem solving (path coefficient = .48), and inhibition was less important (path coefficient = .07).

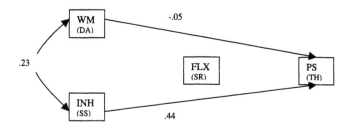

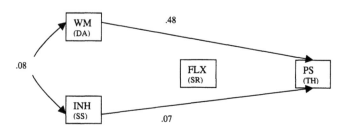

FIGURE 4   Model 8, Multiple Group Comparison Model; Top: Age ≤ 4; Bottom: Age > 4.

DISCUSSION

Path analysis was used to compare different models of executive function organization in preschool children, a population from which it can be difficult to obtain complete data on comprehensive neuropsychological batteries. Performance on a working memory task and on an inhibition task predicted performance on a complex problem-solving task, the TOH, as well as did models that included performance on a task designed to measure mental flexibility. Path analysis may be a powerful tool by which to investigate relations among executive functions or other neuropsychological abilities in populations where it is difficult to obtain complete data on a large battery of measures, such as certain clinical populations, young children, or older adults. Path analysis has many of the same capabilities as structural equation modeling, including modeling complex relations among variables, comparing complicated models to simpler, nested models, and conducting multiple-group comparisons to determine whether a model fits the observed data from different groups equally well.

Substantively regarding neuropsychology, these results provide preliminary support for those theories that are predicated on a dualistic notion of executive functions (e.g., Diamond, 1988; Roberts & Pennington, 1996), that is, where the contributions of working memory and inhibition are central. Indeed, these constructs accounted for 29% of the variance in complex problem solving, as indicated by the TOH score, a substantial portion of performance. Furthermore, the relation between working memory and inhibition was important, consistent with Roberts and Pennington's view of a competitive balance between these two processes. However, there are other ways to conceptualize this balance, for example, with reciprocal causation, which also is consistent with some theories of prefrontal function (e.g., Fuster, 1989). Such models were not investigated here, as they can be difficult to fit, do not change the amount of variance explained in the dependent construct, and are best attempted with a full structural model that includes multiple indicators of the constructs of interest.

The benefits of directly comparing more complex models are apparent. Flexibility does not appear to mediate the relation between working memory, inhibition, and problem solving, at least in preschool children. In preschool children, mental flexibility may be less differentiated from working memory and inhibition than in school-age children and, therefore, not an important contributor to problem-solving abilities in the preschool age range. Complex problem solving and planning tasks may not demand significant mental flexibility until the child can solve problems successfully that require a larger repertoire of plans and schema (Bull et al., 2004). Alternatively, the simpler, more "motoric" flexible search behavior measured by SR (Kaufmann et al., 1989) may not adequately measure the more "cognitive" flexibility of EF. In fact, recent evidence from adult neuroimaging studies suggests that flexible switching between extradimensional categories (e.g., position to shape) activates prefrontal systems, whereas intradimensional shifts (one location vs. the other) do not (Dias, Robbins, & Roberts, 1996, 1997). However, this issue has not been studied in normal children, let alone those of preschool age. Clearly, longitudinal studies are necessary to characterize these ontogenetic relations in young children and how they map onto subsequent executive functions during the school-age years.

In contrast to a study of adults in which only inhibition contributed to TOH performance (Miyake et al., 2000), here the inhibition-only model was rejected. In preschool children, working memory contributed to complex problem solving, as did inhibition. For young children, the requirement of maintaining the task rules and their performance relative to the goal state may engage working memory to a greater extent, in comparison to the adults studied by Miyake et al. However, more complicated models of executive organization were not considered. The integration of these micro- and macrolevel constructs appears to be a fruitful avenue to explore and may yield important insights into the nature of cognitive organization and mechanisms of cognitive development.

In a related vein, the working memory-only model also was rejected. Although some theorists have emphasized the centrality of working memory in executive control (e.g., Kimberg & Farah, 1993), such a position was not supported here, at least in this age range. This evidence must be considered preliminary given the limitations of the path model, where only one test is selected to primarily measure each construct. For example, if all of the selected tests actually measured only working memory, the observed differences between the models would simply reflect differing construct validity among the selected test instruments. Given the diverse evidence of the validity of these tasks as indicators of the constructs that make up differing aspects of executive control (e.g., Espy, 1997; Espy et al., 2001, 1999; Goldman et al., 1971; Mishkin, 1964; Miyake et al., 2000), this explanation seems unlikely.

Interestingly, the best fitting model that included inhibition and working memory as predictors of problem solving did not fit the data from younger and older children equally well. Inhibition was a stronger determinant of problem solving in younger children, whereas working memory was more important in older children. These findings may represent the different maturational timetable of these abilities. Inhibitory control may develop more rapidly in younger children, with more protracted development in working memory (e.g., Espy, 1997; Espy et al., 2001, 1999; Welsh et al., 1991). As a result, older children may bring to bear their better developed working memory to solve the more difficult, complex TOH problems, which in turn, demand more working memory for correct solution. However, these analyses were exploratory. The recommended approach is to develop and test competing models on the basis of theory or on results from an initial sample, and in the latter case, to further validate and confirm the results on a separate sample. At a minimum, a larger sample size would be required to fully test whether there are age-related differences in executive function organization.

The sample for this study included a disproportionate number of college-educated families. Although such a demographic was consistent with the local area from which children were recruited, the mean education level was higher than national expectations. It will be important to determine whether a similar pattern of executive function organization is consistent across children of varying socioeconomic circumstances. In fact, the multiple-group comparison approach demonstrated here with respect to age could be used to test the equivalency of model fit across diverse groups of children.

Although the strength of the path-analysis approach is in the ability to test structural models, there also are inherent limitations. Most importantly, performance on a single test instrument never is a pure measure of the intended construct. Although tests were chosen to primarily measure a given construct on the basis of empirical evidence and theoretical rationale, these instruments may not measure fully the hypothesized executive process. Specifically, successfully using information from a previously correct retrieval to guide performance on the next trial on DA inevitably requires a degree of inhibition, whereas successful SS Inhibit-condition performance requires maintaining the inhibition rule online. To flexibly shift among mental sets presumably would require both maintaining the rule and inhibiting the incorrect response. Particularly with higher order executive functions, finding "pure" measures of given executive functions has proven difficult. Many of the measures used in this study have been related to the prefrontal cortex in nonhuman animals (e.g., Goldman et al., 1971; Goldman-Rakic, 1987) and in human infants (e.g., Bell & Fox, 1992), with specific performance differences noted among tasks (Espy, 1997; Espy et al., 2001, 1999) that lend a degree of convergent validity. However, exactly what cognitive functions are assessed by these measures in preschool children, and other executive function tests in older children and adults more generally, requires further explication.

Because one inherent assumption of the path model is that the selected test measures the construct of interest, if the measure is not perfectly reliable, the observed path coefficients may misspecify the true relations between constructs. Although it is possible to adjust the path models for measure reliability (i.e., by setting the paths between the construct and the measured variable to the square root of the reliability coefficient), the reliability must be known. Unfortunately, because of the experimental nature of these measures and their relatively new application to exploring cognitive organization in preschool children, reliability estimates were not available. Because a single test is used to measure the construct, vagaries related to the individual tests, such as test order or material-specific differences, may have measurable effects on model results. Although the hypothesized model accounted for a large portion of the variance in complex problem-solving abilities, the amount of residual variance also depends on test reliability, in addition to measurement and subject error, and the influences of other variables not considered in the model, for example, visuospatial ability, which has been related to TOH performance (Roennlund, Loevden, & Nilsson, 2001).

Structural equation modeling allows better assessment of the latent construct of interest by using the shared variance between multiple measures believed to assess the same cognitive construct. Recent advances in missing data techniques, such as multiple imputation (Schafer, 1997), may be useful in the application of structural equation modeling procedures to data from populations where obtaining complete data on large test batteries can be difficult, such as certain clinical populations, young children, and older adults. Some structural equation modeling programs also now include a maximum likelihood estimation routine that allows for data that are missing at random (e.g., Mplus, AMOS). Irrespective of what approach is used, the pattern of missing data must be inspected thoroughly and the assumptions that underlie such procedures considered carefully before employing such approaches. These new techniques may be a valuable method for understanding executive function organization, and cognitive processing more generally, in a wider array of populations and ages.

ACKNOWLEDGMENTS

This research was supported, in part, by grants from the Rita Rudel Foundation, Office of Research Development and Administration, Southern Illinois University; and from the University of Arizona Foundation to Kimberly Andrews Espy.

We thank the staff from the Beginning School, Presbyterian Child Development Center, and the Child Development Laboratory; and the participating families. The assistance of Melanie McDiarmid, Martha Glisky, and Mary Cwik, in data collection; and of Lisabeth DiLalla, in statistical advice, also is appreciated.

REFERENCES

Bell, M. A., & Fox, N. A. (1992). The relations between frontal brain electrical activity and cognitive development during infancy. *Child Development, 63,* 1142–1163.

Borkowski, J. G., & Burke, J. E. (1996). Theories, models, and measurements of executive functioning: An information processing perspective. In G. R. Lyon & N. A. Krasnegor (Eds.), *Attention, memory, and executive function* (pp. 235–262). Baltimore: Brookes.

Bull, R., Espy, K. A., & Senn, T. E. (2004). A comparison of the performance on the Towers of London and Hanoi in young children. *Journal of Child Psychology and Psychiatry, 45,* 743–754.

Cwik, M. (2002). *An examination of the construct validity of the Behavior Rating Inventory of Executive Function–Preschool Version.* Unpublished master's thesis, Southern Illinois University, Carbondale.

Damasio, A. R., & Anderson, S. W. (1993). The frontal lobes. In K. M. Heilman & E. Valenstein (Eds.), *Clinical neuropsychology.* New York: Oxford University Press.

Diamond, A. (1988). Abilities and neural mechanisms underlying AB performance. *Child Development, 59,* 523–527.

Dias, R., Robbins, T. W., & Roberts, A. C. (1996). Dissociation in prefrontal cortex of affective and attentional shifts. *Nature, 380,* 69–72.

Dias, R., Robbins, T. W., & Roberts, A. C. (1997). Dissociable forms of inhibitory control within prefrontal cortex with an analog of the Wisconsin Card Sort Test: Restriction to novel situations and independence from "on-line" processing. *Journal of Neuroscience, 17,* 9285–9297.

Espy, K. A. (1997). The Shape School: Assessing executive function in preschool children. *Developmental Neuropsychology, 13,* 495–499.

Espy, K. A., Kaufmann, P. M., Glisky, M. L., & McDiarmid, M. D. (2001). New procedures to assess executive functions in preschool children. *Clinical Neuropsychologist, 15,* 46–58.

Espy, K. A., Kaufmann, P. M., McDiarmid, M. D., & Glisky, M. L. (1999). Executive functioning in preschool children: Performance on A-not-B and other delayed response format tasks. *Brain and Cognition, 41,* 178–199.

Francis, D. J., Fletcher, J. M., & Rourke, B. P. (1988). Discriminant validity of lateral sensorimotor tests in children. *Journal of Clinical and Experimental Neuropsychology, 10,* 779–799.

Fuster, J. M. (1989). *The prefrontal cortex: Anatomy, physiology, and neuropsychology of the frontal lobe* (2nd ed.). New York: Raven.

Goel, V., & Grafman, J. (1995). Are the frontal lobes implicated in "planning" functions? Interpreting data from the Tower of Hanoi. *Neuropsychologia, 33,* 623–642.

Golden, C. (1978). *Stroop Color Word Test.* Chicago: Stoelting.

Goldman, P. S., Rosvold, H. E., Vest, B., & Galkin, T. W. (1971). Analysis of the delayed-alternation deficit produced by dorsolateral prefrontal lesions in the rhesus monkey. *Journal of Comparative and Physiological Psychology, 77,* 212–220.

Goldman-Rakic, P. S. (1987). Development of cortical circuitry and cognitive function. *Child Development, 58,* 601–622.

Hu, L., & Bentler, P. M. (1999). Cutoff criteria for fit indexes in covariance structure analysis: Conventional criteria versus new alternatives. *Structural Equation Modeling, 6,* 1–55.

Hughes, C. (1998). Executive function in preschoolers: Links with theory of mind and verbal ability. *British Journal of Developmental Psychology, 16,* 233–253.

Kaufmann, P., Leckman, J. M., & Ort, S. I. (1989). Delayed response performance in males with Fragile-X. *Journal of Clinical and Experimental Neuropsychology, 12,* 69.

Kimberg, D. Y., & Farah, M. J. (1993). A unified account of cognitive impairments following frontal lobe damage: The role of working memory in complex, organized behavior. *Journal of Experimental Psychology, General, 122,* 411–428.

Klahr, D., & Robinson, M. (1981). Formal assessment of problem solving and planning processes in preschool children. *Cognitive Psychology, 13,* 113–148.

Korkman, M., Kemp, S. L., & Kirk, U. (2001). Effects of age on neurocognitive measures of children ages 5 to 12: A cross-sectional study on 800 children from the United States. *Developmental Neuropsychology, 20,* 331–354.

Levin, H. S., Culhane, K. A., Fletcher, J. M., Mendelsohn, D. B., Lilly, M. A., Harward, H., et al. (1994). Dissociation between delayed alternation and memory after pediatric head injury: Relationship to MRI findings. *Journal of Child Neurology, 9,* 81–89.

Lezak, M. D. (1995). *Neuropsychological assessment* (3rd ed.). New York: Oxford University Press.

Loehlin, J. C. (1998). *Latent variable models: An introduction to factor, path, and structural analysis* (3rd ed.). Mahwah, NJ: Lawrence Erlbaum Associates, Inc.

Lyon, G. R., & Krasnegor, N. A. (Eds.). (1996). *Attention, memory, and executive function.* Baltimore: Brookes.

Mishkin, M. (1964). Perseveration of central sets after frontal lobe lesion in monkeys. In J. M. Warren & K. Akert (Eds.), *The frontal granular cortex and behavior* (pp. 219–241). New York: McGraw-Hill.

Miyake, A., Friedman, N. P., Emerson, M. J., Witzki, A. H., Howerter, A., & Wagner, T. D. (2000). The unity and diversity of executive functions and their contributions to complex "frontal lobe" tasks: A latent variable analysis. *Cognitive Psychology, 41,* 49–100.

Muthen, L. K., & Muthen, B. O. (1998). *Mplus user's guide.* Los Angeles: Muthen & Muthen.

Owen, A. M., Downes, J., Sahakian, B., Polkey, C., & Robbins, T. R. (1990). Planning and spatial working memory following frontal lesions in man. *Neuropsychologia, 28,* 1021–1034.

Owen, A. M., Doyon, J., Petrides, M., & Evans, A. C. (1996). Planning and spatial working memory: A positron emission tomography study in humans. *European Journal of Neuroscience, 8,* 353–364.

Pedhazur, E. J., & Schmelkin, L. P. (1991). *Measurement, design, and analysis: An integrated approach.* Hillsdale, NJ: Lawrence Erlbaum Associates, Inc.

Pennington, B. F. (1997). Dimensions of executive functions in normal and abnormal development. In N. A. Krasnegor, G. R. Lyon, & P. S. Goldman-Rakic (Eds.), *Development of the prefrontal cortex: Evolution, neurobiology, and behavior* (pp. 265–282). Baltimore: Brookes.

Pennington, B. F., Bennetto, L., McAleer, O., & Roberts, R. J. (1996). Executive functions and working memory: Theoretical and measurement issues. In G. R. Lyon & N. A. Krasnegor (Eds.), *Attention, memory, and executive function* (pp. 327–348). Baltimore: Brookes.

Roberts, R. J., & Pennington, B. F. (1996). An interactive framework for examining prefrontal cognitive processes. *Developmental Neuropsychology, 12,* 105–126.

Roennlund, M., Loevden, M., & Nilsson, L. (2001). Adult age differences in Tower of Hanoi performance: Influence from demographic and cognitive variables. *Aging Neuropsychology and Cognition, 8,* 269–283.

Schafer, J. L. (1997). *Analysis of incomplete multivariate data.* London: Chapman & Hall.

Simon, H. A. (1975). The functional equivalence of problem solving skills. *Cognitive Psychology, 7,* 268–288.

Taylor, H. G., Albo, V. C., Phebus, C. K., & Sachs, B. R. (1987). Postirradiation treatment outcomes for children with acute lymphocytic leukemia: Clarification of risks. *Journal of Pediatric Psychology, 12,* 395–411.

Watanabe, M., Kodama, T., & Hikosaka, K. (1997). Increase in extracellular dopamine in primate prefrontal cortex during a working memory task. *Journal of Neurophysiology, 78,* 2795–2798.

Wechsler, D. (1987). *Wechsler Memory Scale–Revised.* San Antonio, TX: Psychological Corporation.

Welsh, M. C., Pennington, B. F., & Groisser, D. B. (1991). A normative-developmental study of executive function: A window on prefrontal function in children. *Developmental Neuropsychology, 7,* 131–149.

Welsh, M. C., Pennington, B. F., Ozonoff, S., Rouse, B., & McCabe, E. (1990). Neuropsychology of early-treated phenylketonuria: Specific executive function deficits. *Child Development, 61,* 1697–1713.

Welsh, M. C., Satterlee-Cartmell, T., & Stine, M. (1999). Towers of Hanoi and London: Contribution of working memory and inhibition to performance. *Brain and Cognition, 41,* 231–242.

DEVELOPMENTAL NEUROPSYCHOLOGY, 26(1), 465–486
Copyright © 2004, Lawrence Erlbaum Associates, Inc.

The Contribution of Executive Functions to Emergent Mathematic Skills in Preschool Children

Kimberly Andrews Espy, Melanie M. McDiarmid,
Mary F. Cwik, Melissa Meade Stalets, Arlena Hamby,
and Theresa E. Senn
Department of Family and Community Medicine
Southern Illinois University School of Medicine

Mathematical ability is related to both activation of the prefrontal cortex in neuroimaging studies of adults and to executive functions in school-age children. The purpose of this study was to determine whether executive functions were related to emergent mathematical proficiency in preschool children. Preschool children ($N =$ 96) were administered an executive function battery that was reduced empirically to working memory (WM), inhibitory control (IC), and shifting abilities by calculating composite scores derived from principal component analysis. Both WM and IC predicted early arithmetic competency, with the observed relations robust after controlling statistically for child age, maternal education, and child vocabulary. Only IC accounted for unique variance in mathematical skills, after the contribution of other executive functions were controlled statistically as well. Specific executive functions are related to emergent mathematical proficiency in this age range. Longitudinal studies using structural equation modeling are necessary to better characterize these ontogenetic relations.

Recent findings from functional imaging studies in adults highlight the role of the prefrontal cortex in mathematical performance, particularly in actual mathematical calculation (Fullbright et al., 2000; Gruber, Indefrey, Steinmetz, & Kleinschmidt, 2001; Menon, Riveria, White, Glover, & Reiss, 2000; Zago et al., 2001) or reasoning (Prabhakaran, Rypma, & Gabrieli, 2001). In children, impair-

Requests for reprints should be sent to Kimberly Andrews Espy, Department of Family and Community Medicine, MC 6503, Southern Illinois University School of Medicine, 600 Agriculture Dr., Carbondale, IL 62901–6503. E-mail: kespy@siumed.edu

ments in arithmetic skills have been related to frontal activation (H. S. Levin, Scheller, et al., 1996; Miles & Stelmack, 1994); however, such studies have not been conducted in normally-developing youngsters to date.

In school-age children and adolescents, mathematical skills also are related, at least in part, to executive functioning (Bull & Scerif, 2001; Cirino, Morris, & Morris, 2002; Gathercole & Pickering, 2000; McLean & Hitch, 1999). In some of these studies, the central importance of working memory (WM) has been identified (e.g., Gathercole & Pickering, 2000; McLean & Hitch, 1999). However, other executive functions also are related to mathematical proficiency. In a sample of 122 nine-year-old children who scored below the 25% percentile of a standardized mathematical test, time to complete the auditory, written–visual, and color Trail Making Tests also were related to arithmetic performance (McLean & Hitch, 1999). The authors concluded that both spatial WM span and switching between retrieval plans (the central executive; Baddeley & Hitch, 1994) contribute to mathematical proficiency. Bull and Scerif (2001) found that inhibition, WM, and inflexible responding accounted for unique variation in mathematical performance in 7-year-old children, after controlling for the influences of reading proficiency and intelligence scores.

It is not clear whether executive functions are related to mathematical skills earlier in development. Although some have argued that simple mathematical skills are evident in infancy (e.g., Wynn, 1992), there is a marked emergence of informal mathematical skills during the preschool period, that is, those mathematical abilities that are not learned through formal instruction. For example, Gelman and Gallistel (1978) argued that preschool children possess a fundamental understanding of mathematical principles about counting, such as stable order, one-to-one correspondence, and cardinality, although young children may not fully understand the implications of these principles in various enumeration contexts (e.g., Geary, 1994; Sophian, 1996). During the preschool years, there are significant changes in counting skills and arithmetic problem solving (e.g., Baroody, 1992; Sophian, 1996) and in spatial and geometric abilities (e.g., Newcombe & Huttenlocher, 2000), which provide the foundation for later mathematical knowledge and procedural competencies gained through formal instruction in the primary grades and beyond (Geary, 1994; Ginsburg, 1989; Rittle-Johnson & Siegler, 1998).

During this same preschool period, there is a rapid development of executive functions, such as inhibition, WM, and flexibility skills (e.g., Diamond, Prevor, Callender, & Druin, 1997; Espy, 1997; Espy, Kaufmann, McDiarmid, et al., 1999; Hughes, 1998; Jacques & Zelazo, 2001). Therefore, examining the relations between executive functions and emergent arithmetic skills in young children may provide insight into the shared ontogenetic organization of these abilities. One limitation that has hampered such endeavors in young children is the lack of available instruments to assess executive functions, as most standardized preschool tests do not adequately assess diverse executive functions. Tasks adapted from developmental and cognitive neuroscience investigations offer one fruitful method by which to investigate executive functions (e.g., Diamond, 1985; Espy, Kaufmann, & Glisky, 1999; Espy, Kaufmann, McDiarmid, et al., 1999). Such tasks are advantageous because their relation to prefrontal cortical function has been established, at least in well-controlled studies with nonhuman animals or using similar neuroimaging paradigms with adult humans.

For example, the relation between the dorsolateral prefrontal cortex and WM is one of the most consistently demonstrated structure–function relations in neuropsychology (Goldman-Rakic, 1987b). WM in monkeys is affected by both cortical, as well as subcortical, experimental manipulations, as evidenced by alterations in performance on the classic delayed response (DR) paradigm (Goldman-Rakic, 1987a). Corollary tasks that use reversals of reward contingencies (Mishkin, 1964) also are impaired by lesions to structures in the ventromedial–orbitofrontal circuits. Such tasks are well tolerated by preschool children because of the nonverbal nature, simple manual response demands, and doling out of frequent, tangible rewards (Espy, Kaufmann, McDiarmid, et al., 1999). Furthermore, performance on such procedures differs between age groups in normal preschool children (Espy, Kaufmann, Glisky, & McDiarmid, 2001), differs in those with presumed prefrontal dysfunction due to phenylketonuria (Diamond et al., 1997) and prenatal cocaine exposure (Espy, Kaufmann, & Glisky, 1999), and is related to individual differences in resting frontal electroencephalogram signals in normal infants (Fox & Bell, 1990). Such developmental cognitive neuroscience tasks (e.g., Diamond, 1985; Espy, Kaufmann, McDiarmid, et al., 1999; Welsh & Pennington, 1988) provide the potential to tap differing executive functions that may have unique relations to emerging mathematical abilities in this age range.

However, both the nature of the organization of executive function and task measurement issues must be considered (Lyon & Krasnegor, 1996). Although many researchers would agree that executive functions are not unitary (e.g., Miyake, Friedman, Emerson, Witzki, & Howerter, 2000; Welsh & Pennington, 1988), there remains considerable controversy regarding which specific constructs are "executive" per se. Such issues are important in their own right, but also inherently affect how executive functions might be related to other functional outcomes, such as mathematics. Furthermore, the selection of specific tests in research batteries to measure salient executive functions most often is based on face validity alone. Because of the interrelated nature of executive function constructs, measures that are included to tap a single executive function construct inevitably demand multiple executive function abilities for proficient performance.

For example, to maintain information in WM for upcoming responding, other information invariably is inhibited (e.g., Diamond, 1985). To flexibly shift responding in the face of conflicting rules requires maintaining the rule in mind and inhibiting prepotent, previous responses. Equating tests (e.g., Wisconsin Card

Sorting Test [WCST]; Heaton, Chelune, Talley, Kay, & Curtiss, 1993) to constructs (shifting) on the basis of face validity, rather than on the underlying measurement characteristics, easily can lead to erroneous conclusions because of the correlated nature of executive function constructs. Consistent with fractionated executive function models (e.g., Miyake et al., 2000), multiple executive function components or factors are identified; however, the factors typically are not orthogonal or independent, but rather share some common variance. Studies that have used factor-analytic techniques that account for shared variance between test performance (e.g., principal components analysis, exploratory and confirmatory factor analysis) routinely identify WM and inhibition executive function constructs (e.g., Espy, Kaufmann, McDiarmid, et al., 1999; Hughes, 1998; Miyake et al., 2000; Pennington, 1997), and commonly a flexibility or shifting executive function construct (e.g., Espy, Kaufmann, McDiarmid, et al., 1999; Hughes, 1998; Pennington, 1997; Welsh, Pennington, & Groisser, 1991). Other more complex executive function constructs, such as concept formation, planning, problem solving, and judgment, may be identified (e.g., H. S. Levin, Fletcher, et al., 1996; Welsh et al., 1991). Using such analytical procedures to empirically reduce the individual test level data to meaningful, shared executive function constructs may better characterize their contribution to emergent mathematical skills. The purpose of this study, then, was to determine how empirically determined executive functions are related to emergent mathematical proficiency in preschool children. Specifically, inhibitory control (IC), WM, and mental flexibility were hypothesized to predict early mathematical abilities in this age range.

METHOD

Participants

To include a wide spectrum of children with varying mathematical proficiencies, two groups of preschool children participated, typically developing and those born preterm at low neurobiological risk. Typically developing preschool children ($n =$ 66) were between the ages of 2 and 5 years ($M = 4.21$ years, $SD = 0.87$ years) and were participating in a larger normative, cross-sectional study of executive function development in this age range (e.g., Espy et al., 2001). Typically developing preschoolers were delivered in normal newborn nurseries and weighed 7.53 lb at birth on average ($SD = 1.17$ lb). None of these children were diagnosed with any neurological, psychiatric, or developmental disorders, determined on the basis of parental report. There were 38 girls and 28 boys, with 20 typically developing children of non-White minority race/ethnicity. Mean maternal education level was 14.62 years ($SD = 2.13$ years). The mean score on the Picture Vocabulary subtest of the Woodcock–Johnson Psycho-Educational Battery–Revised (WJ–R; Woodcock

& Johnson, 1989), which was used as an estimate of overall intelligence (Sattler, 1992), was 101.61 (SD = 14.12) for the typically developing youngsters.

Preschool children born preterm (n = 30) also were between the ages of 2 and 5 years (M = 3.76 years, SD = 1.05 years) and were participating in an ongoing follow-up study (e.g., Espy et al., 2002) of those born early (M gestational age at birth = 32.23 weeks; SD = 2.0 weeks) and of low birth weight (M = 3.76 lb, SD = 0.91 lb) at a local neonatal intensive care unit. Participation was restricted to low-risk preterm infants (28 to 35 weeks gestational age, with no evidence of Intraventricular Hemorrhage > Grade II, periventricular leukomalacia, seizures, chronic lung disease, or bronchopulmonary dysplasia), to investigate outcome in those who are not at obvious risk for more severe neurodevelopmental sequelae (Hack, Klein, & Taylor., 1995). There were 19 girls and 11 boys, with 5 children born preterm of non-White minority race/ethnicity. Mean maternal education was 14.20 years (SD = 2.16 years) for those born preterm. Preschoolers born preterm obtained a score of 98.87 on the WJ–R Picture Vocabulary subtest (SD = 13.35). There were no differences between the typically developing preschoolers and those born preterm in the proportion of boys and girls, $\chi^2(1, N = 96) = 0.28, p > .05$, in the proportion of children of White versus non-White race/ethnicity, $\chi^2(1, N = 96) = 1.99, p > .05$, in average maternal education level, $F(1, 94) = 0.80, p > .05$, or in the mean WJ–R Picture Vocabulary subtest standard score, $F(1, 94) = 0.80, p > .05$.

Procedure

Preschool children were administered a battery of executive function tests in a single session by a trained child clinical graduate student blind to the experimental hypotheses. A fixed order for test administration was used, where tests that used similar materials were separated (e.g., DR format tasks) and tests with different presentation and response formats were interleaved to yield a fast-paced, interesting assessment experience for the child. Children were assessed individually in a quiet room, while the parent or guardian was present in the room completing study forms. To maintain cooperation and interest, short breaks were used when necessary. Test sessions were videotaped for the purpose of later scoring. Parents received compensation for study participation, and the children received a bag of developmentally appropriate toys, stickers, and small items.

Measures

Applied Problems.   This subtest of the WJ–R (Woodcock & Johnson, 1989) was used to assess emergent mathematical abilities. The WJ–R Applied Problems items are graded in difficulty (empirically determined by Rasch item analyses). Specific mathematical content is mixed, including subitizing, ordinal counting, counting relevant object items among mixed object groups, and simple subtraction and addition calculations. The standard administration was used, where the preschool child is shown the pictorial mathematical problem, and then points or says the answer. The resulting standard score was used in the analyses.

Picture Vocabulary.   Administration of a complete measure of intellectual ability was too time consuming and not directly related to study hypotheses. Because vocabulary typically is the most highly correlated with overall intellectual ability (Sattler, 1992), a standardized vocabulary measure, the WJ–R Picture Vocabulary subtest (Woodcock & Johnson, 1989), was included as an estimate of overall intelligence. The standard score was used in the statistical models.

Because of the fractionated nature of executive function, a battery of tasks was used to assess multiple executive function abilities, including four tasks that use the basic delayed-response setup. For the delayed-response-type tasks, a gray testing board with two drilled lateral wells was used. The wells were covered with two inverted beige coffee cups because they were displaced easily and "neutral" in color and shape. On both tasks, rewards consisted of stickers, M&Ms®, or different cereal bits. Different rewards were used at the beginning of each task. In addition, because young preschoolers are more active and distractible than older children, different rewards also were used when motivation or interest lagged to maximize persistence and facilitate task completion.

Delayed response (DR; Jacobson, Wolfe, & Jackson, 1935).   In this task, the child watched while a reward was hidden in one of the two revealed lateral wells. The cups were replaced simultaneously, and the tray was removed from the child's sight (under the testing table). The examiner counted aloud from 1 to 10 in an engaging manner to distract the child and reduce the use of locational cues that have been shown to improve performance (Diamond, 1988). Then, the testing board was presented to the child after the 10-sec delay. The child was instructed to "Find the reward!" After displacing the selected cup, if correct, the child removed and kept the reward. If the child chose an incorrect location, the examiner encouraged the child to try again on the next trial and did not allow the child to have the reward. Both cups then were removed, and another reward was hidden while the child watched. Rewards were hidden randomly across the left and right wells, in an order consistent across subjects for a total of 17 trials. The total number of correct responses was scored.

DR has been used in many animal studies, but only recently has it been used with humans. Diamond and Doar (1989) concluded that WM and inhibition are necessary to correctly retrieve the reward in DR. DR is similar to A-not-B (Piaget, 1954), which has been demonstrated to load with other measures of WM and inhibition in preschool children (Espy, Kaufmann, McDiarmid, et al., 1999). In DR, the reward is hidden randomly across lateral wells while the child watches, whereas in A-not-B, the reward is hidden is a pattern dependent on the child's response (i.e., the reward is hidden on the same side until the child searches correctly at that location for two consecutive trials, and then the alternate well is baited). DR was selected rather than A-not-B because the number of reversal trials is constant across subjects.

Delayed alternation (DA; Espy, Kaufmann, McDiarmid, et al., 1999).
Adapted from studies with primates (e.g., Goldman, Rosvold, Vest, & Galkin, 1971), DA is considered a measure of WM, consistent with results from studies of nonhuman animals with lesions to dorsolateral prefrontal circuits (Goldman et al., 1971; Watanabe, Kodama, & Hikosaka, 1997) and work in our laboratory with normally developing preschoolers (Espy, Kaufmann, McDiarmid, et al., 1999). This task was similar to DR and used the same testing board. In DA, however, the reward was always hidden out of the child's sight. To achieve optimal rewards, the child had to alternate retrieval between the left and right lateral wells. Because the location of the reward on subsequent trials was dependent on the child's selection on the previous trial, the child had to maintain the previously rewarded location to guide search behavior on the subsequent trial. First, a pretrial was presented where neither well was baited with a reward, to lead the child to alternate among locations from the outset. After the pretrial, the reward was hidden in the location opposite from the child's last correct response after a 10-sec delay. When the child disrupted the alternation by erroneously searching on the same side, the examiner hid the reward at the same location until correct retrieval occurred, thereby resuming the alternating sequence. Sixteen trials were administered. The number of consecutive perseverative errors was recorded to index the degree of breakdown in WM.

Spatial reversal (SR; Kaufmann, Leckman, & Ort, 1989).   Although SR is similar in administration and format to DA, it does not share significant variance (Espy, Kaufmann, McDiarmid, et al., 1999). Maximal performance requires rule-based learning, presumably similar to the WCST (Heaton et al., 1993), and shifting of performance as rule-based contingencies change (Mishkin, 1964). As in DA, the reward in SR was hidden out of the child's sight, and a 10-sec delay between trials was used. The reward was hidden in the same well on each trial until the child achieved four consecutive correct responses. Then, the opposite well was baited until the criterion of four consecutive correct responses was achieved again. If the child responded incorrectly, the reward remained on the target side until four consecutive correct retrievals were achieved. Sixteen trials were administered. Because optimal SR performance requires attaining a maximum number of sets with a minimum of errors, an efficiency score was calculated by dividing the number of sets attained by the number of errors.

Spatial reversal with irrelevant color cues (SRC; Espy, Thompson, & McDiarmid, 2000).   Administered directly after SR, SRC was identical in format, except that the cups used to cover the wells differed in color (blue and yellow). The reward continued to be hidden on the same side until the reward was retrieved from that well for four consecutive correct trials. The colored cups were used as a distractor, such that each colored cup covered the left or right well in a random sequence independent of reward location. Optimal performance required the child to ignore the color of the cup while attending to the side on which the reward was found. The number of correct trials required to obtain the first four-trial set was used as the dependent measure.

Six Boxes (Diamond et al., 1997).   Six Boxes was an experimental task adapted by Diamond et al. (1997) modeled after the Hamilton Search Task (Hamilton, 1911) that has been used to study WM in nonhuman animals (E. D. Levin & Bowman, 1986) and the Self-Ordered Pointing Task used to study WM in adult humans (Petrides, 1995). This task originally included two conditions: verbal–spatial and verbal. However, a third condition, spatial, was added for the purposes of this study as Diamond et al. (1997) found that the 4-year-old children performed at ceiling levels on the verbal–spatial condition. In each condition, rewards (stickers) were hidden in each of six small boxes while the child watched. The child was asked to find a reward each time the boxes were presented, with the array of boxes re-presented to the child until all rewards were found. Between trials, the boxes were hidden behind a screen for a 10-sec delay. In the verbal–spatial condition, differently colored and shaped boxes were used to conceal the reward, and these boxes remained in the same location. Therefore, the child could use verbal and spatial information to find the reward. In the verbal condition, the differently shaped and colored boxes were rearranged out of the child's view during the delay between trials; therefore, the child had to use verbal information (shape–color) to find the reward. The spatial condition used six identical white, square boxes that remained in the same location, thereby necessitating the use of spatial location to correctly retrieve the reward. Because 4- and 5-year-old children perform at ceiling levels on the verbal–spatial condition (Diamond et al., 1997), this condition was not administered unless the participant required more than nine moves to complete the verbal condition. The number of trials to find all rewards was recorded, with an average efficiency score (number of boxes opened divided by number of moves made, averaged across the three conditions) calculated.

Children's Continuous Performance Task (C–CPT).   This computerized task was developed by Kerns and Rondeau (1998) as a modification of similar tasks frequently used to measure attention and IC in older children and adults. Overall task duration was reduced, visual stimuli that were engaging and familiar to preschool children were adopted, and animal noises were included as auditory stimuli. Children attended to a random grayscale display of several common animals on an Apple® laptop, one at a time, for a total duration of 3 min. Each animal was presented for 1.5 sec and accompanied by an animal sound (e.g., dog barking, horse neighing). The animal sounds were selected randomly and independently of the type of animal, such that the sound did not match the animal presented, except by chance occurrences. The child was familiarized with all the animals and the sounds prior to testing. The child then was instructed to press the button on the computer mouse whenever a target animal (sheep) was presented, regardless of the accompanying noise. A brief trial run (25 sec) was conducted at least once with each participant but was repeated if the child seemed to have difficulty understanding the task demands. Although stimuli were presented randomly, a ratio of six distractors to one target was maintained across participants. The percentage of commission errors (responses to nontarget stimuli) relative to the total responses was calculated, as Riccio, Reynolds, and Lowe (2001) suggested that commission errors best measure poor modulation of response inhibition.

Visual Attention (VA).   In this subtest of the NEPSY–A Developmental Neuropsychological Assessment (NEPSY; Korkman et al., 1998), children were instructed to find items that match the target stimuli among a page of targets and distractors. However, unlike the NEPSY administration, all children completed only one trial, the random array of cats, which is common to both the younger and older NEPSY test forms. Time to locate all target stimuli was recorded, with a 3-min maximum allowed. Efficiency scores were calculated by dividing the number of targets identified by the total number of responses (targets and commission errors).

Statue.   In this NEPSY (Korkman et al., 1998) subtest, children stood with their eyes closed and pretended to hold a flag for 75 sec. At standard intervals during the 75 sec, the examiner attempted to distract the child by making varied noises such as knocking on the table or saying, "Ho hum!" For every 5-sec interval, any body movement, eye openings, or vocalizations were recorded. Two points were scored for every error-free time interval. If the child made only one error in an interval, 1 point was given. The total number of points was tallied and used as the dependent measure.

Self-control (Lee, Vaughn, & Kopp, 1983).   In this task, the child was presented at the conclusion of testing with an attractive wrapped gift. The gift was placed on the table in front of the child, and the child was instructed not to touch the gift until the examiner had finished another task. The examiner then engaged in another activity (e.g., reviewing test sheets or interviewing the parent) while surreptitiously observing the child. The latency to touch the gift (with a maximum of 150 sec) was recorded.

Composite scores.   First, the raw scores from each task were transformed into z scores using the overall sample mean and standard deviation (depicted in Table 1). Because a lower percentage of commission errors on the C–CPT, fewer consecutive perseverative errors on DA, and fewer trials to the first set on SRC indicated better performance, the sign of the z scores for these three variables was inverted (multiplied by −1) so that all positive z scores indicated superior performance for the purposes of averaging. Construct composite scores then were calculated as the average of all available z scores for tasks that loaded on that principal component (McDiarmid, 2002) derived from the subjects with complete data on all tasks (49%). Components were determined based on examination of the scree plot and retaining factors with eigenvalues > 1 (Gorsuch, 1983), using a promax extraction that allowed correlated components. The identified components were consistent across the raw and age-residualized scores, with all tests contributing substantively to a single factor. Variables were assigned to factors if the loading exceeded .50.

This data reduction strategy was chosen because of the prevalence of missing data. Not surprisingly, task perseverance of younger children was more variable, leading to more missing data for the younger children. Using factor scores from only children with complete data would limit generalization across the entire preschool age range. Therefore, this strategy of calculating composite scores based on the factor-loading pattern allowed the inclusion of preschoolers with missing data but still accounted for the interrelations among executive function measures.

RESULTS

Sample mean performance on the individual executive function tasks is presented in Table 1. Note the range of performance, with no evidence of floor or ceiling ef-

TABLE 1
Study Sample Executive Function Task Performance

Measure	M	SD	Range
DA maximum consecutive perseverative errors	2.38	1.40	0.00–7.00
Six boxes efficiency score	0.74	0.15	0.42–1.00
VA efficiency score	0.83	0.22	0.21–1.00
C–CPT % commission errors	0.55	0.32	0.00–0.96
DR total correct	13.53	2.67	6.00–17.00
Self control latency	98.54	58.48	0.00–150.00
Statue total score	15.61	9.86	0.00–30.00
SRC trials to first set	7.84	4.39	0.00–16.00
SR efficiency	0.38	0.27	0.00–1.00

Note.   Due to missing data, N = 75 to 96, depending on task. DA = delayed alteration; VA = visual attention subtest; C–CPT = Children's Continuous Performance Test; DR = delayed response; SRC = spatial reversal with irrelevant color cues; SR = spatial reversal.

fects. The results from the principal components analyses are depicted in Table 2. Three factors were extracted, accounting for 60.82% of the variance. The first identified principal component accounted for 26.59% of the variance and was labeled *working memory* (WM), composed of efficiency scores from Six Boxes and VA (both loadings positive in sign), along with the maximum number of consecutive perseverative DA errors (loading negative in sign). The IC composite was composed of the C–CPT percentage commission errors, the total number correct on DR, the latency to touch on Self Control, and the Statue total score, accounting for 19.39% of the variance. Finally, the third identified component (14.84%) was labeled *shift,* composed of the number of trials to the first set on SRC and the SR efficiency score. These executive function composite scores then were computed as described, based on these factor-loading pattern, and then used as the relevant predictors of emergent mathematical skills and in comparisons between groups.

Bivariate correlations between the executive function composite scores and pertinent sample characteristics are depicted in Table 3. Results revealed that both maternal education and child vocabulary score were related to early mathematical competency (the dependent measure) and to some executive function composite scores (the independent variables). Furthermore, the executive function composites were not standardized with respect to age, and therefore, age also was included as a covariate in the predictive models. To test the study hypotheses, several hierarchical regression analyses were conducted. First, each executive function composite was entered in the regression model after controlling for age, with separate analyses for each executive function composite score. Then, similar models were run with each executive function composite score entered after age and the other

TABLE 2
Executive Function Component Structure Identified in Principal
Components Analysis

Task (Variable)	Working Memory	Inhibitory Control	Shifting
DA (maximum consecutive perseverative errors)[a]	.75	—	—
Six boxes (efficiency score)	.74	—	—
VA (efficiency score)	.90	—	—
C–CPT (% commission errors)[a]	—	.61	—
DR (total correct)	—	.58	—
Self-control (latency to touch)	—	.75	—
Statue (total score)	—	.69	—
SRC (trials to first set)[a]	—	—	.65
SR (efficiency score)	—	—	.74

Note. All factor loadings > .50 are displayed. DA = delayed alteration; VA = visual attention subtest; C–CPT = Children's Continuous Performance Test; DR = delayed response; SRC = spatial reversal with irrelevant color cues; SR = spatial reversal.

[a]Reverse scored such that higher scores indicate more optimal performance.

TABLE 3
Bivariate Correlations Among Dependent, Independent, and Covariate
Measures

Variables	IC	WM	Shifting	Age	Mat Ed	WJ–R PVSS
WJ–R APSS	.55****	.31**	−.08	.12	.37***	.57****
IC		.50****	.05	.50****	.20	.36***
WM			−.01	.67****	.24*	.17
Shifting				.07	.00	−.11
Age					.14	.04
Mat Ed						.29**

Note. $N = 96$. IC = inhibitory control composite z score; WM = working memory composite z score; Mat Ed = maternal education level in years; WJ–R = Woodcock–Johnson–Revised Psycho-educational Battery; PVSS = Picture Vocabulary standard score; APSS = Applied Problems standard score.

*$p < .05$. **$p < .01$. ***$p < .001$. ****$p < .0001$.

covariates (i.e., the child's score on the WJ–R Picture Vocabulary subtest and maternal education level) that were included as a block. To determine the relative contribution of each executive function composite beyond that of the two other executive function composites (e.g., unique contribution of WM to mathematical skills, beyond that of IC and shift), models included age and the two covariates, then the two remaining executive function composite scores, and finally, the executive function composite score of interest.

Contained in Table 4 are the results from the regression analyses relating performance on the executive function composites to emergent mathematical abilities. After statistically controlling for the influence of age, higher scores on the IC and on the WM composites were related to greater mathematical proficiency on the WJ–R Applied Problems subtest, $F(1, 93) = 45.13, p < .0001$, and $F(1, 93) = 9.51, p < .001$, respectively. These relations persisted when the influences of the two covariates, maternal education level and child's score on the WJ–R Picture Vocabulary subtest, also were included in the models; for IC, $F(1, 91) = 25.36, p < .0001$, and for WM, $F(1, 91) = 4.52, p < .05$. In both models, the IC composite accounted for the largest portion of the variance in preschool mathematical skills, 32% in the only age-controlled model and 14% in the age- and covariate-controlled model, respectively. The relation between the IC composite score and the WJ–R Applied Problems subtest standard score is depicted in Figure 1. The inclusion of the covariates affected the relation between WM composite performance and early mathematical skills more than that of IC composite scores and mathematics, as the difference in the proportion of variance attributed to WM was reduced by 80% between the two models, in contrast to a 50% reduction for IC. The magnitude of the unstandardized regression weights indicated that the difference in WJ–R mathematical proficiency was 9.65 points between children who scored

TABLE 4
Contributions of Executive Functions in Emergent Mathematics Skills

Variables	$R^2\Delta$	F	b	β
1. Age controlled				
1 a. Inhibitory control	.32****	45.13	13.70****	0.65****
1 b. Working memory	.17***	9.51	8.61***	0.41***
1 c. Shifting	.01	0.77	−2.05	−0.09
2. Age + covariates controlled				
2 a. Inhibitory control	.14****	25.36	9.65****	0.46****
2 b. Working memory	.03*	4.52	5.02***	0.24*
2 c. Shifting	.00	0.14	−0.70	−0.03
3. Age + covariates + other EF composites controlled				
3a. Inhibitory control	.12****	22.18	9.23****	0.44**
3 b. Working memory	.01	0.17	2.85	0.14
3 c. Shifting	.00	0.45	−1.12	−0.05

Note. $N = 96$. Covariates = maternal education and child picture vocabulary subtest standard score. EF = executive functioning. Each model was run separately for each dependent variable.
*$p < .05$. **$p < .01$. ***$p < .001$. ****$p < .0001$.

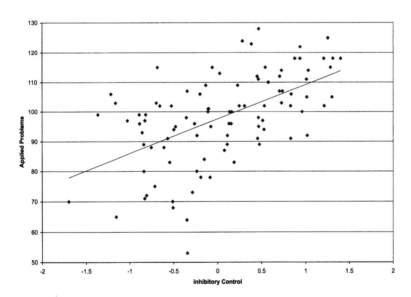

FIGURE 1 Woodcock-Johnson-R Applied Problems standard score as a function of IC z score in preschool children.

at the mean (expected score = 98.24) on the IC composite and those who scored 1 *SD* below the mean (expected score = 88.59), after accounting for child age, maternal education level, and child vocabulary score. Correspondingly, the difference in expected score on the WJ–R Applied Problems subtest between children who scored at the mean on the WM composite and those who scored 1 *SD* lower was –5.02 points. Shift composite scores were unrelated to WJ–R mathematical proficiency in the age-controlled $F(1, 93) = 0.77, p > .05$, and age- and covariate-controlled models, $F(1, 91) = 0.14, p > .05$.

Because scores on the executive function composites were intercorrelated, further analyses were conducted to examine the unique contribution of each executive function composite, beyond that of the remaining executive functions. The models included age, the two covariates, the remaining two executive function composite scores, and finally, the executive function composite score of interest. These results are displayed in the bottom of Table 4. Only performance on IC composite accounted for unique variability (12%) in emergent mathematical abilities on the WJ–R, beyond that of both WM and shift composite scores, $F(1, 89) = 22.18, p < .0001$. The difference in WJ–R Applied Problems scores between children who scored at the mean and those who scored 1 *SD* below the mean was –9.23 points. Neither WM, $F(1, 89) = 1.69, p > .05$, nor shift, $F(1, 89) = 0.45, p > .05$, composite scores were related independently and uniquely to emergent mathematical abilities.

DISCUSSION

Specific executive functions, namely WM, IC, and shifting, were determined empirically, based on shared variance across individual tests. In turn, executive functions were related to emergent mathematical proficiency in preschool children. Both IC, and to a lesser extent WM, contributed substantively to mathematical performance in this age range. These findings provide a developmental link to similar relations between executive function and mathematical performance previously reported in school-age children (e.g., Bull & Scerif, 2001; Gathercole & Pickering, 2000; McLean & Hitch, 1999). Given the differences in age range, methods used, and design between this study and others, the consistency of the relation of executive functions and mathematical performance is persuasive.

Specifically, the contribution of IC to early mathematical skills was central in preschoolers. Here, the magnitude of the relation to mathematics was large, even when the effects of child age, estimated child verbal intelligence, and maternal education level were controlled statistically. Furthermore, IC predicted emergent mathematical skills in preschool children when the influences of WM and shifting were removed, still accounting for 12% of mathematical skill variability. In contrast, Bull and Scerif (2001) found that in 7-year-old children, inhibition (assessed by Stroop Interference scores) accounted for only 2% of the unique variance (marginally significant) in mathematical performance, after controlling for estimated intelligence, reading skills, WM, and perseverative responding. These relative differences in the magnitude of the effect of IC are particularly salient, as in both studies, the predictive models accounted for a comparable overall percentage of mathematical performance variability (R^2 = 52% in our study, R^2 = 62% in Bull & Scerif, 2001).

In preschool children, IC typically is measured by tasks that require inhibition of a motor response. For example, pushing a button when a target animal is presented, but not pressing the response key when the animal's sound is paired with the incorrect animal picture; maintaining a still posture despite distractions; inhibiting reaching for an enticing gift; and inhibiting searching at a previously rewarded location. In contrast, in school-age children, inhibition more often is measured by tasks that require a stronger cognitive inhibitory component, such as the Stroop Interference that was used by Bull and Scerif (2001). The relations between the more primitive, "motorically"-based IC and the later, more "cognitive" inhibition is not clear. Ruff and Rothbart (1996) conceptualized IC as a developmental precursor to the cognitive inhibition, but such relations have not been demonstrated empirically. Until such relations are clarified further with longitudinal designs, the ontogenetic relation between IC and the developmental of mathematical competency will not be elucidated fully.

Several investigators (Bull & Scerif, 2001; Gathercole & Pickering, 2000; McLean & Hitch, 1999) have noted the role of WM in mathematics in older school-age children. In preschoolers, WM accounted for significant variance in early mathematical proficiency, when the influences of child age, estimated child verbal intelligence, and maternal education level were controlled. However, in this age range, WM skills were correlated substantially with IC (r = .50, p < .0001), limiting the amount of unique variance in emergent mathematical skills that could be accounted for by WM. The high correlation between performance on the IC and WM composites in the preschool children studied here differs from the nonsignificant relation (magnitude not reported) between WM and inhibition in school-age children reported by Bull and Scerif (2001). In preschool children, IC and WM may be more "intertwined" or less differentiated, reducing the unique contribution to mathematical proficiency in comparison to that of older children.

Unfortunately, other investigators who have examined the relation between WM and mathematical performance in school-age children (Gathercole & Pickering, 2000; McLean & Hitch, 1999) did not include tests that were designed to measure other specific executive functions. Instead, in these studies, the Baddeley and Hitch (1994) model was used, where WM was parsed into the central executive, visual spatial sketch pad, and phonological loop. Complicating the characterization of the relation between WM and executive function abilities is the lack of a shared definition of executive function. For example, in

Gathercole and Pickering (2000), counting span (Case, Kurland, & Goldberg, 1982) was chosen to assess the central executive, and other more visual spatial tasks were used to measure the visuospatial sketch pad. In McLean and Hitch (1999), Corsi blocks (Milner, 1971), another span-type task, was chosen as a measure of the visuospatial sketch pad, where several Trail Making Test-type tasks were used to measure the central executive. Finally, Bull and Scerif (2001) used counting span to measure WM. Span tasks probably tap short-term memory storage capacity rather than WM per se, when WM is defined as maintaining information online for further processing or responding (Fuster, 1989).

Interestingly, shifting or mental flexibility did not contribute to mathematical skills in preschool children. These findings are in contrast to those reported for school-age children (Bull & Scerif, 2001; McLean & Hitch, 1999). Mental flexibility may have contributed more to mathematical abilities in older children, given the necessity for the child to flexibly apply different mathematical procedures (e.g. borrowing, carrying) to obtain correct mathematical solutions. More complex mental flexibility skills also may be later developing and, thus, may be less related to mathematical performance in preschool children. However, the measurement of cognitive flexibility in preschool children has proved to be challenging. Reversal task performance may discriminate only those with severe disturbances in flexibly shifting between response sets, for example, children diagnosed with severe disorders such as autism (McEvoy, Rogers, & Pennington, 1993). Other measures that focus on concept formation may prove to be more useful in this regard (e.g., Jacques & Zelazo, 2001; Smidts, Jacobs, & Anderson, this issue).

These observed relations may be related to the type of mathematical problems that preschool children can solve. In school-age children even as young as age 7 years, mathematical problems likely require maintaining information online for subsequent processing and responding. For example, children must recall mathematical facts to use for carrying and borrowing. In contrast, mathematical problems for preschool children involve counting and simple regrouping, which, at least on the surface, do not demand as much WM skills to achieve adequate proficiency. In fact, most of the early items from the WJ–R Applied Problems subtest can be solved with knowledge of small-quantity numbers (National Institute of Child Health and Human Development, 2002). Not surprisingly, more proficient performance on these simple problems likely requires more basic IC, as was observed here. Using multiple measures of mathematical abilities will be important to determine how executive functions are related to more complex mathematical skills that involve, for example, reasoning, time calculation, and measurement. Longitudinal studies that dynamically relate the development of executive control and mathematical skill development in multiple arenas across primary grades is necessary.

One strength of the approach used here is the empirical derivation of the composites (McDiarmid, 2002) to assess the executive functions of interest. Three components were extracted, labeled as WM, IC, and mental flexibility, consistent with other studies in older children (e.g., Kelly, 2000; H. S. Levin, Fletcher, et al., 1996; Pennington, 1997; Welsh et al., 1991). Generally, the measurement pattern was consistent with expectations, although the loading of DR with the other instruments on the IC factor was somewhat surprising, as was the loading of the NEPSY VA subtest on the WM factor. Although this observed measurement pattern was derived empirically, the labels applied are a matter of individual preference and judgment. The labels were applied on the basis of previous findings and historical context; however, other labels from other frameworks also might easily describe the derived factors. Furthermore, another disadvantage of this statistical approach is that the loading pattern results are test specific, where the specific pattern might have varied if different dependent variables, even from the same task, had been selected for inclusion.

What is needed are systematic studies that use measurement model approaches to better characterize executive function organization in children (e.g. confirmatory factor analysis), similar to what was initiated by Miyake et al. (2000) in college students. Although the executive function composites used here were derived empirically, structural equation modeling approaches are preferred, which can more accurately represent the relations among observed test performance and the latent constructs. Such studies are more difficult to conduct in young children who cannot complete long batteries of tests that are necessary to fully define the latent constructs, commonly resulting in missing data that limits participant inclusion. This issue was apparent here, where the executive function components were calculated from subjects with complete data only, not surprisingly, largely in older preschool participants. A different loading pattern might have resulted if all children could have been included in these analyses. Because missing data is a common occurrence in studies with young children and those with clinical conditions, the use of imputation procedures (e.g., Allison, 2001; Schafer, 1997) or different modeling estimation procedures that are not used commonly in neuropsychology may be necessary to fully use data from such participants. These procedures must be applied with care, however, as the underlying cognitive construct also may be rapidly maturing, in some cases, leading to different loading patterns at different ages. Only by understanding executive function organization in different age ranges will it be possible to better describe the resultant relations to other functional outcomes, such as mathematical proficiency.

Another study limitation is the sampling strategy. Children born preterm at low risk for neurodevelopmental sequelae were sampled to increase performance variability and power to detect relations between executive function and emergent mathematics by including children more likely to experience later mathematical difficulties. The observed findings, including the resulting test to construct loading pattern, might have differed in a more homogenous sample. All children included here were born at 28 weeks gestation or more, with a much lower risk of adverse cognitive sequelae than those born earlier in gestation or at lower birth weights (Hack et al., 1995). Therefore, these findings likely do not represent how executive function may relate to emergent mathematical ability in preschool children born preterm, more broadly. Future studies that focus exclusively on the relation between executive function and emergent mathematical skills in those born preterm across the full spectrum of neurobiological risk are critical to better understand outcome in this important population.

The relation between executive function and mathematical proficiency suggests an important role of prefrontal cortical circuits in this age range, consistent with findings from recent imaging studies in adults and children relating to various mathematical skills and frontal lobe function (Fullbright et al., 2000; Gruber et al., 2001; H. S. Levin, Scheller, et al., 1996; Menon et al., 2000; Miles & Stelmack, 1994; Prabhakaran et al., 2001; Zago et al., 2001). However, without direct measurement of brain function and concurrent behavioral assessment in this age range, the specific areas that contributed to emergent mathematical proficiency in preschool children are unknown. Because of the technical limitations of the use of functional imaging methods with young children, high-density sensor array, event-related potential methods may be more suitable tools by which to examine such relations in young children.

More generally, the use of developmental and cognitive neuroscience paradigms in preschool children offer the opportunity to better assess more discrete neuropsychological skills that are related to functional outcome, such as emergent mathematical proficiency. However, there may be test-specific issues, such as test administration order that were not controlled here, which may have affected the noted findings. Nevertheless, such methods are particularly appealing, as the relation of test performance to specific brain areas may be stronger than more traditional general ability measures. Although the neuropsychological structure in preschool children likely is less differentiated than in older children, these methods are useful in highlighting executive function performance discrepancies that relate to functional academic outcome. Even in modern investigations that focus on direct brain measurement with highly specialized and technical methods, the careful description of behavior–behavior relations across the developmental context (Fletcher & Taylor, 1984) still is relevant today.

ACKNOWLEDGMENTS

This research was supported, in part, by the Pediatric Neuropsychology/Developmental Cognitive Neuroscience Award from the Rita Rudel Foundation and the Special Research Program Award from the Southern Illinois University Office of Research Development and Administration to Kimberly Andrews Espy.

We thank the participating families, undergraduates who assisted in various laboratory tasks associated with this study, and Diana Mitchell for her assistance with data collection.

REFERENCES

Allison, P. (2001). *Missing data.* Thousand Oaks, CA: Sage.

Baddeley, A. D., & Hitch, G. J. (1994). Developments in the concept of working memory. *Neuropsychology, 8,* 485–493.

Baroody, A. J. (1992). The development of preschoolers' counting skills and principles. In J. Bideau, C. Meljac, & J. Fischer (Eds.), *Pathways to number* (pp. 99–126). Hillsdale, NJ: Lawrence Erlbaum Associates, Inc.

Bull, R., & Scerif, G. (2001). Executive functioning as a predictor of children's mathematics ability: Inhibition, switching, and working memory. *Developmental Neuropsychology, 19,* 273–293.

Case, R., Kurland, D. M., & Goldberg, J. (1982). Operational efficiency and the growth of short-term memory span. *Journal of Experimental Child Psychology, 33,* 386–404.

Cirino, P. T., Morris, M. K., & Morris, R. D. (2002). Neuropsychological concomitants of calculation skills in college students referred for learning difficulties. *Developmental Neuropsychology, 21,* 201–218.

Diamond, A. (1985). Development of the ability to use recall to guide action, as indicated by infants' performance on AB. *Child Development, 56,* 868–883.

Diamond, A. (1988). Abilities and neural mechanisms underlying AB performance. *Child Development, 59,* 523–527.

Diamond, A., & Doar, B. (1989). The performance of human infants on a measure of frontal cortex function, the delayed response task. *Developmental Psychobiology, 22,* 271–294.

Diamond, A., Prevor, M. B., Callender, G., & Druin, D. P. (1997). Prefrontal cortex cognitive deficits in children treated early and continuously for PKU. *Monographs of the Society for Research in Child Development, 62*(4), 1–205.

Espy, K. A. (1997). The Shape School: Assessing executive function in preschool children. *Developmental Neuropsychology, 13,* 495–499.

Espy, K. A., Kaufmann, P. M., & Glisky, M. L. (1999). Neuropsychological function in toddlers exposed to cocaine in utero: A preliminary study. *Developmental Neuropsychology, 15,* 447–460.

Espy, K. A., Kaufmann, P. M., Glisky, M. L., & McDiarmid, M. D. (2001). New procedures to assess executive functions in preschool children. *Clinical Neuropsychologist, 15,* 46–58.

Espy, K. A., Kaufmann, P. M., McDiarmid, M. D., & Glisky, M. L. (1999). Executive functioning in preschool children: Performance on A-not-B and other delayed response format tasks. *Brain and Cognition, 41,* 178–199.

Espy, K. A., Stalets, M. M., McDiarmid, M. D., Senn, T. E., Cwik, M. F., & Hamby, A. F. (2002). Executive functions in preschool children born preterm: Applications of cognitive neuroscience paradigms. *Child Neuropsychology, 8,* 83–92.

Espy, K. A., Thompson, E., & McDiarmid, M. D. (2000). *Spatial reversal with irrelevant color cues.* Unpublished test.

Fletcher, J. M., & Taylor, H. G. (1984). Neuropsychological approaches to children: Towards a developmental neuropsychology. *Journal of Clinical Neuropsychology, 6,* 39–56.

Fox, N. A., & Bell, M. A. (1990). Electrophysiological indices of frontal lobe development: Relations to cognitive and affective behavior in human infants over the first year of life. *Annals of the New York Academy of Sciences, 608,* 677–698.

Fullbright, R. K., Molfese, D. L., Stevens, A. A., Skudlarski, P., Lacadie, C. M., & Gore, J. C. (2000). Cerebral activation during multiplication: A functional MR imaging study of number processing. *American Journal of Neuroradiology, 21,* 1048–1054.

Fuster, J. M. (1989). *The prefrontal cortex: Anatomy, physiology, and neuropsychology of the frontal lobe.* (2nd ed.). New York: Raven.

Gathercole, S. E., & Pickering, S. J. (2000). Working memory deficits in children with low achievements in the national curriculum at 7 years of age. *British Journal of Educational Psychology, 70,* 177–194.

Geary, D. C. (1994). *Children's mathematical development.* Washington, DC: American Psychological Association.

Gelman, R., & Gallistel, C.R. (1978). *The child's understanding of number.* Washington, DC: American Psychological Association.

Ginsburg, H. P. (1989). *Children's arithmetic* (2nd ed.). Cambridge, MA: Harvard University Press.

Goldman, P. S., Rosvold, H. E., Vest, B., & Galkin, T. W. (1971). Analysis of the delayed-alternation deficit produced by dorsolateral prefrontal lesions in the rhesus monkey. *Journal of Comparative and Physiological Psychology, 77,* 212–220.

Goldman-Rakic, P. S. (1987a). Circuitry of primate prefrontal cortex and regulation of behavior by representational memory. In F. Plum & V. Mountcastle (Eds.), *Handbook of physiology* (Vol. 5, pp. 373–417). Bethesda, MD: American Physiological Association.

Goldman-Rakic, P. S. (1987b). Development of cortical circuitry and cognitive function. *Child Development, 58,* 601–622.

Gorsuch, R. L. (1983). *Factor analysis* (2nd ed.). Hillsdale, NJ: Lawrence Erlbaum Associates, Inc.

Gruber, O., Indefrey, P., Steinmetz, H., & Kleinschmidt, A. (2001). Dissociating neural correlates of cognitive components in mental calculation. *Cerebral Cortex, 11,* 350–359.

Hack, M., Klein, N. K., & Taylor, H. G. (1995). Long-term developmental outcomes of low birth weight infants. *Future of Children, 5,* 176–196.

Hamilton, G. V. (1911). A study of trial and error reactions in mammals. *Journal of Animal Behavior, 1*(1), 33–66.

Heaton, R. K., Chelune, G. J., Talley, J. L., Kay, G. G., & Curtiss, G. (1993). *Wisconsin Card Sorting Test manual.* Odessa, FL: Psychological Assessment Resources.

Hughes, C. (1998). Executive function in preschoolers: Links with theory of mind and verbal ability. *British Journal of Developmental Psychology, 16,* 233–253.

Jacobson, C. F., Wolfe, J. B., & Jackson, T. A. (1935). An experimental analysis of the functions of the frontal association areas in primates. *Journal of Nervous and Mental Disease, 82,* 1–14.

Jacques, S., & Zelazo, P. D. (2001). The Flexible Item Selection Task (FIST): A measure of executive function in preschoolers. *Developmental Neuropsychology, 20,* 573–591.

Kaufmann, P. M., Leckman, J. M., & Ort, S. I. (1989). Delayed response performance in males with Fragile-X. *Journal of Clinical and Experimental Neuropsychology, 12,* 69.

Kelly, T. P. (2000). The development of executive function in school-aged children. *Clinical Neuropsychological Assessment, 1,* 38–55.

Kerns, K. A., & Rondeau, L. A. (1998). Development of a continuous performance test for preschool children. *Journal of Attention Disorders, 2,* 229–238.

Korkman, M., Kirk, U., & Kemp, S. (1998). *NEPSY: A developmental neuropsychological assessment manual.* San Antonio, TX: Psychological Corporation.

Lee, M., Vaughn, B. E., & Kopp, C. B. (1983). Role of self-control in the performance of very young children on a delayed-response memory-for-location task. *Developmental Psychology, 19,* 40–44.

Levin, E. D., & Bowman, R. E. (1986). Long-term lead effects on the Hamilton Search Task and delayed alternation in monkeys. *Neurobehavioral Toxicology & Teratology, 8,* 219–224.

Levin, H. S., Fletcher, J., Kufera, J., Harward, H., Lilly, M., Mendelsohn, D., et al. (1996). Dimensions of cognition measured by the Tower of London and other cognitive tasks in head-injured children and adolescents. *Developmental Neuropsychology, 12,* 17–34.

Levin, H. S., Scheller, J., Grafman, J., Martinkowski, K., Winslow, M., & Mirvis, S. (1996). Dyscalculia and dyslexia after right hemisphere injury in infancy. *Archives of Neurology, 53,* 88–96.

Lyon, G. R., & Krasnegor, N. A. (Eds.). (1996). *Attention, memory and executive function.* Baltimore: Brookes.

McDiarmid, M. D. (2002). *The relation between low-level lead exposure and attention in preschool children.* Unpublished doctoral dissertation, Southern Illinois University, Carbondale.

McEvoy, R. E., Rogers, S. J., & Pennington, B. F. (1993). Executive function and social communication deficits in young autistic children. *Journal of Child Psychology and Psychiatry and Allied Disciplines, 34,* 563–578.

McLean, J. F., & Hitch, G. J. (1999). Working memory impairments in children with specific arithmetic learning difficulties. *Journal of Experimental Clinical Psychology, 74,* 240–260.

Menon, V., Riveria, S. M., White, C. D., Glover, G. H., & Reiss, A. L. (2000). Dissociating prefrontal and parietal cortex activation during arithmetic processing. *Physical Review Letters, 85,* 520–524.

Miles, J., & Stelmack, R. M. (1994). Learning disability subtypes and the effects of auditory and visual priming on visual event-related potentials to words. *Journal of Clinical & Experimental Neuropsychology, 16,* 43–64.

Milner, B. (1971). Interhemispheric differences in the localization of psychological processes in man. *British Medical Bulletin, 27,* 272–277.

Mishkin, M. (1964). Perseveration of central sets after frontal lesions in monkeys. In J. M. Warren & K. Akert (Eds.), *The frontal granular cortex and behavior* (pp. 219–241). New York: McGraw-Hill.

Miyake, A., Friedman, N. P., Emerson, M. J., Witzki, A. H., & Howerter, A. (2000). The unity and diversity of executive functions and their contributions to complex "frontal lobe" tasks: A latent variable analysis. *Cognitive Psychology, 41,* 49–100.

National Institute of Child Health and Human Development (2002, October). Workshop, "Early Childhood Education and School Readiness," Baltimore, MD.

Newcombe, N., & Huttenlocher, J. (2000). *Making space: The development of spatial representation and reasoning.* Cambridge, MA: MIT Press.

Pennington, B. F. (1997). Dimensions of executive functions in normal and abnormal development. In N. A. Krasnegor, G. R. Lyon, & P. S. Goldman-Rakic (Eds.), *Development of the prefrontal cortex* (pp. 265–281). Baltimore: Brookes.

Petrides, M. (1995). Impairments on nonspatial self-ordered and externally ordered working memory tasks after lesions of the mid-dorsal part of the lateral frontal cortex in the monkey. *Journal of Neuroscience, 15,* 359–375.

Piaget, J. (1954). *The construction of reality in the child.* New York: Basic Books.

Prabhakaran, V., Rypma, B., & Gabrieli, J. D. E. (2001). Neural substrates of mathematical reasoning: A functional magnetic resonance imaging study of neocortical activation during performance of the necessary arithmetic operations test. *Neuropsychology, 15,* 115–127.

Riccio, C. A., Reynolds, C. R., & Lowe, P. A. (2001). *Clinical applications of continuous performance tests: Measuring attention and impulsive responding in children and adults.* New York: Wiley.

Rittle-Johnson, B., & Siegler, R. S. (1998). The relationship between conceptual and procedural knowledge in learning mathematics: A review. In C. Donlan (Ed.), *The development of mathematical skills* (pp. 75–110). East Sussex, England: Psychology Press.

Ruff, H. A., & Rothbart, M. K. (1996). *Attention in early development: Themes and variations.* New York: Oxford University Press.

Sattler, J. M. (1992). *Assessment of children* (3rd ed.). San Diego: Sattler.

Schafer, J. L. (1997). *Analysis of incomplete multivariate data.* London: Chapman & Hall.

Smidts, D. P., Jacobs, R., & Anderson, V. (2004/this issue). The Object Classification Task for Children (OCTC): A measure of concept generation and mental flexibility in early childhood. *Developmental Neuropsychology, 26,* 385–401.

Sophian, C. (1996). *Children's numbers.* Boulder, CO: Westview.

Watanabe, M., Kodama, T., & Hikosaka, K. (1997). Increase in extracellular dopamine in primate prefrontal cortex during a working memory task. *Journal of Neurophysiology, 78,* 2795–2798.

Welsh, M. C., & Pennington, B. F. (1988). Assessing frontal lobe functioning in children: Views from developmental psychology. *Developmental Neuropsychology, 4,* 199–230.

Welsh, M. C., Pennington, B. F., & Groisser, D. B. (1991). A normative-developmental study of executive function: A window on prefrontal function in children. *Developmental Neuropsychology, 7,* 131–149.

Woodcock, R. W., & Johnson, M. B. (1989). *Woodcock–Johnson Psycho-Educational Battery–Revised.* McAllen, TX: DLM.

Wynn, K. (1992). Addition and subtraction by human infants. *Nature, 358,* 749–750.

Zago, L., Pesenti, M., Mellet, E., Crivello, F., Mazoyer, B., & Tzourio-Mazoyer, N. (2001). Neural correlates of simple and complex mental calculation. *Neuroimage, 13,* 314–327.

DEVELOPMENTAL NEUROPSYCHOLOGY, 26(1), 487–512
Copyright © 2004, Lawrence Erlbaum Associates, Inc.

Executive Functions Following Traumatic Brain Injury in Young Children: A Preliminary Analysis

Linda Ewing-Cobbs, Mary R. Prasad,
and Susan H. Landry
Department of Pediatrics
University of Texas Health Science Center at Houston

Larry Kramer
Department of Radiology
University of Texas Health Science Center at Houston

Rosario DeLeon
Department of Psychology
University of Houston

To examine executive processes in young children with traumatic brain injury (TBI), we evaluated performance of 44 children who sustained moderate-to-severe TBI prior to age 6 and to 39 comparison children on delayed response (DR), stationary boxes, and spatial reversal (SR) tasks. The tasks have different requirements for holding mental representations in working memory (WM) over a delay, inhibiting prepotent responses, and shifting response set. Age at the time of testing was divided into 10- to 35- and 36- to 85-month ranges. In relation to the community comparison group, children with moderate-to-severe TBI scored significantly lower on indexes of WM/inhibitory control (IC) on DR and stationary boxes tasks. On the latter task, the Age × Group interaction indicated that performance efficiency was significantly reduced in the older children with TBI relative to the older comparison group; performance was similar in younger children irrespective of injury status. The TBI and comparison groups did not differ on the SR task, suggesting that shifting response set was not significantly altered by TBI. In both the TBI and comparison groups, performance improved with age on the DR and stationary boxes tasks. Age at testing was

Requests for reprints should be sent to Linda Ewing-Cobbs, Department of Pediatrics, University of Texas Health Science Center, 7000 Fannin, Suite 2401, Houston, TX 77030. E-mail: linda.ewing-cobbs@uth.tmc.edu not significantly related to scores on the SR task. The rate of acquisition of working memory (WM) and IC increases steeply during preschool years, but the abilities involved in shifting response set show less increase across age groups (Espy, Kaufmann, & Glisky, 2001; Luciana & Nelson, 1998). The findings of our study are consistent with the rapid development hypothesis, which predicts that skills in a rapid stage of development will be vulnerable to disruption by brain injury.

Executive functions exert a major influence on the most complex aspects of thought. Executive functions refer to a group of related but separable higher order cognitive abilities, including planning, impulse control, WM, maintenance of mental set, attentional control (Roberts & Pennington, 1996), as well as development and implementation of strategies for problem solving (Pennington, 1994). Recent studies of executive functions emphasize the interaction of a core set of prefrontal processes involving WM and inhibitory control (IC) of prepotent motor responses (Roberts & Pennington, 1996). *Working memory* is viewed as the active, online maintenance of relevant information to guide behavior and cognition (Baddeley, 1986; Goldman-Rakic, 1987), while ignoring irrelevant information and inhibiting prepotent responses (Bjorklund & Harnishfeger, 1990; Dempster, 1991; Diamond, 1990). *Inhibitory control* has been defined as a resource that prevents irrelevant information from entering or being maintained in WM and facilitates suppression of incorrect prepotent responses (Diamond, 1991; Hasher & Zacks, 1998). Barkley (1997b) characterized three types of IC: (a) overriding a prepotent response, (b) resisting interference, and (c) stopping an ongoing motor response. Working memory and IC are viewed as independently contributing to problem solving (Miyake, 2001) and to competence in other cognitive areas, such as reading (Chiappe, Hasher, & Siegel, 2000), written language (Swanson & Berninger, 1996), and mathematics (Bull & Scerif, 2001; Geary, 1993; Marzocchi, Lucangeli, De Meo, Fini, & Cornoldi, 2002). Executive functions in general, and WM and IC in particular, are commonly viewed as dependent on distributed neural networks involving the prefrontal cortex that coordinate component processes across time and space (Constantinidis, Williams, & Goldman-Rakic, 2002; Roberts & Pennington, 1996).

Recent analyses of executive function tasks in adults suggested that the core functions of inhibition, shifting set, and updating information in WM are partially distinguishable but are not completely independent (Miyake et al., 2000). In this article, we discuss studies of changes occurring in these core executive functions during infancy and the preschool years. Assessment techniques derived from developmental neuroscience models of executive processes are used to identify possible deficits in WM, IC, and shifting response set in infants and young children with traumatic brain injury (TBI).

Developmental increases in WM have been attributed to alterations in capacity as well as to increased efficiency of managing resources. Recent studies have examined the developmental trajectory of WM in infants, young children, and adolescents. Diamond's elegant studies suggested different developmental trajectories for the emergence of WM and IC. Diamond and Goldman-Rakic (1989) administered the A not B task, which was linked to functioning of the dorsolateral prefrontal cortex in nonhuman primate studies, to normal infants and children. The task requires the child to (a) watch as a reward is hidden in one of two locations, (b) remember where the reward is hidden during a brief delay in which the location is shielded from view, and (c) to select the correct location when the shield is removed. A correct response requires the child to inhibit the prepotent response of reaching to a location previously associated with a reward when the reward location changes. Significant improvement occurs from 7 to 12 months of age associated with increases in the ability to hold information in WM. To examine WM and IC in older children, Diamond and colleagues used a Directional Stroop task that varied WM and IC load (Diamond, O'Craven, & Savoy, 1998). Between 4 and 22 years of age, marked improvements in IC were noted with less striking improvement in WM (Diamond, 2001). Using a modified version of Diamond's Directional Stroop task, Roncadin (2002) determined that WM span did not increase with age; rather, improvements were related to increases in performance efficiency. Working memory and IC were closely related in younger children. Both Roncadin, and Luciana and Nelson (1998), attributed improvements in WM in older children to enhanced activation and inhibition resources, such as faster response speed and use of executive strategies.

Developmental cognitive neuroscience models of WM have been guided by animal models and functional imaging studies that implicate the involvement of prefrontal cortex in WM tasks. Several tasks that were linked to functioning of the dorsolateral or orbitofrontal prefrontal cortex in animal models, human lesion studies, or functional imaging studies have been applied to normal and clinical populations of children. Delayed response (DR), self-ordered pointing, and object reversal tasks have been used most frequently. These tasks all require holding mental representations in WM over a delay and prepotent activation of a currently nonrewarding response (Roberts & Pennington, 1996).

As previously described, Diamond and Goldman-Rakic (1989) extended the A not B and DR procedures to infants. The stationary boxes task (Petrides & Milner, 1982) is a variant of a self-ordered pointing task requiring the child to keep track of his or her history of searching multiple boxes for rewards and to inhibit return to a previously rewarded location. Self-ordered pointing tasks have been linked to prefrontal cortical functioning in children, adult humans, and nonhuman primates (Diamond, Prevor, Callender, & Druin, 1997; Petrides & Milner, 1982). Although self-ordered pointing tasks require the same basic WM processes involved in DR tasks, they impose a larger memory load and require serial self-ordering of internal representations (Levy & Goldman-Rakic, 2000). The degree of involvement of WM and IC in completion of the stationary boxes task is not well-understood. Diamond and colleagues (Diamond, 2001) confirmed that successful completion of DR and self-ordered pointing tasks is dependent on prefrontal cortex. Prefrontal ablation reduces performance on both tasks. In contrast, depletion of prefrontal dopamine by excitotoxic lesions damaging cell bodies, but not fibers, or by clinical conditions such as phenylketonuria producing low levels of dopamine, disrupts performance only on the DR task, which requires both WM and IC (Collins, Roberts, Dias, Everitt, & Robbins, 1998; Diamond, 2001). Bryan and Luszcz (2001) reported that performance on a self-ordered pointing task in adults ages 17 to 88 was related to speed of processing and to measures of perseveration but not to indexes of WM. Adults with prefrontal lesions can solve the task using spatial strategies that do not rely on WM (Diamond et al., 1997); however, it is not clear whether young children are able to develop similar strategies for task completion or whether they are more reliant on active maintenance of trials in WM due to immaturity of other executive functions.

The spatial reversal (SR) task (Kaufmann, Leckman, & Ort, 1989), which was modeled after object reversal tasks, was developed to assess set shifting and cognitive flexibility. Object reversal tasks have been linked to the orbital frontal cortex (Mishkin, 1964). There are few developmental studies examining shifting response set in childhood. SR tasks do not share significant variability with A not B or DR tasks; successful performance may be more reliant on cognitive flexibility and ability to determine the underlying task rules and less reliant on WM and IC (Espy, McDiarmid, & Glisky, 1999). In contrast to other tasks used to assess executive functions in young children, scores from the SR task showed little change over the preschool years (Espy, Kaufmann, & Glisky, 2001).

WM and IC are disrupted by TBI sustained during childhood. Recent investigations of WM in children and adolescents with TBI used N-back tasks, which manipulate memory load by requiring the child to hold specific information in mind over a predetermined number of trials (e.g., respond when a target letter is identical to the letter presented 1 or 2 trials earlier; Braver et al., 1997). Children with severe TBI had decreased hits and increased false alarms on N-back tasks assessing phonological and semantic WM, which were interpreted as indicating reduced WM and decreased IC (Levin et al., 2002). Performance improved with age, which is consistent with other studies showing improvement in WM and IC with development (Bjorklund & Harnishfeger, 1990; Gathercole & Baddeley, 1990; Luciana & Nelson, 1998; Roncadin, 2002).

Several studies have examined inhibitory processes using the stop-signal task in children with TBI. The stop-signal task is a two-choice reaction-time task; when a stimulus appears to the left or right of the fixation point, children respond by pressing a key on the same side as the stimulus. They are told to inhibit responding whenever they hear a stop-signal, which is adjusted dynamically relative to the child's performance (Logan, Cowan, & Davis, 1984). Konrad and colleagues (Konrad, Gauggel, Manz, & Scholl, 2000a, 2000b) found that chil-

dren with TBI had a primary deficit in inhibition of prepotent and on-going responses related to structural brain damage. Schachar, Levin, Max, Purvis, and
Chen (2004) identified significant disruption in response inhibition in a subset of
children with severe chronic TBI who also developed secondary attention deficit
hyperactivity disorder. Despite behavioral evidence of impaired response inhibition, the presence of frontal lobe lesions has not been consistently related to the
performance of children with TBI on WM and IC tasks (Dennis, Guger,
Roncadin, Barnes, & Schachar, 2001).

Assessment of executive functions following TBI in infants and young children is complicated by differences in the external cause of the injury. Severe TBI
in infants is frequently caused by child abuse and is often associated with a different pattern of intracranial findings than in accidental injuries (Ewing-Cobbs et
al., 1998). In comparison to children with accidental TBI, those with abusive or
inflicted TBI were more likely to have multiple extra-axial hemorrhages and
signs of preexisting brain abnormality such as mild cerebral atrophy. Intra-
parenchymal hemorrhage, shear injury, and skull fractures were more frequent
after accidental TBI, whereas subarachnoid hemorrhage and infarct or edema occurred with comparable frequency in both groups (Ewing-Cobbs, et al., 2000).
General cognitive functioning is significantly reduced after moderate-to-severe
TBI in young children. Forty-five percent of children with inflicted TBI and 5%
of children with accidental TBI scored in the deficient range when evaluated 1 to
3 months after injury (Ewing-Cobbs et al., 1998). Nearly half of the children
with inflicted TBI also had difficulty in regulation of affect, frustration toler-
ance, attention, and adaptation to change (Ewing-Cobbs, Prasad, Kramer, &
Landry, 1999). Both injury severity and the presence of abusive TBI were significantly related to long-term cognitive outcomes (Prasad, Ewing-Cobbs, Swank,
& Kramer, 2002).

In contrast to the distinct recovery curves in older children and adolescents that
indicate rapid improvement in a variety of skills in the first 6 months after TBI, the
recovery curves of young children are comparatively flat, suggesting limited recovery of function (Anderson & Moore, 1995; Ewing-Cobbs et al., 1998). Relative
to school-age children and adolescents, young children appear to be particularly
vulnerable to the effects of TBI as indicated by lower scores on measures of intelligence (Anderson et al., 1997; Anderson, Catroppa, Morse, Haritou, & Rosenfeld,
2000; Ewing-Cobbs, Miner, Fletcher, & Levin, 1989), speeded perceptual motor
tasks (Thompson et al., 1994), sustained and selective attention (Dennis,
Wilkinson, Koski, & Humphreys, 1995), metacognition and executive functions
(Dennis, Barnes, Donnelly, Wilkinson, & Humphreys, 1996; Levin et al., 1996;
Levin, Song, Ewing-Cobbs, Chapman, & Mendelsohn, 2001), language and dis-
course (Chapman, Levin, Matejka, Harward, & Kufera, 1995; Ewing-Cobbs,
Levin, Eisenberg, & Fletcher, 1987), and word decoding (Barnes, Dennis, &
Wilkinson, 1999).

Due to the rapid growth of prefrontal regions in infants and young children (Chugani, 1998; Huttenlocher & Dabholkar, 1997; Matsuzawa et al., 2001; Webb, Monk, & Nelson, 2001), early childhood may represent a developmental stage during which executive functions are particularly vulnerable to the effects of TBI. Skills in a rapid stage of development appear to be more vulnerable to the effects of acquired brain injury than well-consolidated skills (Dennis, 1988; Ewing-Cobbs et al., 1987). Therefore, WM, IC, and other executive functions that develop rapidly during the preschool years may be vulnerable to disruption by TBI. Skills that show less growth during the same developmental stage may show less disruption.

The purpose of this article is to apply developmental cognitive neuroscience models of executive processes to infants and young children with TBI. We selected tasks believed to reflect constructs of WM, IC, and shifting response set. We hypothesized that

1. Young children with TBI would show performance reductions on tasks requiring WM, IC, and set shifting relative to typically developing children. Performance was expected to be more disrupted by TBI on the DR and stationary boxes tasks, which have greater age-related increase in performance across the preschool years, than on the SR task, which shows less change.

2. Indexes of executive function would show higher scores in preschoolers relative to infants and toddlers.

3. General cognitive function and maternal education would explain a modest amount of variability in executive function scores.

METHOD

Participants

Study participants were enrolled in a longitudinal, prospective study of outcome following early TBI. The sample was composed of 44 children who sustained moderate-to-severe TBI prior to age 6 years. Severe brain injury was defined as Glasgow Coma Scale (GCS; Teasdale & Jennett, 1974) scores of 8 or less. Moderate TBI was defined as GCS scores ranging from 9 to 15 with positive CT or MRI findings indicating parenchymal injury or extra-axial hemorrhage. As in our previous studies (Ewing-Cobbs et al., 1997, 1998; Prasad et al., 2002) the GCS was modified to reflect the abilities of children from birth to 35 months of age. The motor scale item "following commands" was modified to include spontaneous movements in infants 0 to 6 months of age and goal-directed movements in children 7 to 35 months of age. The verbal scale items "confused" and "oriented" were regarded as equivalent to "cries" and "cries to indicate needs." A pseudoscore of 1 was assigned if periorbital swelling or intubation precluded the assessment of eye opening or verbal output; use of pseudoscores does not significantly affect score distributions (Marion & Carlier, 1994). To examine serial scores in children treated with sedatives and/or paralytics, the child's hourly GCS scores were recorded, and the best level of response was coded for each 24-hr period. The lowest postresuscitation GCS scores were comparable in the younger and older groups, $F(1, 42) = 1.83, p > .1$, suggesting similar impairment of consciousness in both age groups. Based on the GCS score, 32% of the young children and 42% of the older children had severe TBI. Inclusion criteria included (a) moderate-to-severe brain injury, (b) no known premorbid neurological or metabolic disorders, (c) no history of reported prior TBI, and (d) gestational age greater than 32 weeks.

Thirty-nine comparison children were recruited from children born at the hospitals at which the TBI children had been hospitalized, federally subsidized clinics, and from community notices. Exclusion criteria included gestational age less than 32 weeks, developmental delay, and known neurological disorders. The comparison children were screened for attainment of appropriate developmental milestones prior to enrollment in the study.

The sample was divided into 2 age groups. The younger group ranged from 11 months to 35 months (2 years) of age and the older group was 36 months to 71 months at the time of testing. Table 1 contains the basic demographic information for the TBI and comparison groups. Girls made up 68% of the TBI and 54% of the comparison groups, respectively, $\chi^2(1, N = 83) = 0.31, p > .1$. Ethnicity was similar across the groups, $\chi^2(3, N = 83) = 6.10, p < .1$. The level of maternal education was significantly higher for the comparison group than for the TBI group, $F(1, 83) = 14.51, p = .0001$.

Each of the 44 children with TBI underwent acute structural MRI or CT scanning within 2 days of admission. Findings from these scans were used to identify preexisting abnormalities. Most children had multiple scans during their hospitalization and findings from these scans were also used to characterize acute and subacute injuries (see Table 2). Seven children had negative scans or findings of skull fracture with no extra-axial or parenchymal lesions. In the remaining children, extra-axial lesions were visualized frequently in both anterior and posterior regions. The number of extra-axial lesions was distributed as follows: 42 subdural, 11 epidural, and 16 subarachnoid hemorrhages. Parenchymal lesions consisted of hemorrhagic contusions (8), edema (8), shear injuries (18), and atrophy (10). Consistent with previous studies (Ewing-Cobbs et al., 1998), atrophy on acute scans was visualized exclusively in children with inflicted TBI. Detailed information about the CT or MRI findings is presented in Table 3; 30% of the children had lesions that could be classified as being strictly anterior or posterior, and 30% of the children had bilateral lesions.

Based on the Child Protection Committee assessment at each hospital, 41% of the children in the younger and 32% of children in the older group were diagnosed with putative inflicted TBI; accidental injury was assumed for other children who

TABLE 1
Demographic Information for Traumatic Brain Injury and Comparison Groups

Variables	TBI Young[a]		TBI Older[b]		Comparison Young[b]		Comparison Older[c]	
Age at Test (in months; M, SD)	22.55	5.26	61.00	12.66	22.62	7.53	57.92	15.59
Maternal education (M, SD)*	12.44	2.17	12.29	1.46	13.96	2.42	14.23	1.74
IQ score (M, SD)	80.83	16.70	89.58	16.75	93.11	9.61	100.85	12.68
Ethnicity (n)								
African American	3		6		11		4	
White	12		8		10		8	
Hispanic	3		6		4		1	
Multi	0		6		1		0	
Gender (n)								
Girls	8		13		14		7	
Boys	10		13		12		6	

Note. TBI = traumatic brain injury.

[a]$n = 18$. [b]$n = 26$. [c]$n = 13$.

*$p < .0001$.

494

TABLE 2
Type and Number of Lesions on Acute Structural Neuroimaging Scans

| | Location of Neuroimaging Scan Finding | | | | | |
| | Anterior | | | Posterior | | |
Type of Lesion	Left	Right	Interhemispheric	Left	Right	Interhemispheric
Extraaxial hemorrhage						
Subdural	7	5	6	11	7	6
Epidural	3	2	—	4	2	—
Subarachnoid	2	1	2	4	4	3
	Left	Right	Subcortical	Left	Right	Subcortical
Parenchymal injury						
Contusion	2	2	0	1	3	0
Edema	2	1	0	3	2	0
Shear	4	2	0	2	2	8
Atrophy	2	2	1	2	2	1

had witnessed injuries and medical findings that were compatible with the cause of injury. Children with inflicted brain injury had a higher frequency of multiple extra-axial hemorrhages and preexisting mild cerebral atrophy. Because of the relatively small sample size, children were not separated by the external cause of injury for statistical analyses (i.e. inflicted vs. accidental TBI).

Procedures

Informed consent was obtained from the parent or guardian of each child. The minimal interval to testing was 1 month. Injury-to-test-interval data are presented in Table 3. The assessment of executive functions was completed an average of 11.3 months after injury in the younger children with TBI and 26.8 months after injury in the older children. Many of the older TBI group were enrolled in a longitudinal study of TBI and, thus, had been participants in the study for a few years before the executive function tasks were administered. The tasks were administered individually to each child in a single session by a trained psychometrician. To enhance children's interest in the testing, rewards on search tasks included small food items (M&Ms®, Fruit Loops®) and stickers. Executive function tasks were only administered to those children who were able to comply with and follow the instructions given by the examiner. The number of children completing each task varied slightly due to age restrictions and occasional difficulties engaging children's interest in specific tasks. The lower age limit for stationary boxes and DR was 10 months, whereas the lower age limit for SR was 15 months.

TABLE 3
Neurologic Information for Traumatic Brain Injury Group

Variables	Age at Test			
	Young[a]		Older[b]	
Age at injury (in months; M, SD)	11.2	9.4	34.2	22.2
Injury–test interval (in months; M, SD)	11.3	9.1	26.8	26.9
1–3 months (n)	8		6	
4–6 months (n)	0		1	
7–12 months (n)	3		1	
1+ years (n)	7		16	
GCS score (M, SD)	10.2	4.9	10.5	4.5

Note.   GCS = Glasgow Coma Scale.
[a]n = 18. [b]n = 24.

General Cognitive and Executive Function Measures

General cognitive ability.   The Bayley Scales of Infant Development–II (BSID–II; Bayley, 1993) were employed for children ages 10 to 42 months of age. Children ages 43 to 85 months were administered the Stanford–Binet Intelligence Scale–IV (SBIV; Thorndike, Hagen, & Sattler, 1986). The BSID has a mean score of 100 and standard deviation of 15, whereas the SBIV has a mean score of 100 and a standard deviation of 16. The scores from the SBIV were converted to a standard deviation of 15, thereby placing both tasks on the same scale. As there are no tests of general cognitive ability that span the age range in this study, we created a composite score using the age-appropriate measure for each child. We have successfully used this strategy in our previous studies in this age range (Ewing-Cobbs et al., 1997, 1998; Prasad et al., 2002). The composite scores correlated .823 when the same test was given and correlated .805 when the child switched from the BSID to the SBIV at adjacent visits (Ewing-Cobbs et al., 1997). In this study, the TBI group performed significantly lower on measures of general cognitive ability in both age groups than normal comparison children, $F(1, 77) = 12.21$, $p = .0008$, as presented in Table 1.

Delayed response (Diamond & Goldman-Rakic, 1989; Jacobsen, 1935).
Successful completion of this task requires WM and IC (Diamond et al., 1997; Goldman-Rakic, 1987). The child watched the examiner hide a reward under one of two cups. The cups were shielded by a screen for 5 sec to delay the child's response and to block vision of the cups. The child then attempted to retrieve the reward by selecting one of the two cups. The order of hiding the reward was varied on a random, predetermined schedule for a total of 10 trials. The child received 1

point for each correct reach. Dependent variables included the number of total correct reaches, which ranged from 0 to 10. The number correct on Trials 1 to 5 and trials 6 to 10 was also examined.

Stationary boxes.   The Stationary boxes task is a WM task based on self-ordered pointing procedures (Diamond et al., 1997; Petrides & Milner, 1982) that requires the child to keep track of which boxes from a fixed array of identical boxes they have searched for a reward. All boxes are baited in view of the child. After each search, the lid is replaced, the boxes are screened for 5 sec, and the next search trial begins. The child attempts to retrieve all rewards using the fewest number of reaches. The child must search the array of boxes and keep track of the locations searched but inhibit returning to a location previously associated with a reward.

Depending on age, either the three-, six-, or nine-box array was used. Age groupings were 10 to 30 months for the three-box array, 31 to 59 months for the six-box array, and the nine-box array was for children over the age of 60 months. Because the number of boxes administered varied by age, the raw scores were converted to ratio scores to adjust for the number of boxes and the number of reaches. The search efficiency score was created by dividing the number of correct boxes by the number of reaches. Therefore, if a child received the six-box version and completed six boxes in nine reaches, the search efficiency score would be .67. If the child required only six reaches, the efficiency score would be 1.00. Dependent variables included (a) search efficiency—the number of correct boxes divided by the number of reaches, and (b) perseverative or nonperseverative errors. *Perseverative errors* were the number of reaches to a previous location on consecutive trials divided by the number of boxes. *Nonperseverative errors* consisted of the number of reaches to a previous location that were separated by at least one trial; error scores were also divided by number of boxes.

Spatial reversal (Kaufmann et al., 1989).   The spatial reversal (SR) task examined the child's ability to develop a simple response set to retrieve a reward over multiple trials. A reward is hidden under each of two cups behind a screen out of the child's view. After the screen is raised, the child selects a cup and retrieves the reward. The screen is lowered and another reward is placed under the cup the child selected and removed from underneath the other cup. The side of hiding remains the same until the child successfully locates the reward on four consecutive trials, which constitutes a response set. Without warning, the cup under which the reward is hidden is then reversed until the child makes four more consecutive correct reaches. The procedure is repeated for a total of 20 trials. Dependent variables were the number of correct responses on Trials 2 to 19, number of perseverative errors (consecutive incorrect responses), number of sets of four consecutive correct responses, and number of set breaks (loss of set after two consecutive correct responses).

Design and Analysis

The design was a 2 (TBI vs. comparison group)× 2 (age 11 to 35 months at time of testing vs. 36 to 71 months at time of testing) factorial. Dependent variables were the raw scores from the executive function tasks.

The distribution of number correct, ratio, and error scores was examined. Number correct and ratio scores across all tasks met the assumption of normality (i.e., skew, kurtosis, outliers). For the number correct, analysis of covariance (ANCOVA), with age at the time of testing as a covariate, was used to examine group differences in executive functions. Because error scores were found to be highly skewed on SR and stationary boxes tasks, chi-square was used. The error scores were residualized for age at testing, and the residual scores were used in the nonparametric analyses. Error scores were not calculated for DR.

Controlling for the influence of demographic variables, including age and general cognitive scores, on other dependent measures obtained from clinical populations is controversial (Adams, Brown, & Grant, 1985; Barkley, 1997a). As previously noted, the executive function variables were not standardized by age. Therefore, age at testing was used as the covariate in ANCOVAs, and the scores were residualized for age in chi-square analyses. We did not control for the effect of general cognitive scores on the executive function variables. Because both sets of variables are altered by brain injury, removing the influence of general cognitive function on other cognitive variables may remove a portion of the variance that is specifically associated with the effects of brain injury. We used hierarchical regression analyses to investigate possible explanatory relations of general cognitive functioning and executive function variables.

Hierarchical regression analyses were performed to examine the relative contributions of demographic and injury variables to prediction of performance on normally distributed variables from the executive function tasks. Order of entry for the variables was theoretically driven. For all models, age at testing and the presence or absence of TBI were entered on the first step as these variables have been shown to be strongly related to a variety of executive processes during the preschool years (Espy et al., 2001; Ewing-Cobbs et al., 1999). The child's level of general cognitive functioning and maternal education were entered on Step 2. Intellectual functioning may be related to performance on some executive functioning tasks (Welsh, Pennington, & Groisser, 1991) and familial factors have been shown to be related to cognitive development (Breslau et al., 2001). The predicted variables were the total score for each of the three measures.

Power analysis was conducted using a Monte Carlo procedure to control for unequal cell sizes. Using an alpha of .05 and a moderate effect size of .5 SDs (Cohen, 1988), this sample size yielded a power estimate of .60 for the main effects. Due to limited power and the exploratory nature of this pilot study, we did not correct for Type I error (experiment-wise error). By correcting for Type I error, we would incur the risk of greater Type II error, which would greatly limit the identification of possible variables sensitive to the effects of early brain injury that may inform future studies.

RESULTS

Analysis of Group and Age Effects

Delayed Response.   Descriptive statistics for dependent variables from the executive function tasks for the younger and older TBI and comparison children are provided in Table 4. The range of correct responses for the DR task varied from 0 to 10. To examine performance accuracy across trials, scores from the total task, the first five trials, and the last five trials were examined. The total DR score varied with age at testing, $F(1, 74) = 7.02$, $p = .01$, but not with the presence or absence of brain injury, $F(1, 74) = 3.17$, $p = .079$. Both groups had comparable scores on the first five trials, $F(1, 74) = 0.77$, $p = .98$. However, the TBI group had fewer correct responses on the last five trials than the comparison children, $F(1, 74) = 5.04$, $p = .028$, suggesting a performance decrement over the course of the task.

Stationary boxes.   Search efficiency was defined as the number of boxes presented to the child divided by the number of reaches to obtain the rewards. The Age at testing × TBI interaction was significant, $F(1, 76) = 4.59$, $p = .036$. Although performance was similar in young children irrespective of the presence of brain injury, older children with TBI searched the array of boxes less efficiently than the comparison group. Chi-square analysis revealed no significant group differences for number of perseverative errors, number of random errors, or the proportion of perseverative to random errors (all $ps > .348$). Figures 1 and 2 show the relations of age and presence or absence of brain injury with search efficiency and rate of perseverative errors.

Spatial reversal.   The normally distributed scores from the SR task, including the total score, trials to completion of the first set, number of sets established, and number of set breaks were examined. Significant Age × Group interactions were not obtained for any of these variables (all $ps > .293$). In addition, there were no significant main effects for age at testing (all $ps > .401$) or for TBI (all $ps > .317$). For the perseverative error score, chi-square analyses revealed no significant effects of TBI, $\chi^2(1, N = 65) = .318$, $p = .57$. A trend for older children to make fewer errors was obtained, $\chi^2(1, N = 65) = 3.28$, $p = .07$.

TABLE 4
Descriptive Statistics for Executive Function Variable

	Age at Test							
	Younger				Older			
	TBI[a]		Comparison[b]		TBI[b]		Comparison[c]	
Task	M	SD	M	SD	M	SD	M	SD
Delayed response								
Total score	6.35	2.34	7.54	1.64	8.68	2.06	8.83	1.40*
Trials 1–5	3.59	1.33	3.83	0.96	4.41	0.96	4.50	0.67
Trials 6–10	2.76	1.30	3.71	0.95	4.27	1.24	4.33	0.89***
Stationary boxes								
Efficiency ratio	0.37	0.18	0.42	0.22	0.65	0.20	0.88	0.21****
Perseverative errors	0.36	0.23	0.27	0.19	0.04	0.06	0.01	0.03**
Spatial reversal								
Total score	10.44	3.17	10.75	2.90	13.00	1.76	11.92	2.71
Number of sets	1.62	1.12	1.73	1.00	1.68	1.02	2.12	0.83
Set breaks	1.00	1.15	0.65	0.80	1.39	1.09	1.00	1.41
Perseverative errors	3.61	3.94	4.24	3.82	1.15	1.30	1.75	1.51

Note. Significant probability levels as follows: age, $*p = .01$ and $**p = .005$; group, $***p = .05$; Age × Group, $****p = .05$.
[a]$n = 18$. [b]$n = 26$. [c]$n = 13$.

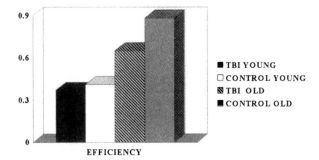

FIGURE 1   A significant Age by Group interaction indicated that the efficiency of searching for rewards in the Stationary Boxes task was reduced in the children with TBI who were 36–85 months of age at the time of testing relative to comparison children of the same age. Search efficiency was comparable in the younger TBI and comparison groups.

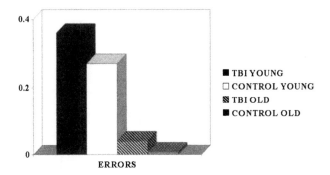

FIGURE 2   Perseverative errors decreased significantly with age; the presence of TBI did not significantly affect the error rate.

Correlational and Hierarchical Regression Analyses

To examine interrelations between executive function variables, we employed partial correlation analysis controlling for age at testing. As seen in Table 5, the total scores for each task were not significantly correlated with scores from the other two tasks. However, total scores were significantly correlated with within-task variables. DR Trials 6 to 10 were significantly related to the stationary boxes search efficiency, $r = .25$, $p = .05$, and perseverative error, $r = .26$, $p = .05$, ratio scores. These variables may share variance associated with WM. The SR total score was correlated with within-task measures of set breaks and perseverative errors. Consistent with findings of Espy et al. (1999), the SR total score was not significantly correlated with measures from other tasks and may reflect variance asso-

TABLE 5
Partial Correlation Coefficients for Executive Function Variables Controlling for Age

Variables	1	2	3	4	5	6	7	8
Delayed response								
1. Total								
2. Trial 1–5	0.85***							
3. Trial 6–10	0.89***	0.51***						
Stationary boxes								
4. Efficiency ratio	0.17	0.04	0.25*					
5. Perseverative ratio	-0.21	0.09	-0.26*	-0.48***				
Spatial reversal								
6. Total	0.03	-0.08	0.12	0.22	-0.24			
7. Number of sets	0.04	0.01	0.05	0.28	-0.08	0.64***		
8. Perseverative errors	-0.06	0.05	-0.14	-0.17	0.28*	-0.93***	-0.43***	

$*p < .05.$ $**p < .01.$ $***p < .005.$

ciated with generating rules and maintaining a mental set over trials. The perseverative error scores from the stationary boxes and SR tests were also significantly correlated, $r = .28$, $p = .05$, suggesting that perseverative responding was related across tasks.

Hierarchical regression analyses were performed on the normally distributed variables to examine relations between demographic and injury predictors with the executive function measures. For all models, age at testing and the presence or absence of TBI were entered on the first step. The child's general cognitive functioning and maternal education were entered on the second step. The predicted variables were the total score for each of the three measures as well as component scores reflecting more specific indexes of each task. Table 6 contains the beta weights for each variable as well as the total R^2 for the model.

Delayed response. For the variables entered on the first step, age at testing was a significant predictor of total correct, accounting for 25% of the variance, $t(1, 72) = 4.84$, $p < .0001$. Presence or absence of TBI was not a significant predictor,

TABLE 6
Hierarchical Regression Models of Executive Function Variables

Task	Step 1		Step 2		
	Model R^2	β	$R^2\Delta$	β	R^2 Total
Delayed response total	.25****				
Age at testing		.50****			
Presence or absence of TBI		−.16			
Cognitive functioning			.05	.19**	.30****
Maternal education				−.02	
Delayed response 6–10	.25****				
Age at testing		−.53****			
Presence or absence of TBI		−.22			
Cognitive functioning			.09	.24*	.33****
Maternal education				.12	
Stationary boxes efficiency					
Age at testing		.72****			
Presence or absence of TBI		−.19*			
Cognitive functioning			0	.13	.48****
Maternal education				−.03	
Spatial reversal total	.18***				
Age at testing		.40****			
Presence or absence of TBI		.06	0		−.18***
Cognitive functioning				.00	
Maternal education				.05	

Note. TBI = traumatic brain injury.
*$p < .05$. **$p < .01$. ***$p < .005$. ****$p < .0001$.

$t(1, 72) = -.52, p = .12$. Variables entered on the second step contributed an additional 5% of variance; the child's level of cognitive functioning accounted for a significant amount of variance, $t(1, 68) = 2.50, p = .01$. Maternal education was not significant, $t(1, 68) = -.15, p = .88$.

Performance on the last five trials of the DR task was predicted by age at testing, $t(1, 72) = 5.21, p < .0001$ and presence or absence of brain injury, $t(1, 72) = -2.19, p = .032$. The first step accounted for 24% of the variance in the dependent measure. In the second step, cognitive functioning was also a significant predictor, $t(1, 68) = 2.10, p = .04$, accounting for an additional 5% in variance, yielding an R^2 total score of .33. The level of maternal education did not enhance prediction of scores.

Stationary boxes.   In the first step, age at testing accounted for a significant amount of variance in the search efficiency score, $t(1, 74) = 8.26, p < .0001$. The presence or absence of TBI was also a significant predictor of variance, $t(1, 74) = -2.22, p = .03$. The second step did not increase the predictive ability of the model significantly. Neither level of cognitive functioning, $t(1, 70) = 1.34, p = .18$, nor maternal education, $t(1, 70) = -.32, p = .75$, were significant.

Spatial reversal.   Age at testing accounted for a significant amount of variance in the first step of the model, $t(1, 62) = 3.32, p = .0015$. Presence or absence of TBI, $t(1, 62) = .47, p = .64$, was not a significant factor in the first step, which accounted for 18% of the variance in total scores. Neither the child's cognitive level, $t(1, 58) = -.03, p = .97$, nor maternal education, $t(1, 58) = 40, p = .69$, significantly enhanced prediction in the second step. For the number of set breaks, none of the models generated accounted for a significant amount of the variance.

DISCUSSION

TBI in young children was associated with specific difficulty on tasks with prominent requirements for WM and IC. In relation to a community comparison group, children with moderate-to-severe TBI had lower scores on indexes of WM and IC as indicated by significant group effects on the DR and stationary boxes tasks. In contrast, both groups had comparable levels of performance on the SR task, suggesting that the index of shifting response set used in this study was not significantly affected by early brain injury. Therefore, the hypothesis that the TBI group would score lower than the comparison group on all executive function tasks was partially supported. As expected, performance was more disrupted on the tasks with significant developmental changes reported in normative samples. Thus, performance was more disrupted on the DR and stationary boxes tasks than on the SR task, which shows less developmental change in this age range.

Age at testing was also related to task performance. Although analyses for all dependent variables were adjusted for age at testing, improved performance with increasing age was noted on two of the three tasks. In both the TBI and comparison groups, increased accuracy was noted on the DR and stationary boxes tasks total scores. The total correct SR score did not differ significantly between the two age-at-testing groups. The hypothesis that older children would score higher than younger children on the executive function measures was fully supported for indexes of WM and IC. However, the relation between the SR total score and age at testing was less consistent. Although the group comparison was not significant using age as a dichotomous variable, age at testing did account for a significant amount of variance when examined as a continuous variable in regression analyses.

Luciana and Nelson (1998) noted that young children were able to perform easy items on WM tasks, which implies that improvements in performance unfold with development rather than appearing as an all-or-none phenomenon. Improved performance with increasing age was related to improvements in WM capacity as well as to improvements in more general executive functions, such as the ability to efficiently sequence motor responses and to develop a strategy for responding (Luciana & Nelson, 1998). As indicated by studies of the unfolding of executive functions during infancy and preschool years, the developmental trajectories of WM and IC increase steeply during preschool years, whereas the abilities involved in shifting response set and generating rules show less developmental change (Diamond, 2001; Espy et al., 2001; Luciana & Nelson, 1998).

The findings of this study are generally consistent with the rapid development hypothesis, which predicts that skills in a rapid stage of development will be vulnerable to disruption by TBI (Dennis, 1988; Ewing-Cobbs et al., 1987). The significant Age at testing × Group interaction on the stationary boxes task revealed that the older children with TBI showed significantly less efficient searching behavior than the older comparison children. The performance of the TBI group became significantly less efficient over trials on the DR task. Therefore, our hypothesis that tasks showing significant growth during preschool years would be more disrupted by TBI than tasks showing less growth was supported. Additional research is needed to ascertain whether performance declines after TBI reflect a failure to develop age-appropriate strategies, attentional difficulties, inefficiencies in inhibition resources, inefficiencies storing, updating, and monitoring information in WM, or all of these. The finding of decreasing response accuracy on the DR over the trials emphasizes the need to examine the influence of time and variability of performance to characterize maintenance of information over time, and the level of activation at a given moment that influences consistency of responding on executive function tasks (Roberts & Pennington, 1996). Task characteristics, such as the length of time that mental representations are held in WM prior to responding are critical variables requiring additional study. All of the tasks used in this study had fixed, brief delay periods. Although some studies have used similar delays (e.g., McEvoy, Rogers, & Pennington, 1993), other studies have used longer delay intervals (e.g., Diamond, 1991). Use of longer delays may provide more sensitive estimates of WM efficiency.

Predictors of the executive function variables used in this study were examined, including age at testing, the presence of TBI, the child's level of general cognitive functioning, and the influence of maternal education. As expected, age at testing accounted for significant variability in raw scores and ratio scores across the measures. Age at testing was related to performance on multiple variables derived from all three tasks and accounted for from 18% to 44% of unique variance. The substantial increases in scores with increasing age on the DR and stationary boxes tasks likely reflect the growth of WM and IC. As age increased, more accurate performance and fewer errors were noted on search tasks requiring holding prior patterns of responses online in WM. The presence of TBI contributed unique variance to prediction of search efficiency on stationary boxes and DR tasks. Additional research is needed to characterize whether these findings reflect difficulties in components of WM, IC, or maintaining mental representations of rules to guide response strategies.

Children with TBI performed significantly lower than normal comparison children on measures of general cognitive functioning. The relation between general cognitive functioning and specific indexes of executive functions was inconsistent. Our hypothesis that the child's level of general cognitive function and maternal education would explain variability in executive function variables received limited support. After accounting for the influence of age and brain injury, the child's level of general cognitive functioning accounted for significant incremental variation only on the DR task, which assesses WM and IC. In typically developing children, indexes of general cognitive functioning have not shown strong relations with measures of executive functions after controlling for age in young children (Espy et al., 1999) or in samples of older children (Levin et al., 1991; Welsh et al., 1991). Maternal education has been related to children's intellectual scores (Breslau et al., 2001). In this study, maternal education did not yield significant incremental prediction of any of the executive function variables. Measures of the family environment, such as indexes of the overall level of family functioning, may moderate the outcomes of children with severe TBI (Yeates et al., 1997). Additional research is clearly needed to examine the relation between family resources and the development of executive functions in young children after TBI.

The measures used in this study have promise for contributing to the clinical assessment of infants and preschool-age children. Despite the wide age range in this study, few floor or ceiling effects were obtained. DR and stationary boxes tasks were attempted successfully by the youngest children, who were 10 to 12 months of age at assessment. Floor effects were not problematic in children less than 25 months of age. In the comparison group, the percentages correct for the total scores on each task were as follows: 30% correct for stationary boxes, 55% correct for

SR, and 68% correct for the DR total scores. In children older than 60 months of age at testing, ceiling effects were noted only on the DR task; performance improved from an average of 85% correct in children from 48 to 60 months of age to 92% correct in comparison children older than 60 months of age. The percentage correct scores were 80% for SR and 85% for stationary boxes, suggesting continued sensitivity in these tasks for children older than 60 months of age.

The pattern of performance of the TBI group on the executive function tasks suggested some degree of sensitivity and specificity. Several variables were sensitive to the effects of brain injury. Children with TBI had performance decrements on tasks presumably assessing WM or IC, whereas brain injury did not significantly reduce indexes of shifting response set. Studies using similar measures to examine executive functions in children with autism found intact WM on DR and stationary boxes and impaired set shifting and increased perseverative errors on SR (Griffith, Pennington, Wehner, & Rogers, 1999; McEvoy et al., 1993; Ozonoff & Strayer, 2001). Espy and Glisky (1999) reported that toddlers exposed to cocaine during gestation made more perseverative errors and showed consecutive perseverations over trials on A not B, which is a prototype DR task. Further research examining performance on these executive function tasks in different clinical populations may identify specific cognitive subskills that are vulnerable to disruption by different acquired and developmental brain abnormalities.

To our knowledge, this is the first study of executive functions in infants and young children with TBI. Longitudinal studies are clearly needed to further characterize the nature of change over time in components of executive functions in infants and young children who incur TBI. This is particularly important because fundamental deficits in areas such as WM are related to difficulties in a host of other cognitive and social–emotional domains. WM deficits represent a major contributor to cognitive difficulties in school-age children and adolescents with TBI (Brookshire, Chapman, Song, & Levin, 2000; Chapman et al., 1995; Hanten, Levin, & Song, 1999; Turkstra & Holland, 1998). In addition, inefficiencies in WM or IC or both may adversely affect the acquisition of later developing skills in areas such as language, reading, mathematics, and written language. Young children with TBI are clearly at risk for significant difficulties in numerous cognitive areas (Anderson et al., 1997; Ewing-Cobbs et al., 1997); deficits in WM and related processes will adversely influence the development and deployment of new skills. Additional research is needed to determine whether WM deficits after early TBI manifest primarily as difficulty manipulating phonological or visuospatial information, deficits in IC, or whether they also reflect a more general deficit in resource capacity and allocation.

This study is limited by the small sample size and moderate power to detect group differences. The small sample size precluded assessing the relation of TBI severity and neuroimaging findings to indexes of WM and other executive functions. The sample encompassed a wide range of ages and included children with both inflicted and accidental TBI. The biomechanics involved in inflicted brain injury are quite distinct, and these children may perform differently on executive function tasks than children with accidental brain injury. It will be important to distinguish the performance of these two groups of children in future studies. Future studies should compare performance of children at specific ages. The development of specific components of executive functions in children with TBI should be examined in a longitudinal design. Moreover, the effect of early-onset dysfunction in fundamental skills such as WM on later developing cognitive and social abilities should be a focus of investigation. Within the context of developmental neuroscience models, future studies should examine interrelations between tasks providing multiple indexes of WM, IC, shifting, planning, and processing speed to better characterize the changes in performance attributable to variations in age at injury and the nature of the brain injury. Information on abilities that are spared versus those that are adversely affected by early brain injury may enhance our understanding of the relation between brain development and the emergence of executive functions. In this study, reduced performance on tasks tapping WM in the TBI group was notable, given the relatively small number of acute focal prefrontal parenchymal lesions visualized on neuroimaging scans. Longitudinal studies incorporating structural and functional neuroimaging studies should be integrated with developmental findings to characterize the impact of age at the time a child sustains diffuse or multifocal injury on the subsequent development of component skills involved in later developing executive functions.

ACKNOWLEDGMENTS

Preparation of this manuscript was supported, in part, by the National Institute of Neurological Disorders and Stroke Grant R01 NS 29462, Accidental and Nonaccidental Pediatric Brain Injury.

The assistance of the participating families and Harris County Children's Protective Services is gratefully acknowledged.

REFERENCES

Adams, K. M., Brown, G., & Grant, I. (1985). Analysis of covariance as a remedy for demographic mismatch of research subject groups: Some sobering simulations. *Journal of Clinical and Experimental Neuropsychology, 7,* 445–462.

Anderson, V. A., & Moore, C. (1995). Age at injury as a predictor of outcome following pediatric head injury: A longitudinal perspective. *Child Neuropsychology, 1,* 187–202.

Anderson, V. A., Morse, S. A., Klug, G. L., Catroppa, C., Haritou, F., Rosenfeld, J., et al. (1997). Predicting recovery from head injury in young children: A prospective analysis. *Journal of the International Neuropsychological Society, 3,* 568–580.

Anderson, V. A., Catroppa, C., Morse, S., Haritou, F., & Rosenfeld, J. (2000). Recovery of intellectual ability following traumatic brain injury in childhood: Impact of injury severity and age at injury. *Pediatric Neurosurgery, 32,* 282–290.

Baddeley, A. (1986). *Working memory.* Oxford, England: Oxford University Press.

Barkley, R. A. (1997a). *ADHD and the nature of self-control.* New York: Guilford.

Barkley, R. A. (1997b). Behavioral inhibition, sustained attention, and executive functions: Constructing a unifying theory of ADHD. *Psychological Bulletin, 121*(1), 65–94.

Barnes, M. A., Dennis, M., & Wilkinson, M. (1999). Reading after closed head injury in childhood: Effects on accuracy, fluency, and comprehension. *Developmental Neuropsychology, 15,* 1–24.

Bayley, N. (1993). *Bayley Scales of Infant Development–Second Edition.* San Antonio, TX: Psychological Corporation.

Bjorklund, D., & Harnishfeger, K. (1990). The resources construct I cognitive development: Diverse sources of evidence and a theory of inefficient inhibition. *Developmental Review, 10* (1), 48–71.

Braver, T. S., Cohen, J., Nystron, L. E., Jonides, J., Smith, E. E., & Noll, D. C. (1997). A parametric study of prefrontal cortex involvement in human working memory. *NeuroImage, 5,* 49–62.

Breslau, N., Chilcoat, H. D., Susser, E. S., Matte, T., Liang, J.-Y., & Peterson, E. L. (2001). Stability and change in children's intelligence quotient scores: A comparison of two socioeconomically disparate communities. *American Journal of Epidemiology, 154,* 711–717.

Brookshire, B., Chapman, S. B., Song, J., & Levin, H. S. (2000). Cognitive and linguistic correlates of children's discourse after closed head injury: A three-year follow-up. *Journal of International Neuropsychological Society, 6,* 741–751.

Bryan, J., & Luszcz, M. A. (2001). Adult age differences in self-ordering pointing task performance: Contributions from working memory, executive function and speed of information processing. *Journal of Clinical and Experimental Neuropsychology, 23,* 608–619.

Bull, R., & Scerif, G. (2001). Executive functioning as a predictor of children's mathematics ability: inhibition, switching, and working memory. *Developmental Neuropsychology, 19,* 273–293.

Chapman, S. B., Levin, H. S., Matejka, J., Harward, H., & Kufera, J. A. (1995). Discourse ability in children with brain injury: Correlations with psychosocial, linguistic, and cognitive factors. *Journal of Head Trauma Rehabilitation, 10*(5), 36–54.

Chiappe, P., Hasher, L., & Siegel, L. S. (2000). Working memory, inhibitory control, and reading disability. *Memory & Cognition, 25*(1), 8–17.

Chugani, H. T. (1998). A critical period of brain development: Studies of cerebral glucose utilization with PET. *Preventative Medicine, 27,* 184–188.

Cohen, J. (1988). *Statistical power analysis for the behavioral sciences* (2nd ed.). Hillsdale, NJ: Lawrence Erlbaum Associates, Inc.

Collins, P., Roberts, A. C., Dias, R., Everitt, B. J., & Robbins, T. W. (1998). Perseveration and strategy in a novel spatial self-ordered task for nonhuman primates: Effect of excitotoxic lesions and dopamine depletions of the prefrontal cortex. *Journal of Cognitive Neuroscience, 10,* 332–354.

Constantinidis, C., Williams, G. V., & Goldman-Rakic, P. S. (2002). A role for inhibition in shaping the temporal flow of information in prefrontal cortex. *Nature Neuroscience, 5,* 175–179.

Dempster, F. N. (1991). Inhibitory processes: A neglected dimension of intelligence. *Intelligence, 15,* 157–173.

Dennis, M. (1988). Language and the young damaged brain. In T. Boll & B. K. Bryant (Eds.), *The master lecture series: Clinical neuropsychology and brain function: Research measurement and practice* (pp. 89–123). Washington, DC: American Psychological Association.

Dennis, M., Barnes, M. A., Donnelly, R. E., Wilkinson, M., & Humphreys, R. P. (1996). Appraising and managing knowledge: Metacognitive skills after childhood head injury. *Developmental Neuropsychology, 12,* 77–103.

Dennis, M., Guger, S., Roncadin, C., Barnes, M. A., & Schachar, R. (2001). Attentional-inhibitory control and social-behavioral regulation after childhood closed head injury: Do biological, developmental, and recovery variables predict outcome? *Journal of the International Neuropsychological Society, 7,* 683–692.

Dennis, M., Wilkinson, M., Koski, L., & Humphreys, R. P. (1995). Attention deficits in the long term after childhood head injury. In S. H. Broman & M. E. Michel (Eds.), *Traumatic head injury in children* (pp. 165–187). New York: Oxford University Press.

Diamond, A. (1990). Developmental time course in human infants and infant monkeys, and the neural bases, of inhibitory control in reaching. In A. Diamond (Ed.), *The development and neural bases of higher cognitive functions* (pp. 637–676). New York: Annals of the New York Academy of Sciences.

Diamond, A. (1991). Guidelines for the study of brain–behavior relationships during development. In H. S. Levin, H. M. Eisenberg, & A. L. Benton (Eds.), *Frontal lobe function and dysfunction* (pp. 339–378). New York: Oxford University Press.

Diamond, A. (2001). A model system for studying the role of dopamine in prefrontal cortex during early development in humans: Early and continuously treated phenylketonuria (PKU). In C. Nelson & M. Luciana (Eds.), *Handbook of developmental cognitive neuroscience* (pp. 433–472). Cambridge, MA: MIT Press.

Diamond, A., & Goldman-Rakic, P. S. (1989). Comparison of human infants and infant rhesus monkeys on Piaget's AB task: Evidence for dependence on dorsolateral prefrontal cortex. *Experimental Brain Research, 74*(1), 24–40.

Diamond, A., O'Craven, K. M., & Savoy, R. L. (1998). Dorsolateral cortex contributions to working memory and inhibition as revealed by fMRI. *Society for Neuroscience Abstracts, 24,* 1251.

Diamond, A., Prevor, M. B., Callender, G., & Druin, D. P. (1997). Prefrontal cortex cognitive deficits in children treated early and continuously for PKU. *Monographs of the Society for Research in Child Development, 62*(4).

Espy, K. A., & Glisky, M. L. (1999). Neuropsychologic function in toddlers exposed to cocaine in utero: A preliminary study. *Developmental Neuropsychology, 15,* 447–460.

Espy, K. A., Kaufmann, P. M., & Glisky, M. L. (2001). New procedures to assess executive functions in preschool children. *Clinical Neuropsychologist, 15*(1), 46–58.

Espy, K. A., McDiarmid, M., & Glisky, M. L. (1999). Executive functioning in preschool children: Performance on A-Not-B and other delayed response format tasks. *Brain and Cognition, 41,* 178–199.

Ewing-Cobbs, L., Fletcher, J. M., Levin, H. S., Francis, D. J., Davidson, K., & Miner, M. E. (1997). Longitudinal neuropsychological outcome in infants and preschoolers with traumatic brain injury. *Journal of the International Neuropsychological Society, 3,* 581–591.

Ewing-Cobbs, L., Kramer, L., Prasad, M., Canales, D. N., Louis, P. T., Fletcher, J. M., et al. (1998). Neuroimaging, physical, and developmental findings after inflicted and noninflicted traumatic brain injury in young children. *Pediatrics, 102,* 300–307.

Ewing-Cobbs, L., Levin, H. S., Eisenberg, H. M., & Fletcher, J. M. (1987). Language functions following closed-head injury in children and adolescents. *Journal of Clinical and Experimental Neuropsychology, 9,* 575–592.

Ewing-Cobbs, L., Miner, M. E., Fletcher, J. M., & Levin, H. S. (1989). Intellectual, motor, and language sequelae following closed head injury in infants and preschoolers. *Journal of Pediatric Psychology, 14,* 531–547.

Ewing-Cobbs, L., Prasad, M., Kramer, L., & Landry, S. H. (1999). Inflicted traumatic brain injury: Relationship of developmental outcome to severity of injury. *Pediatric Neurosurgery, 31,* 251–258.

Ewing-Cobbs, L., Prasad, M., Kramer, L., Louis, P. T., Baumgartner, J., Fletcher, J. M., et al. (2000). Acute neuroradiologic findings in young children with inflicted or noninflicted traumatic brain injury. *Child's Nervous System, 16,* 25–34.

Gathercole, S. E., & Baddeley, A. (1990). The role of phonological memory in vocabulary acquisition: A study of young children learning new words. *British Journal of Psychology, 81,* 439–454.

Geary, D. C. (1993). Mathematical disabilities: Cognitive, neuropsychological and genetic components. *Psychological Bulletin, 114,* 345–362.

Goldman-Rakic, P. S. (1987). Development of cortical circuitry and cognitive functions. *Child Development, 58,* 642–691.

Griffith, E. M., Pennington, B. F., Wehner, E. A., & Rogers, S. J. (1999). Executive functions in young children with autism. *Child Development, 70,* 817–832.

Hanten, G., Levin, H. S., & Song, J. (1999). Working memory and metacognition in sentence comprehension by severely head-injured children: A preliminary study. *Developmental Neuropsychology, 16,* 393–414.

Hasher, L., & Zacks, R. T. (1998). Working memory, comprehension, and aging: A review and new view. In G. H. Bower (Ed.), *The psychology of learning and motivation: Advances in research and theory* (pp. 193–225). New York: Academic.

Huttenlocher, P. R., & Dabholkar, A. S. (1997). Developmental anatomy of prefrontal cortex. In G. R. Lyon & P. S. Goldman-Rakic (Eds.), *Development of the prefrontal cortex: Evolution, neurobiology, and behavior* (pp. 69–84). Baltimore: Brookes.

Jacobsen, C. F. (1935). Functions of frontal association areas in primates. *Archives of Neurology and Psychiatry, 33,* 558–560.

Kaufmann, P. M., Leckman, J., & Ort, S. (1989). Delayed response performance in males with Fragile X. *Journal of Clinical and Experimental Neuropsychology, 12*(1), 69.

Konrad, K., Gauggel, S., Manz, A., & Scholl, M. (2000a). Inhibitory control in children with traumatic brain injury (TBI) and children with attention deficit/hyperactivity disorder (ADHD). *Brain Injury, 14,* 859–875.

Konrad, K., Gauggel, S., Manz, A., & Scholl, M. (2000b). Lack of inhibition: A motivational deficit in children with attention deficit/hyperactivity disorder and children with traumatic brain injury. *Child Neuropsychology, 6,* 286–296.

Levin, H. S., Culhane, K. A., Hartmann, J., Evankovich, K., Mattson, A. J., Harward, H., et al. (1991). Developmental changes in performance on tests of purported frontal lobe functioning. *Developmental Neuropsychology, 7,* 377–395.

Levin, H. S., Fletcher, J. M., Kufera, J. A., Harward, H., Lilly, M. A., Mendelsohn, D., et al. (1996). Dimensions of cognition measured by the Tower of London and other cognitive tasks in head-injured children and adolescents. *Developmental Neuropsychology, 12,* 17–34.

Levin, H. S., Hanten, G., Chang, C., Zhang, L., Schachar, R., Ewing-Cobbs, L., et al. (2002). Working memory after traumatic brain injury in children. *Annals of Neurology, 52*(1), 82–88.

Levin, H. S., Song, J., Ewing-Cobbs, L., Chapman, S. B., & Mendelsohn, D. (2001). Word fluency in relation to severity of closed head injury, associated frontal brain lesions, and age at injury in children. *Neuropsychologia, 39,* 122–131.

Levy, R., & Goldman-Rakic, P. S. (2000). Segregation of working memory functions within the dorsolateral prefrontal cortex. *Experimental Brain Research, 133*(1), 23–32.

Logan, G., Cowan, W. B., & Davis, K. A. (1984). On the ability to inhibit thought and action: A model and a method. *Journal of Experimental Psychology, 10,* 276–294.

Luciana, M., & Nelson, C. (1998). The functional emergence of prefrontally-guided working memory systems in four- to eight-year-old children. *Neuropsychologia, 36,* 273–293.

Marion, D. W., & Carlier, P. M. (1994). Problems with initial Glasgow Coma Scale assessment caused by prehospital treatment of patients with head injuries: Results of a national survey. *Journal of Trauma, 36*(1), 89–95.

Marzocchi, G. M., Lucangeli, D., De Meo, T., Fini, F., & Cornoldi, C. (2002). The disturbing effect of irrelevant information on arithmetic problem solving in inattentive children. *Developmental Neuropsychology, 21,* 73–92.

Matsuzawa, J., Matsui, M., Konishi, T., Noguchi, K., Ruben, C. G., Bilker, W., et al. (2001). Age-related volumetric changes of brain gray and white matter in healthy infants and children. *Cerebral Cortex, 11,* 335–342.

McEvoy, R. E., Rogers, S. J., & Pennington, B. F. (1993). Executive function and social communication deficits in young autistic children. *Journal of Child Psychology and Psychiatry, 34,* 563–578.

Mishkin, M. (1964). Perseveration of central sets after frontal lobe lesion in monkeys. In J. M. Warren & K. Akert (Eds.), *The frontal granular cortex and behavior.* New York: McGraw-Hill.

Miyake, A. (2001). Individual differences in working memory: Introduction to the special section. *Journal of Experimental Psychology: General, 130*(1), 163–168.

Miyake, A., Friedman, N., Emerson, M., Witzki, A., Howerter, A., & Wager, T. D. (2000). The unity and diversity of executive functions and their contributions to complex "frontal lobe" tasks: A latent variable analysis. *Cognitive Psychology, 41,* 49–100.

Ozonoff, S., & Strayer, D. L. (2001). Further evidence of intact working memory in autism. *Journal of Autism and Developmental Disorders, 31,* 257–263.

Pennington, B. F. (1994). The working memory function of the prefrontal cortices: Implications for developmental and individual differences in cognition. In M. M. Haith, J. Benson, R. J. Roberts, & B. F. Pennington (Eds.), *Future oriented processes in development* (pp. 243–289). Chicago: University of Chicago Press.

Petrides, M., & Milner, B. (1982). Deficits on subject-ordered tasks after frontal- and temporal-lobe lesions in man. *Neuropsychologia, 20,* 249–262.

Prasad, M., Ewing-Cobbs, L., Swank, P. R., & Kramer, L. (2002). Predictors of outcome following traumatic brain injury in young children. *Pediatric Neurosurgery, 36,* 4–74.

Roberts, R. J., & Pennington, B. F. (1996). An interactive framework for examining prefrontal cognitive processes. *Developmental Neuropsychology, 12,* 105–126.

Roncadin, C. (2002). *Working memory and cognitive inhibition in typical and head injured children: Normal and aberrant developmental trajectories.* Unpublished doctoral dissertation, York University, Toronto, Ontario, Canada.

Schachar, R., Levin, H. S., Max, J. E., Purvis, K., & Chen, S. (2004). Attention deficit hyperactivity disorder symptoms and response inhibition after closed head injury in children: Do preinjury behavior and injury severity predict outcome? *Developmental Neuropsychology, 25,* 179–198.

Swanson, H. L., and Berninger, V. W. (1996). Individual differences in children's working memory and writing skill. *Journal of Experimental Child Psychology, 63,* 358–385.

Teasdale, G., & Jennett, B. (1974). Assessment of coma and impaired consciousness: A practical scale. *Lancet, 2,* 81–84.

Thompson, N. M., Francis, D. J., Stuebing, K. K., Fletcher, J. M., Ewing-Cobbs, L., Miner, M. E., et al. (1994). Motor, visual-spatial, and somatosensory skills after closed head injury in children and adolescents: A study of change. *Neuropsychology, 8,* 333–342.

Thorndike, R. L., Hagen, E. P., & Sattler, J. M. (1986). *Stanford–Binet Intelligence Scale: Fourth Edition.* Itasca, IL: Riverside.

Turkstra, L. S., & Holland, A. L. (1998). Assessment of syntax after adolescent brain injury: Effects of memory on test performance. *Journal of Speech, Language, and Hearing, 41,* 137–149.

Webb, S. J., Monk, C. S., & Nelson, C. A. (2001). Mechanisms of postnatal neurobiological development: Implications for human development. *Developmental Neuropsychology, 19,* 147–171.

Welsh, M. C., Pennington, B. F., & Groisser, D. B. (1991). A normative-developmental study of executive function: A window on prefrontal function in children. *Developmental Neuropsychology, 7,* 131–149.

Yeates, K. O., Taylor, H. G., Drotar, D., Wade, S. L., Klein, S., Stancin, T., et al. (1997). Preinjury family environment as a determinant of recovery from traumatic brain injuries in school-age children. *Journal of the International Neuropsychological Society, 3,* 617–630.

DEVELOPMENTAL NEUROPSYCHOLOGY, 26(1), 513–540

Impaired Neuropsychological Functioning in Lead-Exposed Children

Richard L. Canfield
Division of Nutritional Sciences
College of Human Ecology
Cornell University

Mathew H. Gendle
Department of Psychology
Elon University

Deborah A. Cory-Slechta
Department of Environmental and Occupational Medicine
UMDNJ–Robert Wood Johnson Medical School

Neuropsychological functions were assessed in 174 children participating in a longitudinal study of low-level lead exposure. At age 5½ years, children were administered the Working Memory and Planning Battery of the Cambridge Neuropsychological Testing Automated Battery. Measures of sociodemographic characteristics of the family, prenatal and perinatal risk, quality of caregiving and crowding in the home, and maternal and child intelligence were used as covariates to test the hypothesis that children with higher lifetime average blood lead concentrations would perform more poorly on tests of working memory, attentional flexibility, and planning and problem solving. The lifetime average blood lead level in this sample was 7.2 micrograms per deciliter (μg/dL; range: 0–20 μg/dL). Children with greater exposure performed more poorly on tests of executive processes. In both bivariate and multivariate analyses, children with higher lifetime average blood lead concentrations showed impaired performance on the tests of spatial working memory, spatial memory span, intradimensional and extradimensional shifts, and an analog of the Tower of London task. Many of the significant associations remained after controlling for children's intelligence test scores, in addition to the other covariates.

Requests for reprints should be sent to Richard L. Canfield, Division of Nutritional Sciences, College of Human Ecology, Cornell University, Savage Hall, Ithaca, NY 14853. E-mail: rlc5@cornell.edu

These findings indicate that the effects of pediatric lead exposure are not restricted to global indexes of general intellectual functioning, and executive processes may be at particular risk of lead-induced neurotoxicity.

Inorganic lead may be the most widespread neurotoxic pollutant on the planet, and investigations into the effects of lead exposure on children's cognitive and behavioral functioning are numerous (Pocock, Smith, & Baghurst, 1994). Eliminating lead from gasoline and paint has resulted in a sharp decline in the average blood lead levels of the U.S. population. Only a generation ago, the average blood lead level of U.S. residents was nearly 15 micrograms per deciliter (μg/dL); today it is approximately 2 μg/dL (Centers for Disease Control and Prevention [CDC], 1982, 2001). A concentration of 10 μg/dL or greater of lead in whole blood is currently defined as a level of concern by the CDC and the World Health Organization (WHO; CDC, 1991; WHO, 1995), but there is no evidence of a threshold value following which lead has no detectable effects on children's intellectual functioning.

This lack of evidence is perhaps not unexpected because there have been few investigations of children with lead levels below 10 μg/dL (Canfield et al., 2003). When such children have been the focus of study, the findings suggest that a unit increase in blood lead in the 0 to 10 μg/dL range is more detrimental to children's intellectual functioning than an equivalent increase within the 10 to 20 μg/dL range (Bellinger, Stiles, & Needleman, 1992; Canfield et al., 2003; Lanphear, Dietrich, Auinger, & Cox, 2000). From the perspective of the recent past, a blood lead concentration of 10 μg/dL can be considered low, but according to some estimates such an exposure is 200 to 600 times higher than in preindustrial humans (Flegal & Smith, 1995). Thus, it remains unclear at what level lead can be considered to carry negligible risk.

Numerous prospective studies have documented that within the 10 to 30 g/dL range, children with higher blood lead score lower on various tests of psychometric intelligence (Baghurst et al., 1992; Bellinger et al., 1992; Dietrich, Berger, Succop, Hammond, & Bornschein, 1993; McMichael et al., 1988; Pocock et al., 1994; Wasserman et al., 1997), but it has long been suspected that lead has more specific effects on particular cognitive functions (Bellinger, 1995; Bellinger, Hu, Titlebaum, & Needleman, 1994; Cory-Slechta, 1995). There is some evidence supporting this view. Patterns of subtest performance on measures of psychometric intelligence are suggestive of more pronounced effects on visual–spatial skills (Bellinger et al., 1991; Dietrich et al., 1993; McMichael et al., 1988; Wasserman et al., 1997), attention (Bellinger et al., 1994), and executive functions (Bellinger et al., 1994) than on verbal abilities or knowledge base. Studies using traditional neuropsychological tests have tended to support this view (Baghurst et al., 1995; Stiles & Bellinger, 1993).

Executive and complex cognitive functions are known to involve mediation by both cortical and subcortical structures of the brain. The mesocorticolimbic system includes projections that integrate functions in hippocampus, prefrontal cortex, and nucleus accumbens (ventral striatum), with these circuits using dopamine and glutamate as primary neurotransmitters (Doyere, Burette, Negro, & Laroche, 1993; Gurden, Tassin, & Jay, 1999; Thierry, Gioanni, Degenetais, & Glowinski, 2000). Experimental studies have shown that lead exposure disrupts these systems, establishing both a neuroanatomical and neurochemical basis for its effects on cognitive function. Lead, for example, results in changes in dopamine receptors and dopamine release in nucleus accumbens, even though the other major dopamine system of the brain, the nigrostriatal pathway, is unaffected (Pokora, Richfield, & Cory-Slechta, 1996; Zuch, O'Mara, & Cory-Slechta, 1998). Alterations of glutamate receptors in nucleus accumbens of rats can actually mimic the effects of lead on learning (Bauter, Brockel, Pankevich, Virgolini, & Cory-Slechta, 2003). Numerous studies also report lead-induced changes in hippocampal function, including changes in glutamate release, receptor binding, and long-term potentiation, presumed to be an electrophysiological correlate of learning (Lasley & Gilbert, 1996, 2002; Lasley, Green, & Gilbert, 1998).

In this study, we examined the association of lead exposure with specific cognitive functions in a cohort of preschool-age children with predominantly low-level lead exposure. The children were followed prospectively beginning at age 6 months (Canfield, Espy, Henderson, & Cory-Slechta, 2002; Canfield et al., 2003; Canfield, Kreher, Cornwell, & Henderson, 2003; Lanphear et al., 1999), using the Working Memory and Planning Battery of the Cambridge Neuropsychological Test Automated Battery (CANTAB, Cambridge Cognition Limited, Cambridge, England). The CANTAB is a computerized testing battery that uses a touch screen interface that places few demands on language comprehension, production, or complex motor skills, making it suitable for use with children and nonhuman primates (Fray & Robbins, 1996). The individual tests that make up the Working Memory and Planning Battery have been derived from common clinical assessments and have been shown to detect subtle cognitive impairments during the asymptomatic phases of several frontosubcortical disorders (Fray & Robbins, 1996). The CANTAB was developed within the theoretical frameworks of Baddeley and Shallice (Baddeley, 1986; Shallice & Burgess, 1993) and was validated and standardized with comparative studies of humans and monkeys, functional neuroimaging, and studies of various clinical populations with localized lesions or neuropsychiatric conditions involving damage to frontal circuits (Robbins, 1996).

The CANTAB has been used to measure executive functions in children as young as 4 years (Luciana & Nelson, 1998) and has been used to detect subtle cognitive alterations in children from at-risk populations, including neonatal intensive care unit survivors (Luciana, Lindeke, Georgieff, Mills, & Nelson, 1999), children with autism children (Hughes, Plumet, & Leboyer, 1999), and children with attention deficit hyperactivity disorder (ADHD; Kempton et al., 1999). It has also been used with adolescents and adults to measure the detrimental effects of neurotoxic exposure to gasoline vapors (Maruff, Burns, Tyler, Currie, & Currie, 1998) and inorganic mercury in adolescents and adults (O'Carroll, Masterton, Dougall, Ebmeier, & Goodwin, 1995). Because the CANTAB appears to be a promising tool for detecting the effects of neurotoxicants, assessing cognitive functions in children, and providing insights into the neural systems underlying neurocognitive impairments, we believed that it could be a powerful instrument for investigating subtle cognitive deficits that may be associated with very low level lead exposure in our cohort of young children.

METHOD

Participants

Participants were originally enrolled at 5 to 7 months of age for a study of lead dust control efficacy (Lanphear et al., 1999) and were invited to participate in a 5-year neurobehavioral study when the children were 24 to 30 months of age. Of the 276 children in the original cohort, data from 46 participants were excluded from this study because they were born prematurely (< 37 weeks gestation), had low birth weight (< 2,500 grams), Down syndrome, speech or hearing pathology, or had a previous diagnosis of ADHD. Three children died prior to this assessment, and data from an additional 14 were excluded because parents were short-term custodians, lacked English proficiency, or had relocated or declined to participate. Data from the 4 children who had lifetime average blood lead levels between 20 and 30 μg/dL were treated as outliers and were also excluded. Of the 230 children who were eligible to participate at 5½ years, complete data for one or more cognitive tests and all covariates were available for 174 children. Of the 56 children who were eligible but were not included in analysis, 24 were missing covariates and 32 did not participate in this assessment. The University of Rochester Medical Center Institutional Review Board approved the study protocol.

Parents were compensated for their participation with $25 vouchers to a local supermarket. Participating families were also given various health department pamphlets providing information about the prevention, detection, and treatment services for various child health problems, including lead exposure.

Apparatus

Children were assessed at 5½ years of age using the Working Memory and Planning Battery of the computerized CANTAB testing system. The CANTAB uses a touch-sensitive screen for presenting stimuli and recording the child's responses. The following six tasks were chosen because of their proposed sensitivity to executive dysfunction (Fray & Robbins, 1996).

Procedure

Before testing began, the examiner demonstrated to the child how the touch screen system worked and, using scripts provided in the CANTAB manual, prepared the child before each task. Instructions were given in American English rather than the British English commands provided in the manual. Several of the tasks are very challenging for young children, leading them to make many errors. These errors prolonged the approximately 1-hr testing period, and appeared to be a cause of frustration that resulted in some children not completing all tasks. Also contributing to differences in the number of cases included in a given analysis was variation in the availability of covariate measures for individual children.

Motor screening task (MOT).   Complete data for MOT and the associated covariates were available for 152 children. MOT was designed to act as a training procedure to ensure accurate pointing and recording of responses by the touch screen, and as a measure of motor speed and control. The child was presented with a series of crosses that appeared in random locations on the monitor. After the examiner demonstrated the correct touching procedure (using the forefinger of the dominant hand to touch the cross, without using excessive force), the child completed 10 trials. Mean latency to respond was the metric of interest.

Big–little circle task (BLC).   BLC tests the ability to follow an explicit rule. One large and one small circle were displayed, and the child was instructed to touch the smaller circle of the pair. After 20 trials, the child was instructed to point to the larger circle. Two measures were derived from BLC, the overall percentage of correct touches ($n = 170$) and the mean latency for correct touches ($n = 156$).

Spatial span task (SSP).   SSP is a sequential spatial memory task. Ten randomly arranged white squares are presented, then, one at a time, some number of the squares change color and then return to white. Following the color changes, a tone signals when to begin touching the boxes, which are to be touched in the same order as originally presented. The number of boxes in the sequence increases from two at the beginning of the test to a final sequence length of nine, with three trials at each sequence length. The positions and colors of the target boxes are altered for each trial to minimize proactive interference. Three measures were derived from this task. The longest sequence recalled was defined as the *maximum span length* for a given child ($n = 158$). *Total errors* were defined as the number of times the child touched an incorrect box ($n = 171$), and *nonsequence errors* were defined as the number of times the child selected a box that was not part of the sequence for that trial ($n = 171$).

Spatial working memory task (SWM).   SWM draws on spatial memory abilities and encourages the use of efficient search strategies. An array of boxes (two-dimensional opaque colored squares) is presented on the monitor, and the child's task is to find tokens (smaller colored squares) contained within a subset of these boxes. Touching a box revealed whether it contained a token. If the child was correct, then he or she could move the token to the right side of the screen to fill a container. The trial ended when the container was filled, and the next trial began with a new visual array. The child was specifically instructed that a box contains only one token and that once it is removed no additional tokens will be found in that box until a new trial begins. After demonstrating the task, sets of two- and three-box trials were used for training and practice. Test trials commenced with four-box problems and then progressed to six box problems. Although eight box problems were also available, they were not attempted by any of the children. The assessment consisted of four trials at each level (four, six, and eight boxes). CANTAB software provides dependent variables representing three error types:

1. Searching in a box previously found to be empty.
2. Searching in a box previously found to contain a token.
3. Repeatedly returning to search in a box that initially contained a token and was subsequently found to be empty during the same trial (i.e., a type of perseveration to a particular box that encompasses both error Types 1 and 2).

A strategy score for the SWM task (Owen, Downes, Sahakian, Polkey, & Robbins, 1990) is also provided. Owen et al. (1990) suggested that following a predetermined search sequence by beginning with a specific box and returning to this box once a token has been found (to begin anew in the search for another token hidden within the array) is a successful and efficient strategy for this task. An estimate of the use of this strategy is obtained by counting the number of times the participant begins a new search with the same box.

Intradimensional–extradimensional shift task (IED).   IED is a test of selective attention and attentional set shifting, and it shares many design features of the widely used Wisconsin Card Sorting Test (WCST; Berg, 1948). The IED task consists of nine test stages. Stage 1 involves learning a simple visual discrimination. Two color-filled nonsense shapes were presented on the video screen, and the child was instructed that one was the correct shape to touch and that the other was incorrect. The child was shown that by touching a shape, the computer will make a sound and indicate on the screen whether the correct shape has been chosen. At each stage, the child touched shapes and received automated feedback until meeting the learning criterion (six consecutive correct responses). For Stage 2, the task contingencies were reversed such that the previously correct stimulus was now incorrect. The next two stages involved the addition of an irrelevant task dimension (a pattern of white lines adjacent to the familiar shapes in Stage 3, and overlapping the shapes in Stage 4). After the child reached criterion with these compound stimuli, the correct shape was again reversed, but the irrelevant line patterns continued to be presented (Stage 5). Stages 6 and 7 introduced the intradimensional (ID) shift by introducing new shapes and line configurations. As in the previous stages, shape was the only relevant dimension. After meeting criterion with the new exemplars (Stage 6), the correct stimulus was reversed (Stage 7) to the alternate exemplar. Stage 8 introduced the extradimensional (ED) shift for which the child was required to shift attention from the stimulus dimension that had been relevant in the previous 7 stages to the dimension that was previously irrelevant. Stage 9 imposed a reversal of the newly learned discrimination. If the child did not reach criterion after 50 trials for any stage, the test automatically terminated. The duration of the test depended largely on the number of stages a child completed, although individual children also varied in their style of responding (i.e., more promptly or leisurely). Two measures were obtained from the CANTAB software: (a) the number of stages completed, and (b) the total number of trials across all stages.

Stockings of Cambridge task (SOC).   SOC implements a version of the Tower of London task, a widely used test of planning, inhibitory control, and general executive functioning), on the touch screen computer system. In the SOC version, the child was presented with two arrangements of colored circles, one on the upper half of the monitor and one on the lower half. The examiner explained that the circles were colored balls, one on top of another, and that the arrangement in the lower half of the screen was for the child to work with and the computer controlled the upper arrangement (the model). The object of the game was for the child to make his or her arrangement match the model, and to do so using the fewest possible number of moves. The examiner demonstrated how to move a ball's location by first touching it (and thus making it flash) and then touching the target location; the child was then assisted in making the lower pattern match the upper pattern. It was then demonstrated that it was only possible to move one ball at a time, and then only the top ball in each column. Children were told not to start moving the balls until they were sure of which moves they should make, thus encouraging them to plan the entire problem solution before enacting it. They were also informed that if they moved the balls too many times before making an accurate copy of the model, the computer would stop the trial and a new pattern would be presented for them to try again.

During the four training and practice trials, which could be solved using one move, the child was prompted verbally, and by pointing, to touch a particular ball, notice that it was flashing, find the location where it should be moved, and touch the desired location. The child was then given further training on two problems for which the solution required two moves. Following this training period the child was presented with three pairs of test problems, each pair requiring a minimum of 2, 3, 4, and then 5 moves.

To more accurately measure planning time, a yoked control procedure was used to measure the time needed to move the balls when no planning is involved. In this procedure, the computer moved the upper balls in the same order as the child had moved them when solving the previous test problems. The child was instructed to follow the movements in the upper display by touching the balls in the lower display. This motor control procedure was followed by a second identical set of test-and-follow problems.

Initial planning time at each problem level was computed by subtracting the latency to touch the first ball in the no-planning trials from that in the planning trials. Overall planning time for subsequent moves was computed in a similar manner, using the time to complete a given problem after the first ball was selected and then dividing by the number of moves made. If at any point the child made more than double the minimum number of moves, the problem was terminated.

Planning abilities were measured by (a) the number of problems solved in the minimum number of moves, (b) the average number of moves needed to solve each problem, (c) the initial planning time, and (d) the subsequent planning time.

Psychometric Characteristics of CANTAB

There is little information available about the psychometric characteristics of tasks in the CANTAB battery, and we are unaware of any such studies in children. One study of 60- to 80-year-old adults focused specifically on the test–retest reliabilities for measures from the CANTAB and from another neuropsychological test battery (Lowe & Rabbitt, 1998). For both test batteries, many variables had very low reliability. Furthermore, the reliability tended to be lower for tests of executive functions than for tests of what are conventionally thought to involve less complex cognitive processes. For example, tests of simple and choice reaction time and memory scanning speed showed test–retest correlations of .80 or better. Reliabilities for tests in the Working Memory and Planning Battery and the Attention Battery of the CANTAB were somewhat lower, with a median test–retest reliability of .66. Interpreting the meaning of lower reliability for tests of executive functions is not straightforward. As noted by the authors, because novelty and strategy are important characteristics of tests of executive function, task performance will increase abruptly when an individual discovers a useful strategy or correctly infers the implicit rules of the task. For individuals who do not make such discoveries, their performance on retest will be unchanged. Therefore, the test–retest reliabilities may not adequately reflect the psychometric validity of the CANTAB tasks.

Covariate measures.   Over the course of this longitudinal study, extensive information about each child's prenatal and perinatal health, parent and family demographics, and the quality of the home environment was gathered from birth records, maternal interviews, and a home visit. These variables included the child's sex and birth weight, mother's self-identified ethnicity (White or non-White), self-reported date of conception, date of first prenatal visit, self-reported smoking during pregnancy (yes/no), duration of breast-feeding, and whether or not the child was hospitalized in a neonatal intensive care unit (NICU).

Several measures were used to assess qualities of home environment believed to support and encourage cognitive growth in young children. The Home Observation for Measurement of the Environment (HOME) Inventory (Bradley & Caldwell, 1984) was administered during a home visit when the children were 24 months old. The interview portion of the HOME Short Form (HOME–SF) was administered when children were 6 years of age and made available for this study. Both the total HOME score and the HOME cognitive stimulation subscore at age 6 were used in the analysis. Maternal intelligence was assessed when children were 3 years old using the four-test, quick screening battery of the Stanford–Binet Intelligence Scale–IV (SBIV). This battery includes measures of vocabulary, visual–spatial construction, visual memory, and quantitative skills. Marital status, crowding in the home, years of maternal education, yearly income, and the frequency with which the family moved during the previous 3 years were assessed by parental interviews. The child's intelligence was assessed by the SBIV partial composite score from the six-test abbreviated battery administered at age 5 years.

Analysis and quality control of blood samples.   Blood lead was assessed semiannually from 6 to 24 months, and then annually at 36, 48, and 60 months. Blood lead concentration was determined by electrothermal atomization absorption spectrometry (New York State Department of Health, Wadsworth Laboratories, Albany, NY). Lead values are means of six analyses of each blood sample (3 aliquots/day measured on 2 consecutive days). The detection limit was 1 μg/dL (Lanphear et al., 1999). Lifetime (postnatal) average blood lead concentration is the exposure index used in this study. Plotting blood lead as a function of age and then computing the area under the blood lead curve yields a measure of total exposure. Dividing the area by the duration of exposure represents lifetime exposure, which is measured on the μg/dL scale. This value was treated as an untransformed continuous variable in all analyses and was the primary independent variable of interest.

Statistical methods.   General linear, logistic, and mixed model regressions were used to estimate and test parameters in models for estimating the association of lifetime average blood lead and the various cognitive outcomes. Because little is known regarding the effects of social and economic conditions on the development of executive function in children, a combination of conceptual and empirical considerations were used in the selection of covariates. Guided by research and theory about the factors influencing general intellectual development (Bouchard & Segal, 1985; Bradley & Caldwell, 1984), the 15 covariates described previously were considered for inclusion in each regression model. After checking for collinearity, initial models were estimated that included all 15 variables. Several criteria were used to determine the variables that remained in the final models: (a) Blood lead was included in all models; (b) any variable whose removal altered the regression coefficient for blood lead by more than 10% was retained, an approach that is recommended when the decision about which covariates to include does not have a strong theoretical basis (Mickey & Greenland, 1989; Tong & Lu, 2001); (c) a variable was also retained if it was significant at $p < .25$; (d) model reduction began with the covariate having the largest p value; and (e) conceptually important but nonsignificant variables (e.g., maternal intelligence, ethnicity, HOME score) were reentered at various stages of model reduction as a check on model specification. Furthermore, regression diagnostics were carried out for each model by examining model residuals in univariate and bivariate plots. One or more outliers were removed from some models. An alpha level of .05 was used for significance tests, and all tests were two-tailed.

RESULTS

Table 1 provides descriptive information for all children who were eligible to participate in this study, and it compares the children with complete data (those included in one or more analyses) to those who did not participate or had incomplete information on covariate measures. Children included in this analysis did not differ significantly from those not included except that the latter group changed residences more frequently.

Blood Lead Concentrations

Lifetime average blood lead concentrations ranged from 1.4 to 19.9 µg/dL. Four children had lifetime concentrations between 20.5 and 28.7 µg/dL and were not included in the analysis. Figure 1 shows the arithmetic mean blood lead concentrations at each blood draw. Average concentrations in this sample were lowest at age 6 months (3.4 µg/dL), attained a maximum of 9.7 µg/dL at 24 months, and declined to 6.0 µg/dL at 5 years. In this sample, lifetime average blood lead was 7.2 µg/dL at age 5.

TABLE 1
Characteristics of Children Included or Lost to Follow Up

Sample Characteristics	Included[a]		Lost to Follow Up[b]	
	M	SD	M	SD
Child characteristics				
Age in months when tested	66.7	1.2	—	—
% girls	50.6		65.5	
% admitted to NICU	6.9		1.8	
Birthweight in kilograms	3.3	0.5	3.3	0.5
Stanford–Binet partial composite score[c]	90.1	11.3	88.8	7.1
Lifetime average blood lead concentration in μg/dL	7.2	3.6	6.7	2.8
Age at breastfeeding termination[d]	2.8	5.1	2.8	4.8
Maternal and family characteristics				
HOME total score	27.2	7.3	28.3	5.8
Stanford–Binet partial composite score[e]	82.4	12.8	82.4	10.4
% greater than $25,000 yearly income	67.8		75.0	
Estimated time from conception to first prenatal visit in days	95.2	53.5	85.0	44.6
% mothers who smoked prenatally	22.0		27.8	
% married	32.2		18.8	
Household crowding in persons per room	0.8	0.3	0.7	0.2
Average annual moves in previous 3 years[f]	0.7	0.8	1.2	1.4
% self-identified as non-White	74.7		63.6	
% greater than high school education	36.8		37.5	
HOME–SF cognitive stimulation subscore	6.1	1.9	6.0	1.5

Note. NICU = neonatal intensive care unit; HOME = Home Observation for Measurement of the Environment Inventory; HOME–SF = HOME–Short Form. [a]n ranges from 165–174. [b]n ranges from 16–56. [c]Abbreviated battery administered at 5 years old. [d]Value of 0 entered for children not breastfed. [e]4-test quick screening battery administered when the child was 3 years old. [f]Difference is significant at $p < .05$.

Descriptive Characteristics of Dependent Variables

Table 2 provides descriptive characteristics for all of the CANTAB outcomes of interest. N represents the number of cases included in the final regression model for a given outcome, which varied from 30 to 171. The two main reasons for data being missing are incomplete data on one or more covariates in the final model and children missing data on a dependent variable due to a failure to complete the testing protocol.

Associations of Blood Lead and Covariates

Lifetime average blood lead concentration was significantly correlated with 11 of the 15 covariates at $p < .05$ (see Table 3), and it was strongly correlated with child

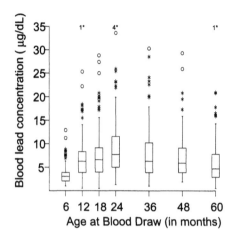

FIGURE 1   Distributions of blood lead concentrations at each assessment. *Note.* The asterisk denotes the number of cases with blood lead concentration > 35 µg/dL. 1 µg/dL = 0.048 mol/L.

IQ. Measures associated with aspects of socioeconomic status were more strongly associated with blood lead than were measures of prenatal and perinatal health.

Associations of Blood Lead and Cognitive Outcomes

Bivariate associations between blood lead and the various cognitive outcomes are shown in Table 4, as are results from covariate-adjusted models.

Motor screening (MOT). The latency data for MOT were positively skewed, typical of nearly all free-response latency measures (Canfield et al., 1997). The sample mean motor latency was 2.0 sec and ranged from 0.7 to 5.0 sec. For purposes of analysis this variable was transformed using the natural log function.

A significant bivariate association was found between lifetime average blood lead and mean motor latency, such that children with higher blood lead concentrations were slower to touch the crosses on the monitor ($r = .27, p = .003$). In a multiple regression model that included maternal IQ, crowding in the home, both HOME scores, and child's age at testing, the association of blood lead and mean motor latency was not significant ($B = 1.6$, standard error [SE] $B = 1.0, p = .111$).

Big–little circle (BLC). The mean latency to touch the correct circle in BLC was also transformed using the natural logarithm. Its association with blood lead was not significant in either the bivariate or multivariate analysis (Table 4). However, the percentage of correct choices in BLC was significantly associated with

TABLE 2
Descriptive Characteristics of the Dependent Variables

CANTAB Task	N	M	SD	Minimum	Maximum
MOT: Mean latency (sec)	152	2.0	0.84	0.75	5.0
BLC: Mean latency (sec)	156	1.2	0.2	0.8	1.8
BLC: % correct	170	92.8	7.4	57.5	100
SSP: Maximum span length	158	2.6	0.7	2	5
SSP: Total errors	171	8.0	3.0	4	19
SSP: Total nontarget errors	171	3.3	1.7	0	8
SWM: Total errors					
4-box problems	166	6.8	3.8	0	20
6-box problems	42	30.1	6.8	14	42
SWM: Strategy score	38	17.2	1.6	13	19
IED: Stages completed	151	6.7	1.8	1	9
IED: Total trials[a]	90	66.4	14.6	46	110
SOC: Problems solved in minimum moves	124	3.4	1.5	1	7
SOC: Mean moves					
2-move problems	134	2.5	0.8	2	5
3-move problems	127	4.8	1.3	3	7
4-move problems	120	6.8	1.5	4	9
5-move problems	31	8.6	1.5	6	12
SOC: Mean initial thinking time (sec)[b]					
2-move problems	130	7.0	8.2	0.4	51.1
3-move problems	125	9.7	10.8	0.2	79.0
4-move problems	119	9.0	7.4	0.3	36.3
5-move problems	31	5.3	4.3	11.5	19.8
SOC: Mean subsequent thinking time (sec)[b]					
2-move problems	114	2.8	4.1	0.4	22.6
3-move problems	113	5.4	7.7	0.1	50.5
4-move problems	112	5.3	5.1	0.6	40.1
5-move problems	30	3.3	3.6	0.4	15.9

Note. CANTAB = Cambridge Neuropsychological Testing Automated Battery; MOT = motor screening test; BLC = big–little circle task; SSP = spatial span test; SWM = spatial working memory task; IED = intradimensional–extradimensional shift task; SOC = Stockings of Cambridge task.
[a]Computed only for children completing Stage 7. [b]Natural log transform used in all analyses.

blood lead in the bivariate analysis ($r = -.34$, $p < .0001$), and the association remained highly significant in a model including marital status and NICU admission as covariates (Table 4). Children with higher blood lead levels were less likely to touch the correct circle.

Spatial span (SSP). A significant bivariate association between lifetime average blood lead concentration and span length suggested that children with

TABLE 3
Bivariate Pearson Correlations Between Lifetime
Average Blood Lead Concentration and Covariates

Covariate	Correlation With PbB[a]
Child IQ	−.48****
Neonatal intensive care unit admission	.06
Maternal IQ	−.41****
HOME total	−.48****
HOME Cognitive stimulation subscore	−.30****
Duration of breastfeeding	−.19**
Cigarette smoking during pregnancy	.12*
Household income	−.42****
Average moves per year	.23***
Sex of child	−.16**
Birth weight	−.06
Maternal ethnicity	−.36****
Marital status	−.35****
Maternal education	−.35****
Average crowding in the home	.09
First prenatal visit	.18**

Note. HOME = Home Observation for Measurement of the Environment Inventory.
[a]PbB is the lifetime average blood lead concentration.
*$p < .10$. **$p < .05$. ***$p < .01$. ****$p < .001$.

higher blood lead levels had impaired spatial memory ($r = -.33$, $p < .0001$). Although the maximum span lengths ranged from 2 to 5, very few children achieved spans of 4 or 5 items ($M = 2.6$ items; see Table 2). Logistic regression was used in covariate-adjusted models to assess whether children with a span length of only 2 items ($n = 91$) had higher blood lead levels than children with spans of 3 or more items ($n = 82$). In a model that included maternal intelligence, duration of breast-feeding, ethnicity, first prenatal visit, and family income as covariates, there was no association of lead and span length (see Table 4).

In bivariate analysis there was a significant positive association between blood lead and the number of nontarget errors ($r = .20$, $p = .009$), but a trend in the opposite direction ($r = -.14$, $p = .067$) for total errors (which includes incorrect touches of a previously correct location). These apparently conflicting findings result from the fact that children with higher spatial span lengths have completed more tasks and thus have more opportunities to make errors. Therefore, maximum span length was used as a covariate in multiple regression analyses.

The association of blood lead and total nontarget errors was estimated in a model that included span length, child sex, age at testing, and NICU admission as covariates. Blood lead was significantly and positively related to the number

TABLE 4
Bivariate and Multivariate Associations Between Lifetime Average Blood Lead Concentration and CANTAB Outcomes

CANTAB Outcome	Pearson's r With PbB	B	SE B	p	Covariates Included in Model[a]
MOT: Mean latency	.27***	.016	.010	.111	2***, 3, 4**, 14**, 20
BLC: Mean latency	.10	3.76	4.93	.446	2*, 4, 13, 20*
BLC: % correct	-.34****	-.619	.170	<.001	1, 12
SSP: Maximum span length	-.33****	.012	.015	.453	2**, 5*, 7***, 11, 15**
SSP: Total nontarget errors	.20***	.145	.036	<.001	1*, 9*, 18****, 20*
SSP: Total errors	-.14*	.112	.046	.016	13***, 18****
SWM: Total errors[b] (PbB × Problem)	—	—	—	<.001	5**, 7**, 9*, 10*, 12**, 19****
4-box problems	.13	-.032	.102	.752	
6-box problems	.37**	.456	.179	.016	
SWM: Strategy score	.11	.037	.087	.670	3*, 4, 6, 7***, 10**, 11
IED: Stages completed	-.22***	-.112	.052	.025	1*, 3, 6, 7, 9, 14
IED: Completed ED shift	-.15*c	-.189	.083	.023	3*, 4, 6, 11
IED: Total trials[d]	.28***	1.40	.459	.003	3*, 4****, 8***, 11***, 13
SOC: Problems solved in minimum moves	-.26***	-.083	.043	.057	2, 3, 6, 7, 9
SOC: Mean moves[b]	—	-.050	.019	.009	2*, 6*, 17****, 20
2-move problems	.25***	.050	.031	.106	
3-move problems	.19**	.071	.033	.030	
4-move problems	.08	.035	.034	.297	
5-move problems	.05	.005	.075	.948	
SOC: Mean initial planning time[b]	—	.008	.017	.627	9, 10*, 15, 17****, 20
2-move problems	.13	.032	.023	.160	

(continued)

527

TABLE 4 (Continued)

CANTAB Outcome	Pearson's r With PbB	B	SE B	p	Covariates Included in Model[a]
3-move problems	-.02	-.002	.024	.947	
4-move problems	-.08	-.000	.025	.988	
5-move problems	-.40**	-.058	.051	.257	
SOC: Mean subsequent planning time[b]	—	—	—	.002	2*, 5, 6**, 10*, 11***, 17****, 20***
(PbB × Problem)					
2-move problems	.35****	.142	.029	<.001	
3-move problems	.11	.052	.031	.091	
4-move problems	-.06	-.000	.032	.992	
5-move problems	-.19	-.040	.066	.544	

Note. PbB is the lifetime average blood lead concentration (in μ/dL). CANTAB = Cambridge Neuropsychological Test Automated Battery; MOT = motor screening test; BLC = big–little circle task; SSP = spatial span task; SWM = spatial working memory task; IED = intradimensional–extradimensional shift task; SOC = Stockings of Cambridge task; HOME = Home Observation for Measurement of the Environment Inventory; ED = extradimensional.

[a]Covariate list: 1 = neonatal intensive care unit admission, 2 = Maternal IQ, 3 = HOME total, 4 = HOME cognitive stimulation subscore, 5 = duration of breastfeeding, 6 = cigarette smoking during pregnancy, 7 = household income, 8 = number of moves, 9 = sex of child, 10 = birth weight, 11 = maternal ethnicity, 12 = marital status, 13 = maternal education, 14 = average crowding in the home, 15 = first prenatal visit, 16 = IED stages completed, 17 = SOC level completed, 18 = SSP span length, 19 = SWM problem type, 20 = age at testing. [b]Metric analyzed using mixed model. [c]Pearson's r is reported here for convenience of presentation. A Kruskal–Wallis test of the difference in blood lead levels for children who completed the ED shift task (Stage 8) versus those who completed no more than Stage 7 revealed: $\chi^2(1) = 2.71$, $p = .099$. [d]Includes only children who completed Stage 7.

*$p < .10$. **$p < .05$. ***$p < .01$ ****$p < .001$.

of nontarget errors made (B = .145, SE B = .036, p = .0002). Nontarget errors were also significantly associated with NICU admission, span length, age of testing, and sex.

The blood lead–total SSP errors relation was estimated in a model that controlled for span length and maternal education. Unlike the bivariate correlation, this model revealed a significant positive association between children's blood lead levels and the total number of errors they made in the SSP task (Table 4).

Spatial working memory (SWM).   No children attempted the eight-box problems, 42 completed the six-box problems, and 166 completed the four-box problems. In addition, the frequency of error Types 1 and 3 was insufficient to support separate analyses by error type, and so all errors were combined to form a total errors score. Therefore, total errors and the strategy score were the only two outcomes used for analysis.

The bivariate association of blood lead and total SWM errors was not significant for the four-box problems (r = .13, p = .100) but was significant for the six-box problems (r = .38, p = .012). Adjustment for covariates was carried out in a mixed model that included fixed classification effects for the child's sex and parents' marital status. Blood lead, birth weight, income, and duration of breast-feeding were covariates. Problem type (four vs. six boxes) was also treated as a fixed classification effect, and a random factor represented individual children. Blood lead was not significantly related to total SWM errors in this model; however, post hoc analyses revealed a significant Lead × Problem Type interaction (p = .001). Tests of simple effects revealed a significant lead effect only for the six-box problems, showing that children with higher lifetime average blood lead levels made more errors on the six-box problems of the SWM task (B = .456, SE B = .179, p = .016). Neither the bivariate nor covariate controlled associations between lifetime average blood lead level and the SWM strategy score were significant (see Table 4).

Intradimensional–extradimensional shift (IED).   There are nine stages to the IED task, whereas most children completed Stage 7 (ID shift reversal, n = 145), few completed Stage 8 (ED shift, n = 35). Bivariate analysis showed a trend such that the mean blood lead level for children who successfully completed the ED shift was lower than for those who did not (6.19 μg/dL versus 7.41 μg/dL, Kruskal–Wallis $\chi^2[1, n = 170] = 2.71, p = .099$). Multivariate analysis was carried out using logistic regression in a model that included maternal ethnicity, both HOME scores, and prenatal smoking as covariates. This analysis indicated that for each increase in lifetime average blood lead level of 1 μg/dL, children were 1.2 times less likely to complete the ED shift (95% confidence interval: 1.03, 1.42, see Table 4). It is unclear, however, to what extent the failure to complete Stage 8 was due to task-related fatigue or to an inability to make the ED shift.

Higher blood lead was also associated with the number of stages completed across all nine stages. Bivariate analysis suggested that children with higher blood lead levels completed fewer IED stages ($r = -.22, p = .003$). The multiple regression model included prenatal smoking, income, child sex, NICU admittance, HOME score, and average crowding in the home, revealing that the number of IED stages completed was significantly and inversely related to blood lead level ($B = -.112, SE B = .052, p = .025$).

The total number of trials across all completed stages was analyzed in the 145 children who completed Stage 7 but did not complete the ED shift presented in Stage 8. In this group, every child experienced the same sequence of problems and had the same number of opportunities to reach criterion. Thus, the measure can be thought of as trials to meet the criterion for Stage 7, and all previous stages. Because trials to criterion and errors to criterion are essentially the same measure in this task ($r = .95$), only the trials to criterion variable is presented.

In the bivariate analysis, children with higher blood lead levels took more total trials to reach the criterion of completing stage 7 ($r = .28, p = .003$). A multiple regression model that included both HOME scores, the mean number of times per year the child moved, maternal ethnicity, and maternal education also indicated that children with higher blood lead levels took more trials to complete Stage 7 ($B = 1.40, SE B = .459, p = .003$).

Stockings of Cambridge (SOC).   Bivariate analysis indicated that children with higher blood lead levels required more moves to solve the two- and three-move problems, but there was no significant association for the four- or five-move problems (Table 4). A mixed regression model treated prenatal smoking and SOC problem level as fixed classification effects, individual children as levels of a random factor, and maternal intelligence and child's age at testing as covariates. A significant main effect indicated that children with higher blood lead levels required more trials to complete the SOC problems (Table 4). The interaction of SOC level and blood lead was not significant, although the pattern of correlations suggests that the source of the main effect is a lead-related increase in the number of moves required to solve the 2- and 3-move problems.

The latency distributions for initial and subsequent planning time were transformed using the natural log function. Bivariate analysis revealed a significant association of blood lead and initial planning time only for the five-move problems (Table 4). Thus, for the 31 children who completed these problems, those with higher lead levels took less time to initiate their first move. A mixed model included child sex and SOC problem level as fixed classification effects, birth weight, and time of first prenatal visit as covariates, and children as levels of a random factor. This analysis revealed no significant effect of blood lead, no Lead × SOC problem-level interaction, and no significant effects at individual problem levels.

Blood lead level was systematically related to subsequent planning time in both bivariate and multivariate analyses. Positive bivariate associations with blood lead were significant only for two-move problems (Table 4). A mixed model included prenatal smoking, ethnicity, and SOC problem level as fixed classification effects and individual children as levels of a random factor. Maternal intelligence, duration of breast-feeding, child's age at testing, and birth weight were included as covariates. The main effect of blood lead level was not significant, but there was a significant Lead × SOC problem-level interaction. Analysis of simple effects revealed a significant lead effect only for the two-move problems, indicating that children with higher blood lead levels took longer to complete the easiest problems subsequent to moving the first ball (Table 4).

One way to assess the potential value of these findings is to ask whether they reveal impairments in cognitive functions that are independent of the impairments indicated by intelligence testing. To address this issue, the child's SBIV score was added as a covariate in each of the models described previously. These augmented models were then estimated, but no further model reduction was carried out. The addition of the SBIV score reduced the significance level of blood lead in most models. For three variables (SWM six-box problems, IED stages completed, SOC problems solved in minimum moves) the lead effect was reduced from significance at $p < .05$, to nonsignificance. There were four variables for which the blood lead effect was reduced from significance to marginal significance at $p < .10$ (SSP total errors, IED completed ED shift, SOC mean moves main effect and three-move problems). For SOC initial planning time for two-move problems, a nonsignificant lead effect became marginally significant. The lead effect remained significant for BLC percentage correct, SSP nontarget errors, IED total trials, and SOC subsequent planning time for two-move problems. SBIV was a significant covariate in 8 of the 15 models, but the statistical significance of SBIV and the amount of change in the lead effect for the dependent variables appeared unrelated.

DISCUSSION

These findings reveal that chronic low-level lead exposure is associated with impaired neuropsychological test performance in young children. Children with higher lifetime average blood lead concentrations performed more poorly on several tests designed to measure specific dimensions of neuropsychological functioning. Furthermore, the associations of blood lead and cognitive performance reported here are not attributable to any of a broad range of potential risk–protective factors that may also influence cognitive development and test performance. The risk factors included prenatal and perinatal health, sociohereditary factors such as family income and maternal education and intelligence, measures of cognitive stimulation in the home, and indexes related to family stress, such as crowding in the home or the frequency of moving residences. However, because lifetime lead exposure was highly correlated with several of these risk factors (see Table 3), including them could have resulted in overcontrol for lead exposure and thus an underestimation of the magnitude of the associations with children's performance (Needleman & Bellinger, 1989). After statistical control for these possible confounders, children with higher blood lead levels performed more poorly, on average, on a test that required them to follow an explicit rule and to reverse the rule on instruction (BLC); on two tests of spatial working memory (SSP and SWM); on a test that required them to discover an implicit rule, continue following the rule after irrelevant information is introduced, and also to flexibly reverse the rule, all without explicit instruction at any stage of the problem (IED); and on a test of planning and problem-solving ability (SOC). Lead exposure was unrelated to speed of responding on tasks measuring simple reaction time (MOT) and choice reaction time (BLC). Although the pattern of findings across tasks, and even across variables within a task, is somewhat unclear, the results suggest that lead exposure may be less damaging to sensorimotor functions than to higher cognitive processes such as focused attention, working memory (WM), and other executive functions. It is important to note that whereas such deficits are frequently ascribed to impairments in frontal cortical circuits, they could in addition or alternatively reflect adverse effects of lead on other subcortical regions, including hippocampus, amygdala, and basal ganglia. These regions make up integrated systems that both human and experimental studies confirm are requisite for the mediation of the behavioral processes for which impairments were observed (McGaugh, McIntyre, & Power, 2002; Poldrack & Packard, 2003; Roberts et al., 1990; Rogers, Andrews, Grasby, Brooks, & Robbins, 2000).

Sensorimotor Function

The MOT is comparable to a test of simple reaction time. When a cross is displayed on the screen, the child needs only to encode the location of the cross, program the trajectory of the reach, and issue a go signal. Although the latency to initiate this simple act is positively associated with blood lead in a bivariate correlation, it is also associated with the general intellectual functioning of the child's mother, the degree of cognitive stimulation in the home, and with a known stressor, crowding in the home (Evans, 1978; Evans, Lepore, Shejwal, & Palsane, 1998; Evans, Maxwell, & Hart, 1999). As a result, the lead-related differences in this simple task may result from differences in other aspects of the child's environment, although as noted previously, to the extent that sociodemographic factors are correlated with lead exposure itself, the estimated effects will be attenuated.

The BLC task presents an analog of a choice reaction time paradigm in which the child must make an elementary decision about which of two stimuli to touch. However, only a binary decision must be made. Infants, children, and adults who react more quickly to a simple stimulus onset are found also to have higher IQ scores, either concurrently or later in development (Canfield et al., 1997; Canfield, Wilken, Schmerl, & Smith, 1995; Carlson, Jensen, & Widaman, 1983; Detterman, 1987). BLC latencies were not associated with blood lead in either bivariate or multivariate analyses. Thus, regardless of the association of such measures to indexes of intellectual functioning, it does not appear that low-level lead exposure contributes uniquely to slower sensorimotor performance.

Discovering, Following, and Reversing Rules

Children's performance on tasks requiring rule-based responding was consistently related to their blood lead levels. In the simplest such task, BLC, children were given an explicit rule to follow ("touch the big circle"). After 10 presentations, they were given an explicit instruction to reverse the rule and choose the alternate stimulus ("now touch the little circle"). They were also instructed to choose as quickly as possible without making mistakes. In both bivariate and multivariate models, higher average blood lead levels were associated with making a smaller percentage of correct choices. Given that response latency and percentage correct were inversely related in these data ($r = -.18, p = .017$), higher lead children might have favored speed over accuracy. It is also possible that children with higher blood lead levels had a weaker representation of the explicit rule in WM. A poor representation would result in more errors, especially when rapid responding is required. A third possibility is that the lead-related deficit is due to perseverative responding when the rule was reversed. In addition, lead-exposed children may have been more likely to respond impulsively. Alterations in perseveration and impulsivity have been suggested by other studies of lead exposure in nonhuman animals and children (Brockel & Cory-Slechta, 1998; Cohn, Cox, & Cory-Slechta, 1993; Rice, 1993, 1997; Stiles & Bellinger, 1993). However, such an explanation appears less plausible in our data given that lead-related alterations were not observed for initial thinking time on the SOC task, a putative measure of impulsivity.

Children with higher lead levels also performed more poorly on the IED task. Adult neuropsychological patients with frontal lobe damage have been shown to be impaired on this task (Owen, Roberts, Polkey, Sahakian, & Robbins, 1991), and the IED is similar to the WCST, which has also been shown to be sensitive to alterations in frontal lobe function (Goldman-Rakic, 1987b; Monchi, Petrides, Petre, Worsley, & Dagher, 2001). In this study, children with higher blood lead levels were less likely to complete the ED stage, completed fewer stages overall, and took more trials to meet the performance criterion. This task also involved using and reversing a rule for selecting the correct stimulus. However, because the rule is implicit and must be discovered through trial and error learning, our results for the ID portion of this task reflect the children's ability to use feedback to shift responding to an alternate stimulus, and to shift responding to a new exemplar—both within the original stimulus dimension.

Studies with adults have reported that patients with frontal lesions show a specific impairment on the ED shift stage of the task, which requires a shift of responding to a novel dimension. However, frontal functions are likely to be involved in pre-ED phases of this task in young children. In a study comparing unmedicated and medicated children diagnosed with ADHD to matched controls, Kempton et al. (1999) found that unmedicated children were impaired on both the ID shift portion of the task and the ED shift, relative to controls and to themselves when taking medication. Furthermore, the unmedicated children showed a broader pattern of executive function deficits, including ED shift deficits and slower solution times on the Tower of London analog task (SOC).

In this study, we found that children with higher average blood lead levels required more trials to reach criterion through the ID reversal stage (seven). Given the Kempton et al. (1999) findings, it is likely that the ID shift requires sufficient attentional flexibility in children to qualify it as being a test of frontal functioning. It is noteworthy that the lead effect was substantial for this task. A difference in lifetime average blood lead of 10 μg/dL was associated with nearly a full standard deviation increase in the number of trials to complete Stage 7.

Spatial Working Memory (SWM)

Children with higher average lead levels performed more poorly on tests of SWM. In the span task, children with higher lead levels made more total errors. Blood lead was most highly associated with nontarget errors, those committed by touching boxes that had not been presented as ones in the sequence to be recalled.

There was no association of lead and span length after adjusting for covariates. Although apparently inconsistent with the findings from the error measures, the lack of significance is most likely due to the difficulty of the task and the coarseness of the span length measure. More than half the children demonstrated a span length of only 2, and an additional 38% had a span of 3. Although children with a span of 2 had significantly higher blood lead levels than children with a span of 3 or more, this difference was not significant after controlling for potential confounders in a logistic regression. Error scores provided a more continuous measure of performance difficulties, and children with higher lead levels made more errors. One interpretation of these findings is that the errors represent a deficit in short-term spatial memory, but it is also possible that the higher lead children had more difficulty with the encoding process, were less attentive when the sequence of target boxes were presented, or were deficient in inhibitory control. The fact that the strongest findings were for errors that involved choosing boxes that were not indicated as targets on that trial suggests that children may have allocated insufficient attention to the presentation of the target boxes.

WM impairments were also suggested by children's performance on the SWM task. This task is sensitive to functional alterations in frontal cortex structures central to WM (Goldman-Rakic, 1987a; Owen, Sahakian, Semple, Polkey, & Robbins, 1995). Similar to SSP, this task was difficult for the children, with only 44 completing the six-box problems. However, for these children, an inverse association with blood lead was found, indicating that a difference in lifetime average blood lead of 10 µg/dL was associated with an additional 4.6 errors (two-thirds of a standard deviation) on the six-box problems.

It is possible to dissociate the mnemonic processes involved in performing SWM from the strategic processes through the use of strategy scores (Owen et al., 1990). SWM strategy scores were available only for children who completed the six-box problems, and no association was found between strategy scores and blood lead. Strategy was also unrelated to span length, suggesting that span and strategy may be somewhat independent (Owen et al., 1996), and that lead effects may be present for measures of the mnemonic component involved in SWM, but not for the strategic component. To assess this possibility, we estimated a model in which blood lead and SWM strategy were independent variables and span length was the dependent variable. This analysis revealed that blood lead was significantly associated with span length even after controlling for strategy. According to this analysis, it appears that lead affected basic mnemonic processes, but not the strategic processes often considered to indicate the involvement of higher level executive functions. One caveat is that this analysis pertains only to a particular strategy used to solve SWM, and a fairly sophisticated strategy for a 5-year-old child. The lack of common use of this strategy may have been responsible for the absence of a relation between lead exposure and the strategy score. Again, children of this age may employ executive processes more for the purposes of focusing attention and general behavioral self-regulation. Nevertheless, it is interesting to note that span length and forgetting errors both showed some association with blood lead level, whereas strategy scores did not. It is not possible to determine, however, whether the strategy score is a poor measure of executive functions in these children or whether lead does not affect these strategic processes. The evidence from these data suggesting that lead affects SWM is quite strong, however.

Planning and Problem Solving

The SOC task is widely known as a task of planning and problem-solving ability, and children with higher blood lead levels required more moves to solve the problems. This finding was due primarily to a lead-related increase in the number of moves required to solve the two- and three-move problems. The source of this difficulty did not appear to be a deficit in the children's use of planning prior to beginning a solution—at least as indicated by the time they took before making their first move. One concern with this metric is the assumption that the solution is planned before the first ball is moved. Especially with young children, this assumption may be unwarranted. The source of the lead effects in this task was not related to the time taken to plan the first move; rather, it was associated with the amount of time children took to complete the problem subsequent to making the first move. This suggests that children may have relied on a trial and error strategy, in which each move must be planned individually. Indeed, a poorly planned first move will almost surely make the solution more complicated. As with frontal patients, higher lead children had longer thinking times after they had initiated a solution, possibly because they acted hastily on their first move (Robbins, 1996). It may be relevant that the longer subsequent thinking times seen in frontal patients are not found in patients with temporal lobectomies (Robbins, 1996).

Overall, our findings suggest that chronic low-level lead exposure impairs cognitive processes commonly considered to be core constituents of executive functions: WM, focused attention, attentional flexibility, planning, and problem solving. Our results are in some respects consistent with those from a study of 10-year-old children who were administered a battery of traditional neuropsychological tests (Stiles & Bellinger, 1993). Although the number of significant associations was small relative to the number of tests they administered, Stiles and Bellinger reported significant associations between blood lead concentration at age 2 years and number of perseverative errors on the California Verbal Learning Test. In addition, they reported a significant association between blood lead concentration at 10 years and perseverative errors on the WCST.

Stiles and Bellinger (1993) found that the associations of blood lead and performance on specific neuropsychological tests were less consistent than for global tests that measure a broader compilation of subprocesses (i.e., intelligence and achievement tests). They suggested that this may reflect the idiopathic nature of lead-related cognitive damage. Although the effects of lead exposure are likely to differ across children, our findings suggest a degree of consistency in lead's effects on more specific cognitive processes, effects not wholly redundant with the children's scores on a global test of intelligence (SBIV). For all but three analyses, lead effects remained significant or were only reduced to marginal significance after the addition of the SBIV score. Given that blood lead and SBIV are associated in these data, both in bivariate ($r = .48, p < .0001$) and multivariate models (Canfield et al., 2003), the control for SBIV substantially reduces the variance not only in the CANTAB outcomes, but also in blood lead. It is thus likely that the augmented models represent a case of overcontrol and support the conclusion that exposure to environmental lead is related to alterations in specific cognitive processes.

The findings of this study indicate that chronic low-level lead exposure impairs several cognitive processes related to what are typically referred to as executive functions. The evidence suggests that these effects include what are sometimes thought of as subordinate processes, such as WM and attentional flexibility, as well as the higher level executive functions of planning and problem solving. The neurobiological alterations underlying these impairments in lead-exposed children remain unclear. Investigations that integrate concurrent functional neuroimaging with tests of specific cognitive functions would allow one to correlate the behavioral alterations described in this study with regional differences in metabolic activity. Further refinement of behavioral assessments would also allow for a more in-depth understanding of the nature of the cognitive deficits associated with pediatric lead exposure.

REFERENCES

Baddeley, A. D. (1986). *Working memory.* Oxford, England: Clarendon.

Baghurst, P. A., McMichael, A. J., Tong, S., Wigg, N. R., Vimpani, G. V., & Robertson, E. F. (1995). Exposure to environmental lead and visual-motor integration at age 7 years: The Port Pirie Cohort Study [see comments]. *Epidemiology, 6,* 104–109.

Baghurst, P. A., McMichael, A. J., Wigg, N. R., Vimpani, G. V., Robertson, E. F., Roberts, R. J., et al. (1992). Environmental exposure to lead and children's intelligence at the age of seven years: The Port Pirie Cohort Study. *New England Journal of Medicine, 327,* 1279–1284.

Bauter, M. R., Brockel, B. J., Pankevich, D. E., Virgolini, M. B., & Cory-Slechta, D. A. (2003). Glutamate and dopamine in nucleus accumbens core and shell: Sequence learning versus performance. *Neurotoxicology, 24,* 227–243.

Bellinger, D., Hu, H., Titlebaum, L., & Needleman, H. L. (1994). Attentional correlates of dentin and bone lead levels in adolescents. *Archives of Environmental Health, 49,* 98–105.

Bellinger, D., Sloman, J., Leviton, A., Rabinowitz, M., Needleman, H. L., & Waternaux, C. (1991). Low-level lead exposure and children's cognitive function in the preschool years. *Pediatrics, 87,* 219–227.

Bellinger, D. C. (1995). Interpreting the literature on lead and child development: The neglected role of the "experimental system." *Neurotoxicology and Teratology, 17,* 201–212.

Bellinger, D. C., Stiles, K. M., & Needleman, H. L. (1992). Low-level lead exposure, intelligence and academic achievement: A long-term follow-up study [see comments]. *Pediatrics, 90,* 855–861.

Berg, E. A. (1948). A simple objective technique for measuring flexibility in thinking. *Journal of General Psychology, 39,* 15–22.

Bouchard, T. J., & Segal, N. L. (1985). Environment and IQ. In B. B. Wolman (Ed.), *Handbook of intelligence: Theories, measurements, and applications* (pp. 391–464). New York: Wiley.

Bradley, R. H., & Caldwell, B. M. (1984). The HOME Inventory and family demographics. *Developmental Psychology, 20,* 315–320.

Brockel, B. J., & Cory-Slechta, D. A. (1998). Lead, attention, and impulsive behavior: Changes in a fixed-ratio waiting-for-reward paradigm. *Pharmacology, Biochemistry and Behavior, 60,* 545–552.

Canfield, R. L., Espy, K. A., Henderson, C. R., Jr., & Cory-Slechta, D. A. (2002). *Low-level environmental lead exposure and executive functioning in young children.* Manuscript submitted for publication.

Canfield, R. L., Henderson, C. R., Jr., Cory-Slechta, D. A., Cox, C., Jusko, T. A., & Lanphear, B. P. (2003). Intellectual impairment in children with blood lead concentrations below 10 micrograms per deciliter. *New England Journal of Medicine, 348,* 1517–1526.

Canfield, R. L., Kreher, D. A., Cornwell, C., & Henderson, C. (2003). Low-level lead exposure and executive functioning in young children. *Child Neuropsychology, 9,* 35–53.

Canfield, R. L., Smith, E. G., Brezsnyak, M. P., & Snow, K. L. (1997). Information processing through the first year of life: A longitudinal study using the visual expectation paradigm. *Monographs of the Society for Research in Child Development, 62,* 1–145.

Canfield, R. L., Wilken, J., Schmerl, L., & Smith, E. G. (1995). Age-related change and stability of individual differences in infant saccade reaction time. *Infant Behavior and Development, 18,* 351–358.

Carlson, J. S., Jensen, C. M., & Widaman, K. F. (1983). Reaction time, intelligence, and attention. *Intelligence, 7,* 329–344.

Centers for Disease Control and Prevention. (1982). *Current trends in blood-lead levels in U.S. population* (Morbidity and mortality weekly report). Atlanta, GA: Author.

Centers for Disease Control and Prevention. (1991). *Preventing lead poisoning in young children: A statement by the Centers for Disease Control.* Atlanta, GA: Department of Health and Human Services.

Centers for Disease Control and Prevention. (2001). *National report on human exposure to environmental chemicals* (CAS no. 7439-92-1). Atlanta, GA: Author.

Cohn, J., Cox, C., & Cory-Slechta, D. A. (1993). The effects of lead exposure on learning in a multiple repeated acquisition and performance schedule. *NeuroToxicology, 14,* 329–346.

Cory-Slechta, D. A. (1995). Bridging human and experimental animal studies of lead neurotoxicity: Moving beyond IQ [comment]. *Neurotoxicology and Teratology, 17,* 219–221; discussion 249–251.

Detterman, D. K. (1987). What does reaction time tell us about intelligence? In P. A. Vernon (Ed.), *Speed of information processing and intelligence* (pp. 177–200). Norwood, NJ: Ablex.

Dietrich, K. N., Berger, O., Succop, P. A., Hammond, P. B., & Bornschein, R. L. (1993). The developmental consequences of low to moderate lead exposure: Intellectual attainment in the Cincinnati lead study cohort following school entry. *Neurotoxicology and Teratology, 15,* 37–44.

Doyere, V., Burette, F., Negro, C. R., & Laroche, S. (1993). Long-term potentiation of hippocampal afferents and efferents to prefrontal cortex: Implications for associative learning. *Neuropsychologia, 31,* 1031–1053.

Evans, G. W. (1978). Crowding and the developmental process. In A. Baum & Y. M. Epstein (Eds.), *Human response to crowding* (pp. 117–139). Hillsdale, NJ: Lawrence Erlbaum Associates, Inc.

Evans, G. W., Lepore, S. J., Shejwal, B. R., & Palsane, M. N. (1998). Chronic residential crowding and children's well-being: An ecological perspective. *Child Development, 69,* 1514–1523.

Evans, G. W., Maxwell, L. E., & Hart, B. (1999). Parental language and verbal responsiveness to children in crowded homes. *Developmental Psychology, 35,* 1020–1023.

Flegal, A. R., & Smith, D. R. (1995). Measurements of environmental lead contamination and human exposure. *Reviews of Environmental Contamination and Toxicology, 143,* 1–45.

Fray, P. J., & Robbins, T. W. (1996). CANTAB battery: Proposed utility in neurotoxicology. *Neurotoxicology and Teratology, 18,* 499–504.

Goldman-Rakic, P. S. (1987a). Circuitry of primate prefrontal cortex and regulation of behavior by representational memory. In F. Plum (Ed.), *Handbook of physiology—The nervous system* (Vol. 5, pp. 373–417). Bethesda, MD: American Physiological Society.

Goldman-Rakic, P. S. (1987b). Development of cortical circuitry and cognitive function. *Child Development, 58,* 601–622.

Gurden, H., Tassin, J. P., & Jay, T. M. (1999). Integrity of the mesocortical dopaminergic system is necessary for complete expression of in vivo hippocampal-prefrontal cortex long-term potentiation. *Neuroscience, 94,* 1019–1027.

Hughes, C., Plumet, M. H., & Leboyer, M. (1999). Towards a cognitive phenotype for autism: Increased prevalence of executive dysfunction and superior spatial span amongst siblings of children with autism. *Journal of Child Psychology and Psychiatry, and Allied Disciplines, 40,* 705–718.

Kempton, S., Vance, A., Maruff, P., Luk, E., Costin, J., & Pantelis, C. (1999). Executive function and attention deficit hyperactivity disorder: Stimulant medication and better executive function performance in children. *Psychological Medicine, 29,* 527–538.

Lanphear, B. P., Dietrich, K., Auinger, P., & Cox, C. (2000). Cognitive deficits associated with blood lead concentrations < 10 microg/dL in US children and adolescents. *Public Health Reports, 115,* 521–529.

Lanphear, B. P., Howard, C., Eberly, S., Auinger, P., Kolassa, J., Weitzman, M., et al. (1999). Primary prevention of childhood lead exposure: A randomized trial of dust control. *Pediatrics, 103,* 772–777.

Lasley, S. M., & Gilbert, M. E. (1996). Presynaptic glutamatergic function in dentate gyrus in vivo is diminished by chronic exposure to inorganic lead. *Brain Research, 736,* 125–134.

Lasley, S. M., & Gilbert, M. E. (2002). Rat hippocampal glutamate and GABA release exhibit biphasic effects as a function of chronic lead exposure level. *Toxicological Sciences, 66,* 139–147.

Lasley, S. M., Green, M. C., & Gilbert, M. E. (1998). Biphasic dose-effect relationships induced by chronic lead (Pb) exposure in hippocampal glutamatergic function. *Toxicologist, 42,* 199.

Lowe, C., & Rabbitt, P. (1998). Test/retest reliability of the CANTAB and ISPOCD neuropsychological batteries: Theoretical and practical issues: Cambridge Neuropsychological Test Automated Battery: International Study of Post-Operative Cognitive Dysfunction. *Neuropsychologia, 36,* 915–923.

Luciana, M., Lindeke, L., Georgieff, M., Mills, M., & Nelson, C. A. (1999). Neurobehavioral evidence for working-memory deficits in school-aged children with histories of prematurity. *Developmental Medicine and Child Neurology, 41,* 521–533.

Luciana, M., & Nelson, C. A. (1998). The functional emergence of prefrontally-guided working memory systems in four- to eight-year-old children. *Neuropsychologia, 36,* 273–293.

Maruff, P., Burns, C. B., Tyler, P., Currie, B. J., & Currie, J. (1998). Neurological and cognitive abnormalities associated with chronic petrol sniffing. *Brain, 121*(Pt. 10), 1903–1917.

McGaugh, J. L., McIntyre, C. K., & Power, A. E. (2002). Amygdala modulation of memory consolidation: Interaction with other brain systems. *Neurobiology of Learning and Memory, 78,* 539–552.

McMichael, A., Baghurst, P., Wigg, N., Vimpani, G., Robertson, E., & Roberts, R. (1988). Port-Pirie Cohort Study: Environmental exposure to lead and children's abilities at the age of four years. *New England Journal of Medicine, 319,* 468–475.

Mickey, R. M., & Greenland, S. (1989). The impact of confounder selection criteria on effect estimation. *American Journal of Epidemiology, 129,* 125–137.

Monchi, O., Petrides, M., Petre, V., Worsley, K., & Dagher, A. (2001). Wisconsin Card Sorting revisited: Distinct neural circuits participating in different stages of the task identified by event-related functional magnetic resonance imaging. *Journal of Neuroscience, 21,* 7733–7741.

Needleman, H. L., & Bellinger, D. C. (1989). Type II fallacies in the study of childhood exposure to lead at low doses: A critical and quantitative review. In M. A. Smith, L. D. Grant, & A. I. Sors (Eds.), *Lead exposure and child development: An international assessment* (pp. 293–304). London: Kluwer.

O'Carroll, R. E., Masterton, G., Dougall, N., Ebmeier, K. P., & Goodwin, G. M. (1995). The neuropsychiatric sequelae of mercury poisoning: The Mad Hatter's disease revisited. *British Journal of Psychiatry, 167,* 95–98.

Owen, A. M., Downes, J. J., Sahakian, B. J., Polkey, C. E., & Robbins, T. W. (1990). Planning and spatial working memory following frontal lobe lesions in man. *Neuropsychologia, 28,* 1021–1034.

Owen, A. M., Morris, R. G., Sahakian, B. J., Hodges, J. R., Polkey, C. E., & Robbins, T. W. (1996). Double dissociations of memory and executive functions in self-ordered working memory tasks following frontal lobe excision, temporal lobe excisions or amygdala-hippocampectomy in man. *Brain, 119,* 1597–1615.

Owen, A. M., Roberts, A. C., Polkey, C. E., Sahakian, B. J., & Robbins, T. W. (1991). Extra-dimensional versus intra-dimensional set shifting performance following frontal lobe excisions, temporal lobe excisions or amygdalo-hippocampectomy in man. *Neuropsychologia, 29,* 993–1006.

Owen, A. M., Sahakian, B. J., Semple, J., Polkey, C. E., & Robbins, T. W. (1995). Visuo-spatial short-term recognition memory and learning after temporal lobe excisions, frontal lobe excisions or amygdalo-hippocampectomy in man. *Neuropsychologia, 33,* 1–24.

Pocock, S. J., Smith, M., & Baghurst, P. (1994). Environmental lead and children's intelligence: A systematic review of the epidemiological evidence [see comments]. *British Medical Journal (Clinical Research Ed.), 309,* 1189–1197.

Pokora, M. J., Richfield, E. K., & Cory-Slechta, D. A. (1996). Preferential vulnerability of nucleus accumbens dopamine binding sites to low-level lead exposure: Time course of effects and interactions with chronic dopamine agonist treatments. *Journal of Neurochemistry, 67,* 1540–1550.

Poldrack, R. A., & Packard, M. G. (2003). Competition among multiple memory systems: Converging evidence from animal and human brain studies. *Neuropsychologia, 41,* 245–251.

Rice, D. C. (1993). Lead-induced changes in learning: Evidence for behavioral mechanisms from experimental animal studies. *Neurotoxicology, 14,* 167–178.

Rice, D. C. (1997). Anatomical substrates of behavioral impairment induced by developmental lead exposure in monkeys: Inferences from brain lesions. *American Zoologist, 37,* 409–425.

Robbins, T. W. (1996). Dissociating executive functions of the prefrontal cortex. *Philosophical Transactions of the Royal Society of London. Series B: Biological Sciences, 351,* 1463–1471.

Roberts, A. C., Robbins, T. W., Everitt, B. J., Jones, G. H., Sirkia, T. E., Wilkinson, J., et al. (1990). The effects of excitotoxic lesions of the basal forebrain on the acquisition, retention and serial reversal of visual discriminations in marmosets. *Neuroscience, 34,* 311–329.

Rogers, R. D., Andrews, T. C., Grasby, P. M., Brooks, D. J., & Robbins, T. W. (2000). Contrasting cortical and subcortical activations produced by attentional-set shifting and reversal learning in humans. *Journal of Cognitive Neuroscience, 12,* 142–162.

Shallice, T., & Burgess, P. (1993). Supervisory control of action and thought selection. In A. D. Baddeley & L. Weiskrantz (Eds.), *Attention: Selection, awareness and control* (pp. 171–187). Oxford, England: Clarendon Press.

Stiles, K. M., & Bellinger, D. C. (1993). Neuropsychological correlates of low-level lead exposure in school-age children: A prospective study. *Neurotoxicology and Teratology, 15,* 27–35.

Thierry, A. M., Gioanni, Y., Degenetais, E., & Glowinski, J. (2000). Hippocampo-prefrontal cortex pathway: Anatomical and electrophysiological characteristics. *Hippocampus, 10,* 411–419.

Tong, I. S., & Lu, Y. (2001). Identification of confounders in the assessment of the relationship between lead exposure and child development. *Annals of Epidemiology, 11,* 38–45.

Wasserman, G. A., Liu, X., Lolacono, N. J., Factor-Litvak, P., Kline, J. K., Popovac, D., et al. (1997). Lead exposure and intelligence in 7-year-old children: The Yugoslavia Prospective Study. *Environmental Health Perspectives, 105,* 956–962.

World Health Organization (1995). *International programme on chemical safety.* Geneva, Switzerland: Author.

Zuch, C. L., O'Mara, D. J., & Cory-Slechta, D. A. (1998). Low-level lead exposure selectively enhances dopamine overflow in nucleus accumbens: An in vivo electrochemistry time course assessment. *Toxicology and Applied Pharmacology, 150,* 174–185.

www.ingramcontent.com/pod-product-compliance
Ingram Content Group UK Ltd.
Pitfield, Milton Keynes, MK11 3LW, UK
UKHW020429010325
455677UK00029B/1069